ISSUES IN
SCIENCE
EDUCATION

SCIENCE
TEACHER
RETENTION
Mentoring and Renewal

ISSUES IN
SCIENCE
EDUCATION

SCIENCE
TEACHER
RETENTION
Mentoring and Renewal

Jack Rhoton and Patricia Bowers, Editors

National Science Education Leadership Association
and

National Science Teachers Association
Arlington, Virginia

NATIONAL SCIENCE TEACHERS ASSOCIATION

Claire Reinburg, Director
Judy Cusick, Associate Editor
Carol Duval, Associate Editor
Betty Smith, Associate Editor

Art and Design Linda Olliver, Director
Printing and Production Catherine Lorrain-Hale, Director
    Nguyet Tran, Assistant Production Manager
    Jack Parker, Desktop Publishing Specialist
Publications Operations Erin Miller, Manager
Marketing Holly Hemphill, Director
NSTA Web Tim Weber, Webmaster
Periodicals Publishing Shelley Carey, Director
SciLINKS Tyson Brown, Manager

National Science Teachers Association
Gerald F. Wheeler, Executive Director
David Beacom, Publisher

Copyright © 2003 by the National Science Teachers Association.
All rights reserved. Printed in the United States of America by Kirby Lithographic Co., Inc.

Issues in Science Education
Science Teacher Retention: Mentoring and Renewal
NSTA Stock Number: PB127X4
04 03 02 4 3 2 1

Library of Congress Cataloging-in-Publication Data
Science teacher retention: mentoring and renewal / Jack Rhoton and
Patricia Bowers, editors.
        p. cm.— (Issues in science education)
Includes bibliographical references and index.
ISBN 0-87355-218-0
1. Science teachers—United States. 2. Teacher turnover—United
States—Prevention. I. Rhoton, Jack. II. Bowers, Patricia. III. Series.
Q149 .S314 2003
507'.1273—dc21   2002014842

Contents

Part I.
Complexities Facing Beginning Science Teachers

Richard M. Ingersoll

This chapter summarizes what the best available nationally representative data reveal about the rates of, and reasons for, the turnover of math and science teachers. The results show that contrary to conventional wisdom, the problems schools have adequately staffing classrooms with qualified teachers are not due to increases in student enrollment or increases in teacher retirement. Rather, large numbers of teachers leave teaching for other reasons, such as job dissatisfaction and in order to pursue other careers. These findings suggest that educational policy initiatives will not solve school staffing problems if they do not address the problem of teacher retention.

Edward Britton and Senta Raizen

A National Science Foundation–funded study of beginning science and mathematics teachers in five countries looked at teacher induction systems that are more comprehensive than most in the United States. For example, the New Zealand system provides beginning teachers with paid release time, during which diverse sources of support offer the beginning teachers a repertoire of induction activities. Induction includes attention to science-specific needs such as development of science courses or lessons and hands-on instruction. Facilitated peer support plays an important role.

Part II.
Teacher Retention and Renewal: Programs in Action

catalyst to develop a strong and collaborative partnership between the 14 participating geographically isolated, rural school districts and the local university, San Diego State University–Imperial Valley Campus, to create a multidimensional systemic plan of professional development designed to address the issues of science teacher retention and renewal.

Mentoring and Coaching for Teachers of Science: Enhancing Professional Culture 71
Kathy A. Dunne and Anne Newton

Mentor programs provide an opportunity to foster a professional culture that focuses on improving the teaching, learning, and assessing of science as well as a means to retain highly qualified new and experienced teachers. This chapter outlines key strategies, structures, policies, and practices that contribute to developing and sustaining quality mentor programs; describes different models (mentoring one-on-one, study groups/team mentoring, mentor teacher-leader model, and collaborative mentor networks); and offers a snapshot of one program that exemplifies each model.

Personal Histories Supporting Retention of Beginning Science Teachers 85
Charles J. Eick

Beginning science teachers enter the classroom with an early professional role identity formed from life experiences in science, education, and volunteer/work settings. These experiences, along with teachers' values and beliefs, can support new science teachers' developing pedagogical content knowledge and ability to manage students in inquiry learning. Science teacher preparation programs need to begin addressing supportive backgrounds for entering students. Programs that build upon students' prior experiential learning may be more successful in retention of beginning science teachers.

The Reemerging Cycle of Teacher Supply and Demand: North Carolina Takes Action 93
Gerry M. Madrazo, Jr.

This chapter presents a brief history of teacher shortages, particularly in the fields of science and mathematics. It describes numerous efforts by North Carolina, not only in recruiting individuals into the teaching profession but also in retaining and renewing teachers already in the profession. Through creative professional development, teachers must become passionate about and committed to teaching and learning. Teachers must have the flexibility to transform their classrooms into "inviting learning environments," with administrative and system support—and resources to implement new and innovative ideas.

Collaborative Efforts to Retain New Teachers: A University–School District Partnership 103
Denise K. Crockett, Geneal Cantrell, Shirley A. Ritter, and Michael Svec

The collaborative effort between Furman University and two local school districts, called the

Teacher to Teacher program, provides an avenue for improved teacher retention and mentoring. The partnership creates a community of learners united to address the many challenges that drive first-year teachers out of the profession. The interns in the program are staying in the profession, are feeling supported, and are achieving self-efficacy sooner than traditional first-year teachers.

Part III.
Professional Development and Strategies for Science Teacher Retention and Renewal

Foreword

Rodger W. Bybee
Director, Biological Sciences Curriculum Study (BSCS)

Beginning science teachers have an amazing array of concerns—Can I control the students? What will my classroom be like? Will other teachers and administrators support me?

The list may vary, but the fact that beginning science teachers have many concerns does not. Individuals reading and using *Science Teacher Retention: Mentoring and Renewal* have the insights, opportunities, and in some cases, obligations to respond to the concerns of beginning science teachers in personally and educationally constructive ways. At a minimum, one should avoid perpetuating ideas that reinforce teachers' concerns. For example, as professionals we can *listen* to beginning teachers and accept what has meaning to them. We can respond to their concerns, and we can avoid old shibboleths such as "Don't smile until Thanksgiving," an attitude that assumes that the students will present problems and one must counter with stern and harsh behaviors. This book will help members of the science teaching community to avoid such old myths about science teaching and to recognize and respond to teachers' concerns in ways that have personal meaning for those involved.

How would you describe the results of experiencing lack of respect from students, peers, administrators, and parents? Of having large classes with the least able students? And teaching science in poorly equipped classrooms? While one must recognize the realities of school systems, it is certainly possible to help beginning teachers develop positive and empowering views of their work and profession. My appeal here centers on the need for individuals within school systems to assume responsibility for establishing personal connections with beginning science teachers. Through such personal connections—mentoring relationships—we can give beginning teachers the sense that they are not alone, they have support, and they can resolve some of their concerns. I fear that we may devote initial time and effort to issues that originate within the larger educational systems and not realize that the process of resolving those issues begins with the personal concerns of science teachers.

Consideration of the challenges faced by beginning teachers and the reasons they cite for leaving the profession provides some insights for those interested in, and at some level responsible for, the retention and renewal of beginning teachers. Confronted with numerous challenges, beginning science teachers can very quickly develop perceptions that they are not able, dependable, and helpful. Why do I use this language? This language links the perceptions of beginning teachers and the policies and programs described in this volume. Further, the terms "able," "dependable," and "helpful" suggest goals for our work. In the induction period, we want to develop the knowledge, understandings, and abilities that give beginning teachers the confidence that they are able to teach science, that students can depend on them for a positive educational experience, and that they are helpful when problems arise.

For me, continuing professional development encompasses the variety of policies and programs that address the need for mentoring during the early years of teaching. The late Susan Loucks-Horsley stated, "Professional development is a concerted effort to help [science teachers] understand and change their practices and beliefs as they improve the learning experiences they provide for students within their school and district (Loucks-Horsley 2001, i). To paraphrase this quotation from a great leader, we need a concerted effort to help beginning teachers establish effective practices and perceptions for their work.

This volume, edited by Jack Rhoton and Patricia Bowers, provides background, strategies, and exemplary programs that will help all those in leadership positions to assume the responsibility to retain and renew science teachers and, ultimately, to enhance student learning.

Reference
Loucks-Horsley, S. 2001. Foreword. In *Professional development: Planning and design,* eds. J. Rhoton and P. Bowers. Arlington, VA: National Science Teachers Association.

Preface

Jack Rhoton and Patricia Bowers

The complexities facing beginning science teachers during the past decade have been highlighted by a plethora of reports coupled with concerns about the quality of science teaching in our nation's K–12 classrooms. Various methods to improve science teacher retention and renewal have been proposed, all of which point to three central questions: What are the complexities facing beginning teachers? What mentoring programs are in place to reduce those complexities? How do we go about introducing action strategies and intervention programs to support beginning teachers?

It has been well documented that beginning science teachers face enormous problems during their first years of teaching, yet they receive very little assistance for resolving conflicts and surviving in the educational system. Successful induction programs and continuing professional learning give teachers the support they need to carry out practices that are consistent with the student-centered, inquiry-based learning envisioned in the National Science Education Standards. In this sense, a successful retention and renewal program becomes an important link in the entire professional development process for the teacher.

Beginning with their first teaching assignment, inductees are expected to perform the same duties as veteran teachers, alone in a classroom. Teaching, however, is not a solitary activity. Many interpersonal dynamics affect the teaching and learning of science in a school or even a single classroom. Having a clear set of standards for classroom practice is important to any teacher, but real, long-lasting professional learning involves a great deal more. Teachers face school policies regarding how they spend their time, structural arrangements, cultural norms, and the need for professional learning—all of which factors ultimately affect student learning, either directly or indirectly. Teachers' professional learning can be enhanced or constrained by the setting within which they work and by the opportunities available to them.

Because of the difficult challenges of the first few years of teaching, beginning teachers often feel highly vulnerable and ultimately may decide to leave the teaching profession. As reported in the findings of Richard Ingersoll (see the first chapter), the top reasons why science and mathematics teachers leave teaching include dissatisfaction with their working environments, lack of leadership and respect from principals, lack of classroom autonomy, lack of respect from students, poor support from administrators, and poorly equipped classrooms and laboratories. Another major dissatisfaction among science teachers is poor salary.

Our challenge is to provide beginning teachers with the strategies and resources they need initially and on a continuing basis. Changes in educational practices seldom are implemented quickly, and pervasive and permanent teacher retention and renewal programs are rarely imposed from without. Successful science teacher retention programs involve many participants playing different roles, including teachers, administrators, and science coordinators.

Even though a common vision is emerging about what an effective professional learning program for both beginning and veteran teachers should look like, a large number of teachers have not had an opportunity to participate in such professional learning in their schools. *Science Teacher Retention: Mentoring and Renewal* addresses the issues surrounding professional development for science teachers and discusses practical approaches used by current teacher retention and renewal programs that are working to build effective science programs in our nation's schools.

The impetus for this book is a shared philosophy between the National Science Education Leadership Association (NSELA) and the National Science Teachers Association (NSTA) that beginning teachers need assistance, especially as they struggle with issues related to discipline-specific content, standards-based instructional strategies, and many sociopolitical pressures. Using nontechnical language, this book is intended to be accessible to a broad audience. It is written for science teachers, science department chairs, principals, systemwide science leaders, superintendents, university personnel, policy makers, and other individuals who have a stake in science education.

The book is organized into three sections. The five chapters in Part 1, "Complexities Facing Beginning Science Teachers," set the stage by examining the critical issues of professional learning and science teacher induction programs, what research says about teacher induction and professional learning programs, and needs assessment for beginning teacher assistance programs. Part II, "Teacher Retention and Renewal: Programs in Action," consists of six chapters that vividly describe induction and retention programs that work. The six chapters in Part III, "Professional Development and Strategies for Science Teacher Retention and Renewal," focus on systemic approaches to support teacher retention and renewal programs, and the role of professional development and teacher induction.

Meaningful and sustained change in science teacher retention and renewal is fraught with challenges and pitfalls, all of which demand effective professional learning programs. The task of developing and sustaining healthy professional learning practices for continuing professional learning is simply too complex for any one person to tackle alone. Therefore, this book is directed at all players in the science education community who have a stake in improving science teaching and learning. Moreover, principals and other administrators must create an atmosphere that supports and encourages an ongoing system to improve science teaching and learning. One of the greatest challenges of leadership is to develop a culture that creates "laboratories" of continual improvement. The final determinant of success in this effort will be measured through the quality of science programs delivered to our students.

About the Editors

Jack Rhoton is a professor of science education at East Tennessee State University, Johnson City, Tennessee. Dr. Rhoton currently teaches science education at the undergraduate and graduate levels; he has also taught science at the elementary, middle, and high school levels. He has received numerous awards for service and science teaching and has been an active researcher in K–12 science, especially the restructuring of science inservice education as it relates to improved teaching practices. Dr. Rhoton is president of the National Science Education Leadership Association (NSELA) (2003–2004), president of the Tennessee Academy of Science (TAS) (2002–2003), and editor of the *Science Educator*, a publication of the NSELA. He is also director of the Tennessee Junior Academy of Science (TJAS), and he serves as editor of the TJAS *Handbook and Proceedings*. Dr. Rhoton's special research interest is in the area of professional development and its impact on science teaching and learning. He is widely published and has written and directed numerous science and technology grants. He has received many honors, including the National Science Teachers Association (NSTA) Distinguished Service to Science Education Award and the East Tennessee State University Distinguished Faculty Award.

Patricia Bowers is the associate director of the Center for Mathematics and Science Education at the University of North Carolina at Chapel Hill (UNC-CH), where she provides professional development training for mathematics and science teachers. She also works closely with the UNC-CH Pre-College program, which recruits under-represented groups into math and science fields. She has been the project director for numerous grants, including 21 Eisenhower grants, and has received awards for service and science education, including the National Outstanding Science Supervisor Award from NSELA. Dr. Bowers was a science, mathematics, and reading /language arts coordinator at the system level and worked as a classroom teacher and guidance counselor at the school level. Dr. Bowers is past-president of the North Carolina Science Teachers Association and the North Carolina Science Leadership Association. She is a former district director for both the National Science Education Leadership Association and the National Science Teachers Association and is a current board member of NSELA.

Acknowledgments

This book would not have been possible without the help, advice, and support of a number of people. The members of the NSTA/NSELA Editorial Board—LaMoine Motz, Carolyn Randolph, Susan Sprague, Charlotte Kresge, Emma Walton, Gerry Madrazo, Martha Hauff, and Martha Rhoton—made valuable suggestions for improvements. Our appreciation is extended to Claire Reinburg and Judy Cusick of NSTA Press for their invaluable help in the final production of the book. No volume is any better than the manuscripts that are contributed to it; we appreciate the time and efforts of those whose work lies within the covers of this book.

We also want to thank and acknowledge the support, help, and suggestions of the NSELA Board of Directors. Special thanks to Kenn Heydrick, past president, for his suggestions and guidance in the early stages of the project. The support of president Nick Micozzi and executive director Peggy Holliday in the later stages of the project is gratefully acknowledged.

Finally, we would like to credit people who simply made room in their busy lives for us do this work. We are indebted to the calm, good-natured support of the East Tennessee State University staff: Sherri Tharpe and Judy Suarez. Both of these individuals did excellent work in managing and word processing the drafts of each manuscript.

Introduction

Kenn Heydrick
NSELA President, 2001–2002

Who dares to teach must never cease to learn.

—John Cotton Dana,
1856–1929, American librarian and museum director

What do you think of when you read this quote from John Cotton Dana? His words can help us understand that the United States needs quality teachers who are adventurous, innovative, and courageous when it comes to taking on the challenges of teaching. In addition, teachers should be active learners themselves, seeking to improve their knowledge and skills and using research to modify their teaching practices. Visualize how schools would change if every teacher believed, "Who dares to teach must never cease to learn."

Several national reports indicate that the United States will need about 2 million new teachers in the next ten years. We also have heard that we lose about 50 percent of our teaching faculty after five years of service. To recruit new teacher candidates, we need to improve the size and quality of the applicant pool. We need to seek out language minority populations, promote teaching as a career, and provide financial support for teacher education programs.

On behalf of the National Science Education Leadership Association (NSELA), I am very grateful for the contributions that Jack Rhoton and Patricia Bowers have made with their two previous National Science Teachers Association (NSTA) books on professional development. This book, *Science Teacher Retention: Mentoring and Renewal*, is a wonderful collection of important essays that address quality teachers who seek continuous improvement. The authors have done an exemplary job in helping us focus on a critical issue confronting education today. I am grateful to the authors for extending the goals I worked for during my NSELA presidency—"The 3 R's: Recruit, Retain, and Recognize"—to highlight another important "R": "Renew."

Let's look at three key aspects that confront our educational system.

1. *Assessment Legislation of 2001.* Have you read the No Child Left Behind Act of 2001? Will it be easier to retain and renew our science teachers with the new initiatives in the act? Within the next five years, each state will need to administer at least one science assessment at the elementary level (grades 3–5), the middle school level (grades 6–8), and the high school level (grades 10–12). Measuring the proficiency of students in science is a good thing—and will drive how we recruit, retain, and renew our teachers. Teachers will be held accountable for the academic performance of their students.
2. *Qualified Teachers.* The No Child Left Behind Act of 2001 requires states to ensure that, within four years, all teachers are qualified to teach in their subject

areas. Each local educational agency must make sure that all teachers hired and teaching in a program supported with funds dispersed under certain parts of the law are "highly qualified." Moreover, each state must ensure that *all* teachers teaching in the core academic subjects are "highly qualified" not later than the end of the 2005–2006 school year. Each state must also have an annual increase in the percentage of teachers who are receiving "high-quality professional development" to enable such teachers to become "highly qualified and successful" classroom teachers.

We are at a unique stage in the history of education: We can help shape the meaning of "highly qualified and successful" teachers and "high-quality professional development." As science leaders, we need to strongly advocate for recruiting and retaining individuals who have a solid content background and are able to communicate effectively with students. Again, our professional development programs must truly "renew" the teaching capacity of our professionals.

Have you heard the phrase "You get what you pay for"? One of the leading strategies we must acknowledge and implement is higher pay scales. Our communities typically say, "We value our teachers," but do they really value them enough to raise their salaries? Also, do we pay teachers adequate stipends for the co-curricular activities they sponsor? Remember that the community gets what it pays for.

3. *Eisenhower Funding Eliminated.* At a time when the need for a sustained commitment to science and math education is absolutely critical, many organizations were disappointed that federal funding for innovative new science and math education partnership programs was reduced to $12.5 million. This amount is in sharp contrast to the $485 million Congress appropriated for math and science teacher professional development in FY 2001.

The professional development aspects of "No Child Left Behind" will need to be addressed through new avenues. We must work carefully with our state education agencies to help funnel funds into science education programs. Our global economy depends on scientific and technological advances. We must provide schools with quality teachers who seek continuous improvement.

Please remember that these national developments provide a unique opportunity for us to shape the future. I urge you to be proactive and to collaborate with others on these important issues. It is the hope of NSELA and NSTA that this book will engage more people in the dialogue of how to retain and renew our science teachers. I urge you to share this book with another colleague after you have read it. Get the conversation going—and brainstorm different ways that you can address these issues in your community and state.

Turnover and Shortages among Science and Mathematics Teachers in the United States

Richard M. Ingersoll

Richard M. Ingersoll, a former high school teacher, is currently an associate professor of educa- tion and sociology at the University of Pennsylvania. Dr. Ingersoll's research looks at elementary and secondary schools as workplaces, teachers as employees, and teaching as a job. He is a nationally recognized expert on the problem of out-of-field teaching and has published numer- ous articles on the problems of teacher turnover and teacher shortages. He is also the author of *Who Controls Teachers Work? Power and Accountability in America's Schools* (Harvard Univer- sity Press 2002), which examines the degree to which schools are centralized or decentralized and its impact on school performance.

Few educational problems have received more attention in recent times than the failure to ensure that elementary and secondary classrooms are all staffed with qualified teachers. In the mid-1980s, a series of highly publicized reports began to focus national attention on the coming possibility of severe teacher shortages in elementary and secondary schools (e.g., National Commission on Excellence in Education 1983; National Academy of Sciences 1987). These reports predicted a dramatic increase in the demand for new teachers, primarily because of two con- verging demographic trends: increasing student enrollments and increasing teacher turnover due to a graying teaching force. Subsequent shortfalls of teachers would, in turn, force many school systems to resort to lowering standards to fill teaching open- ings, the net effect of which would inevitably be high numbers of underqualified teachers and lower school performance. More recent reports stressed that shortages would affect some teaching fields more than others. Special education, math, and science, in particular, have been identified as fields with especially high turnover and therefore most likely to suffer shortages (Murnane et al. 1991; Boe, Bobbitt, and Cook 1997; Grissmer and Kirby 1992).

As a result, over the past decade, the inability of schools to adequately staff class- rooms with qualified teachers has increasingly been recognized as a major social

---

This chapter draws from an earlier paper prepared in February 2000 for the National Commission on Mathematics and Science Teaching for the 21st Century, chaired by John Glenn.

problem, has received widespread coverage in the national media, and has been the target of a growing number of reform and policy initiatives (National Commission on Teaching and America's Future 1997). The dominant policy response to school staffing problems has been to attempt to increase the supply of available teachers through a wide range of recruitment initiatives. Some programs, such as Troops-to-Teachers, are designed to entice professionals into mid-career changes to teaching. Others, such as Teach for America, seek to lure the "best and brightest" college graduates into teaching. A wide range of alternative licensing programs are designed to ease entry into teaching. Finally, financial incentives, such as signing bonuses, the forgiving of student loans, housing assistance, and tuition reimbursement have all been instituted to aid recruitment.

Concern over school staffing problems has also given impetus to research on teacher shortages and turnover. However, as numerous analysts have noted, it was difficult, initially, to study these issues because of a lack of accurate data, especially at a nationally representative level, on many of the pertinent issues surrounding teacher supply, demand, and quality. To obtain such data, the National Center for Education Statistics (NCES), the statistical arm of the U.S. Department of Education, designed the Schools and Staffing Survey (SASS) in the late 1980s. This is now the largest and most comprehensive data source available on the staffing, occupational, and organizational aspects of schools. SASS administers survey questionnaires to a random sample of about 55,000 teachers from all types of schools and from all 50 states. In addition, all those teachers who left their teaching jobs in the year subsequent to the administration of the initial survey questionnaire are again contacted to obtain information on their departures. This supplemental study, known as the Teacher Follow-up Survey (TFS) (National Center for Education Statistics 1995), is the largest and most comprehensive data source on teacher turnover in the United States. NCES has administered SASS/TFS on a regular basis; to date, four cycles have been released: 1987–89; 1990–92; 1993–95; and 1999–2001. [The last cycle was not fully released when this chapter was written.]

The Research Project

Over the past decade, I have conducted research, using SASS and TFS, to study a number of issues concerned with teacher turnover, shortages, and quality. This chapter draws from this larger body of research to briefly summarize what the data reveal about the rates of and reasons for teacher turnover. (For more detailed presentations of this research, see Ingersoll 1999, 2001a, 2001b, 2002.)

The data presented here come primarily from the 1995 TFS and represent all teachers for grades K–12 and from both public and private schools. Math and science teachers are the primary focus of this chapter. The latter are those identified by their principals as having their main teaching assignment in either math or science and represent about 11 percent of the total teaching force. About 22 percent of these math/science teachers are employed in elementary or middle schools, another 73 percent are in secondary schools, and about 5 percent are in combined (K–12) schools. Throughout the chapter, I compare the data on math/science teachers with the data for all teachers. To provide a benchmark for both, teachers' rates of turnover are compared to levels of employee turnover in other occupations.

There are two types of teacher turnover. The first, often called *teacher attrition,* refers to those who leave the occupation of teaching altogether. The second type, often called *teacher migration,* refers to those who transfer or move to different teaching jobs in other schools. Research on teacher supply and demand has often emphasized the first type and neglected the second type. Many people assume that teacher migration is a less significant form of turnover because it does not increase or decrease the overall supply of teachers, as do retirements and career changes, and, hence, that it does not contribute to the problem of staffing schools and shortages. From a systemic point of view, this is probably correct. However, from the view-point of those managing schools, teacher migration and attrition have the same effect; in either case it results in a decrease in staff members, who usually must be replaced. Hence, from the schools' perspective, teacher migration can, indeed, contribute to the problem of keeping schools staffed with qualified teachers. For this reason, this chapter will present data on both teacher migration and teacher attrition. Hereafter, I refer to teacher migration as "movers," teacher attrition as "leavers," and total turnover as "departures."

After establishing how many teachers depart from their teaching jobs and how these rates compare with other occupations, this chapter presents statistics on the reasons why teachers move from or leave their teaching jobs. These data are drawn from items in the TFS questionnaire that ask teachers to indicate the reasons (up to three) for their departures, from a list provided in the questionnaire (see Appendix). Data are presented from an additional set of items that asks teachers to indicate the sources (up to three) of their dissatisfaction, if they had indicated dissatisfaction either with teaching, their school, or their salary as a reason for their turnover.

Results
Levels of Turnover

Teaching is a relatively large occupation; it represents 4 percent of the entire nation-wide civilian work force. There are, for example, over twice as many K–12 teachers as registered nurses and five times as many teachers as either lawyers or professors. Moreover, the rate of turnover for teachers appears to be higher than in many other occupations. One of the best known sources of national data on rates of employee turnover, the Bureau of National Affairs, has shown that nationwide levels of employee turnover, gathered from a wide range of occupations, have been quite stable over the past decade, averaging 11 percent per year (Bureau of National Affairs 1998). The employee turnover rate provides an overall benchmark; comparison of the TFS data with the rate for employees in general suggests that teaching has a relatively high turnover rate: 14.5 percent in 1988–89; 13.2 percent in 1991–92;

14.3 percent in 1994–95; and 15.7 in 2000–2001. As a result, numerically, teacher turnover is a large phenomenon; the data show that in 1994–95 over 417,000 teachers, from a force of about 3 million, departed their teaching jobs. Total teacher turnover is about evenly split between migration and attrition; 7 percent of teacher turnovers were movers (migration) and 7.3 percent left the profession altogether (attrition). Interestingly, the turnover rate for math/science teachers—16 percent—is not much higher than for other teachers, and the difference is not statistically significant (see Figure 1).

Figure 1. Percent Annual Employee Turnover, and Percent Annual Teacher Turnover

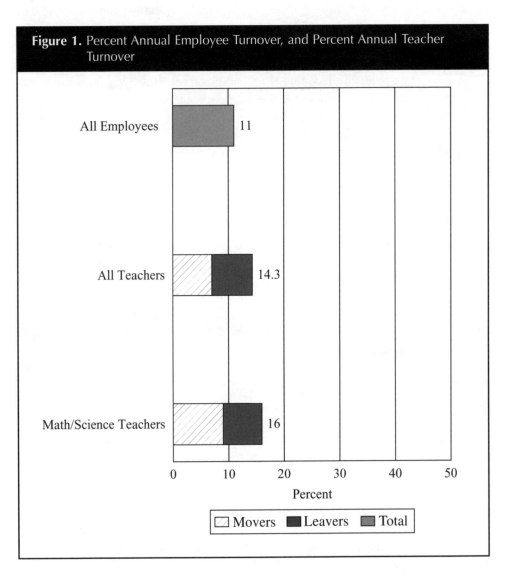

Note: Employee data from Bureau of National Affairs. 1998. BNA's quarterly report on job absence and turnover. *Bulletin to Management.* Washington, DC: Bureau of National Affairs.

Turnover, however, is not equally spread across the teaching force. Teachers' decisions about whether to stay or leave are influenced, in particular, by the length of their teaching experience. Beginning teachers have very high rates of departure; these rates significantly decline through the mid-career period as teachers "settle in," and then rise again in the retirement years. This means that teaching is an occupation that loses many of its newly trained members very early in their careers.

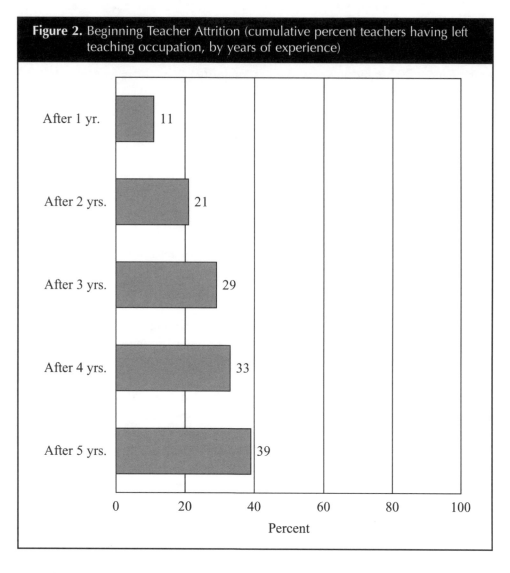

Figure 2. Beginning Teacher Attrition (cumulative percent teachers having left teaching occupation, by years of experience)

Note: The cumulative rates of beginning teacher attrition shown in Figure 2 are only a rough approximation. The data do not follow a particular "class" or cohort of newly hired teachers to ascertain how many remain in teaching after a particular length of time. Instead, the cumulative loss of new teachers was calculated by multiplying the probabilities of turnover for successive years. These cumulative estimates do not account for those who later reenter teaching .

Figure 2, for example, provides a rough estimate of the cumulative losses of beginning teachers from attrition in their first several years of teaching. The data suggest that after just three years, 29 percent of all beginning teachers have left teaching altogether, and after five years, fully 39 percent have left teaching. Because of sample size limitations, it is not possible to make precise estimates of the cumulative losses for math/science teachers alone; however, the data suggest they are slightly higher than the averages depicted in Figure 2.

These high turnover rates account for most of the demand for new teachers, which, in turn, is a driving force behind school staffing problems. The data show that while student enrollments are increasing, the demand for new teachers is not primarily due to these increases. In recent years, the vast majority of new hires have simply been replacements for those who have just departed. For instance, the TFS data show that about 286,200 teachers (excluding within-district transfers) were newly hired by schools just prior to the 1993–94 school year. In the following 12 months, about 213,000 teachers—a figure equivalent to 75 percent of those just hired—left the profession altogether. In short, the demand for new teachers, and the subsequent problems schools face ensuring that classrooms are staffed with qualified teachers, is to a significant extent due to teachers moving from or leaving their jobs at higher rates than in many other occupations. These patterns are chronic; similar results are found in all three cycles of the TFS data from the late 1980s to the mid-1990s and appear to be true for the 2000–2001 data (which were not fully released when this chapter was written).

Reasons for Turnover
This section turns to the reasons behind these relatively high rates of teacher turnover. Table 1 lists the data on teachers' reasons for their leaving—separately for all teachers and math/science teachers and also separately for movers (migration) and leavers (attrition). Note that the column segments in Table 1, displaying percentages of teachers giving various reasons for turnover, each add up to more than 100 percent because respondents could indicate up to three reasons for their departures. The same applies to the columns displaying reasons for dissatisfaction-related turnover. The Table 1 data (but with movers and leavers combined) are also more succinctly illustrated in Figures 3 and 4.

As illustrated in Figure 3 and Table 1, overall, math/science teachers do not greatly differ from other teachers in the reasons why they depart from their teaching jobs. Contrary to conventional wisdom, retirement is not an especially prominent factor. The latter actually accounts for only a small part (13 percent) of total turnover. Of course, if one focuses on attrition alone (only those leaving teaching altogether) retirement is more prominent because, by definition, migration excludes retirement. Even in this case, however, retirement is not an especially prominent factor; retirement accounts for only a quarter of leavers (25 percent). Notably, retirement also does not account for the relatively high rates of turnover by math/science teachers.

Table 1. Percent Teacher Turnover and Percent Teachers Giving Various Reasons for Their Turnover

	All Teachers		Math/Science Teachers	
	Movers	Leavers	Movers	Leavers
Rates of Turnover	7	7.3	9	7
Reasons for Turnover				
Retirement	-	25	-	26
School Staffing Action	34	8	28	11
Family or Personal	36	44	32	45
To Pursue Other Job	29	25	33	21
Dissatisfaction	32	25	48	28
Poor salary	49	61	53	66
Poor administrative support	51	32	57	22
Student discipline problems	22	24	33	21
Lack of faculty influence and autonomy	18	15	11	15
Poor student motivation	12	18	17	32
Poor opportunity for professional advancement	8	5	4	1
Inadequate time to prepare	5	6	3	6
Intrusions on teaching time	5	11	6	12

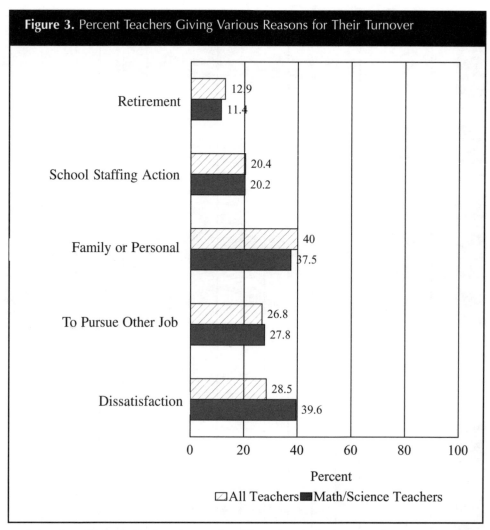

Figure 3. Percent Teachers Giving Various Reasons for Their Turnover

School staffing cutbacks, due to layoffs, school closings, and reorganizations, account for a larger proportion of total turnover than does retirement. Staffing actions more often result in migration to other teaching jobs rather than leaving the teaching occupation altogether (34 percent of migration and 8 percent of attrition). Personal reasons, such as departures for pregnancy, child rearing, health problems, and family moves are more often given as reasons for turnover than are either retirement or staffing actions (36 percent of migration and 44 percent of attrition).

Finally, two related reasons are, collectively, a very prominent source of turnover. About half of all teachers who depart their jobs give as a reason either job dissatisfaction or the desire to pursue another job, in or out of education. Notably, math/science teachers are significantly more likely to move from or leave their teaching jobs because of job dissatisfaction than are other teachers (40 percent of math/science and 29 percent of all teachers).

As illustrated in Figure 4 and Table 1, of those who depart because of job dissatisfaction, the most common reasons given are low salaries, a lack of support from the administration, student discipline problems, lack of student motivation, and lack of influence over school decision-making. Moreover, several factors stand out as *not* serious enough to lead to much turnover: large class sizes, intrusions on classroom time, lack of planning time, and lack of opportunity for professional advancement. These findings were found to be true across different cycles of the data and across different subsets of teacher turnover. In general, similar kinds of dissatisfactions lie behind both teacher migration and teacher attrition. Further analyses of the TFS migration data show that there is a strong flow of teachers from less desirable to more desirable schools. After controlling for the type of school, four factors stand

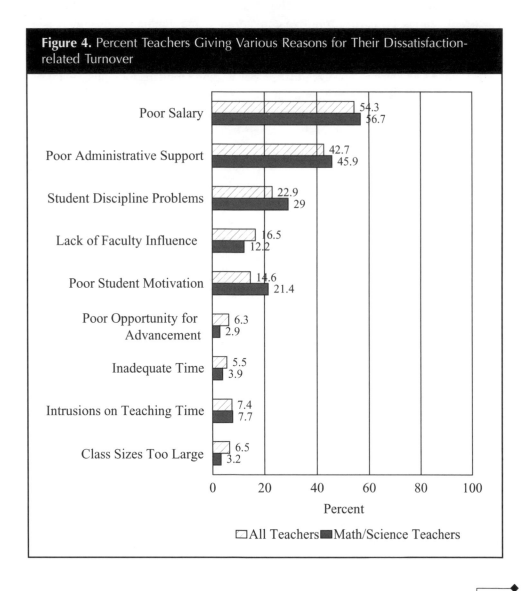

Figure 4. Percent Teachers Giving Various Reasons for Their Dissatisfaction-related Turnover

out as related to both teacher migration and attrition: schools with low salaries, student discipline problems, little support for new teachers, and little faculty input into school decision-making.

In sum, the data indicate that math/science teachers, like other teachers, depart their jobs for a variety of reasons. Retirement accounts for a relatively small number of total departures; a moderate number of departures are due to school staffing actions; a large proportion indicate they depart for personal reasons; and a large proportion also report they depart either because they are dissatisfied with their jobs or in order to seek better jobs or other career opportunities.

Implications

Since the early 1980s, educational policy analysts have predicted that shortfalls of teachers resulting primarily from two converging demographic trends—increasing student enrollments and increasing teacher retirements—would lead to problems staffing schools with qualified teachers and, in turn, lower educational performance.

This analysis indicates, however, that school staffing problems for neither math/science nor other teachers are solely, or even primarily, due to teacher shortfalls caused by increases in student enrollment or increases in teacher retirement. In contrast, the data suggest that large numbers of teachers depart teaching for reasons other than retirement, including job dissatisfaction and the desire to seek better jobs or other careers.

These findings have important implications for educational policy. Supply and demand theory holds that where the quantity of teachers demanded is greater than the quantity of teachers supplied, there are two basic policy remedies: increase the quantity supplied or decrease the quantity demanded. As noted in the beginning of this chapter, teacher recruitment, an example of the former approach, has been and continues to be a dominant approach to addressing school staffing inadequacies. However, this analysis suggests that recruitment programs alone will not solve the staffing problems of schools if they do not also address the problem of teacher retention. In short, recruiting more teachers will not solve staffing inadequacies if large numbers of those teachers then prematurely leave.

What then can be done? From the perspective of this analysis, schools are not simply victims of inexorable demographic trends, and there is a significant role for the management of schools in both the genesis of, and solution to, school staffing problems. Rather than increase the quantity of teacher supply, an alternative solution to school staffing problems, documented by this analysis, is to decrease the demand for new teachers by decreasing turnover. The data suggest that the way to improve teacher retention is to improve the conditions of the teaching job. In schools across the country, significantly lower levels of teacher turnover are found where there is more support from the school administration for new teachers, such as induction and mentoring programs. The same holds for schools with higher salaries, fewer student discipline problems, and enhanced faculty input into school decision-making. In short, if we could improve these aspects of schools, the result would be lower rates of turnover, which, in turn, would diminish school staffing problems and ultimately aid the performance of schools.

Appendix

Definitions of Measures of Reasons for Turnover

In the Teacher Follow-up Survey (TFS), teachers could list up to three choices from a list of 12 reasons for their departures. The 12 reasons are grouped into five categories, as follows:

1. Retirement
2. School Staffing Action (reduction-in-force/lay-off/school closing/reassignment)
3. Family or Personal (family or personal move; pregnancy/child rearing; health; other family or personal reasons)
4. To Pursue Other Job (to pursue another career; to take courses to improve career opportunities in or outside the field of education; for better teaching job)
5. Dissatisfaction (dissatisfied with teaching as a career; dissatisfied with the school; for better salary or benefits)

Those teachers who indicated dissatisfaction, as defined above, as a reason for their departure, could then list up to three choices from a list of 12 reasons for their dissatisfaction. I grouped the 12 reasons into nine categories, as follows:

1. Poor Salary
2. Poor Administrative Support (lack of recognition and support from administration; lack of resources and material/equipment for your classroom; inadequate support from administration)
3. Student Discipline Problems
4. Lack of Faculty Influence and Autonomy (lack of influence over school policies and practices; lack of control over own classroom)
5. Poor Student Motivation (poor student motivation to learn)
6. Poor Opportunity for Professional Advancement
7. Inadequate Time to Prepare (inadequate time to prepare lesson/teaching plans)
8. Intrusions on Teaching Time (intrusions on teaching time—that is, not enough time directly teaching students)
9. Class Sizes Too Large

References

Boe, E., S. Bobbitt, and L. Cook. 1997. Whither didst thou go? *Journal of Special Education* 30: 371–89.

Bureau of National Affairs. 1998. BNA's quarterly report on job absence and turnover. *Bulletin to Management*. Washington DC: Bureau of National Affairs.

Grissmer, D., and S. Kirby 1992. *Patterns of attrition among Indiana teachers, 1965-1987*. Santa Monica, CA: Rand.

Ingersoll, R. 1999. The problem of underqualified teachers in American secondary schools. *Educational Researcher* 28: 26–37. (Also on the American Educational Research Association website: *http://www.aera.net/pubs/er/arts/28-02/ingsoll01.htm*.)

———. 2001a. Misunderstanding the problem of out-of-field teaching. *Educational Researcher* 30(1): 21–22.

———. 2001b. Teacher turnover and teacher shortages: An organizational analysis. *American Educational Research Journal* 38(3): 499–534.

———. 2002. *Out-of-field teaching, educational inequality and the organization of schools: An exploratory analysis*. Seattle, WA: University of Washington, Center for the Study of Teaching and Policy.

Murnane, R., J. Singer, J. Willett, J. Kemple, and R. Olsen. 1991. *Who will teach? Policies that matter.* Cambridge, MA: Harvard University Press.

National Academy of Sciences. 1987. *Toward understanding teacher supply and demand.* Washington, DC: National Academy Press.

National Center for Education Statistics. 1995. *Teacher follow-up survey.* Washington, DC: U.S. Department of Education.

National Commission on Excellence in Education. 1983. *A nation at risk: The imperative for educational reform.* Washington, DC: Government Printing Office.

National Commission on Teaching and America's Future. 1997. *Doing what matters most: Investing in quality teaching.* New York: National Commission on Teaching and America's Future.

Comprehensive Teacher Induction in Five Countries: Implications for Supporting U.S. Science Teachers

Edward Britton and Senta Raizen

Edward Britton, associate director of the National Center for Improving Science Education at WestEd, was co-principal investigator of a recent National Science Foundation–funded study of teacher induction abroad and project director of an international study of high school exit examinations for mathematics and science. He contributed to the science curriculum component of the Third International Mathematics and Science Study and coordinated U.S. participation in an international study of innovations in mathematics and science education through the Organization of Economic Cooperation and Development. He started out in education by teaching science in a junior-senior high school.

Senta Raizen, director of the National Center for Improving Science Education at WestEd, led a National Science Foundation–funded study of teacher induction in other countries. She served on the international steering committee for the Third International Mathematics and Science Study (TIMSS) and co-authored major TIMSS reports. She was principal investigator for an international comparison of high school examinations in mathematics and science, and an international study of innovations in mathematics and science education. Raizen has edited or contributed to over 50 books and written more than 100 articles in the fields of science, mathematics, and technology education.

Educators around the world are realizing that helping new teachers learn more about teaching is an important investment, one that can yield enhanced instruction throughout a teacher's career. From interviews with many of our colleagues from the Third International Mathematics and Science Study (TIMSS), we learned that most had weak or no teacher induction programs in their countries; however, they had a rapidly growing conviction of the need to strengthen the learning of their beginning teachers. U.S. educators and policy makers are also beginning to get the message that novice teachers need more than just a two-day orientation workshop (Britton et al. 2000).

Some countries are ahead of the game in providing more comprehensive teacher induction. WestEd's National Center for Improving Science Education and Michigan State University examined how five countries—France, Japan, New Zealand, Switzerland, and China (specifically, the city of Shanghai)—provide new middle and high school science and mathematics teachers with substantial, ongoing support (Britton et al. 2002). The three-year study was funded by the National Science Foundation. All five countries have support systems for novice teachers that have been established for 10 or more years; New Zealand's system, which has been in place for 25 years, is the oldest among the five countries' systems.

Comprehensive Induction:
Meeting the Many Needs of Beginning Teachers

Addressing the many needs of beginning teachers requires a lot of effort, by a lot of people having different roles and expertise, using a variety of activities tailored to the novices' needs. This tall order is rarely filled around the world, even though research has long documented that novices come with a very wide range of needs. Most induction programs tackle only some kinds of needs—most commonly, helping to improve classroom management or orienting teachers to their school's facilities and procedures.

While induction systems in the studied countries also include the important kinds of support mentioned above, they go beyond support to offer the elements of comprehensive induction programs (as listed in Table 1). They also launch novice secondary teachers into early career learning; for example, they offer detailed understanding of how to plan and teach lessons in their subjects, how to assess student understanding, and how to work with parents. They also promote reflection on teaching, thereby encouraging continuous learning throughout a teacher's career.

Table 1 illustrates the distinctions between what we term "limited" and "comprehensive" teacher induction programs. It is obvious that to address effectively the many diverse needs of beginning teachers, education systems need to commit more effort, more resources, more participation by all sectors of the system, more kinds of people, more kinds of activities, more time in the year, and a longer period of time than traditional induction programs offer.

Illustrating Comprehensive Induction:
School-based Induction in New Zealand

The universal experience of beginning teachers is to encounter pitfalls at every turn. But in many New Zealand schools, beginning science teachers also find help in every direction (Britton, Raizen, and Huntley 2002). New Zealand's national ministry of education requires that schools give first-year teachers 20 percent paid release time, and the ministry provides the funds for it. Typically, that means new teachers are assigned four classes rather than five, which gives them three to five more free periods a week than their more experienced colleagues. In 2002, the government strengthened the induction program by extending 10 percent release time to second-year teachers. And unlike in the United States, new teachers in New Zealand are usually not assigned to the most difficult classes. In addition, all schools in New Zealand must develop an Advice and Guidance (AG) program for their first- and second-year teachers (Moskowitz and Kennedy 1997; Teacher Registration Board 1993, 1997).

Table 1. Key Features of Limited versus Comprehensive Teacher Induction Programs

Program Feature	Limited Induction	Comprehensive Induction
Goals	Focuses on teacher orientation, support, enculturation, retention	Also promotes career learning, enhances teaching quality
Policies	Provides optional participation and modest time, usually unpaid	Requires participation and provides substantial, paid time
Overall program design	Employs limited number of ad hoc induction providers and activities	Plans an induction system involving a complementary set of providers and activities
Induction as a transitional phase	Treats induction as an isolated phase, without explicit attention to teachers' prior knowledge or future development	Considers influence of teacher preparation and professional development on induction program design
Initial teaching conditions	Pays limited attention to initial teaching conditions	Pays attention to assigned courses, students, non-teaching duties
Level of effort	Invests limited total effort, or all effort, in few providers, activities	Requires substantial overall effort
Resources	Does not provide resources sufficient to meet program goals	Provides resources sufficient to meet program goals
Levels of education system involved	Involves some levels of the system, perhaps in isolation	Involves all relevant levels of system in articulated roles
Length of program	One year or less	More than one year
Sources of support	Primarily or solely uses one mentor	Uses multiple, complementary induction providers
Conditions for novices/ providers	Usually attends to learning conditions for novices	Also provides conditions and training for providers
Activities	Uses a few types of induction activities	Uses a set of articulated, varied activities

Figure 1 illustrates that beginning teachers in New Zealand receive help from many sources, especially within their schools but also from outside. Novice science teachers are assigned one primary mentor, usually the science department head. Department heads formally and informally observe beginners' classes, hold one-on-one meetings with them, permit beginners to observe their teaching, arrange for novices to observe other teachers, and alert them to professional development opportunities outside the school.

Every school has an AG coordinator, usually a deputy principal, who is the novices' second main source of support. As administrators, the coordinators have flexible schedules that allow them to meet with beginning teachers for one-on-one meetings whenever the novices have free periods. Coordinators also bring together new teachers on a regular basis, typically every two weeks, to grapple with whatever practical, emotional, or other needs the teachers are facing. Thus, beginning teachers help each other through these facilitated peer support meetings.

Buddy teachers usually are another secondary source of support, and their roles vary. Some buddy teachers help substantively—for example, by observing novices' classes and offering advice. But they can also provide more basic assistance. As one coordinator noted, "I assign a buddy teacher who lives nearby and can give them a ride if need be, bring some work home to them if they're sick, etc."

Although not a formal part of the induction program, other staff members in New Zealand schools also support beginning teachers; these include other science teachers, science department laboratory technicians, and teachers in other subjects. The most common way that other science teachers help is through informal means such as conversations at "interval" and lunchtime. All secondary schools have a 15–20-minute interval in the morning when the entire school faculty comes to the faculty lounge for coffee and refreshments while the pupils have a recess. In our school visits, it appeared that over 90 percent of the teachers regularly show up for these collective breaks. As a result, new teachers have a chance to briefly discuss anything on their minds with virtually any other teacher. A similar phenomenon occurs at lunchtime, although less so because attendance is lower (about 50–80 percent). Beyond the school, regional science advisors and leaders of workshops or short courses at colleges and universities also aid novices.

The following comments by one second-year teacher illustrate the support found by novices in New Zealand.

Four people were especially helpful last year. Dorothy [her department head] was brilliant. Any questions and I'd go straight in and ask, and she was happy to answer. I still do. The second person was Glenda [her buddy teacher], the biology teacher next door. She was the first line of attack because she was next door. I'd run across to her and she was full of advice. The third was Irene, who helped me with astronomy and geology. Mr. Hastings [her AG coordinator] absolutely was looking out for me, and the meetings he ran for all of us [begin-

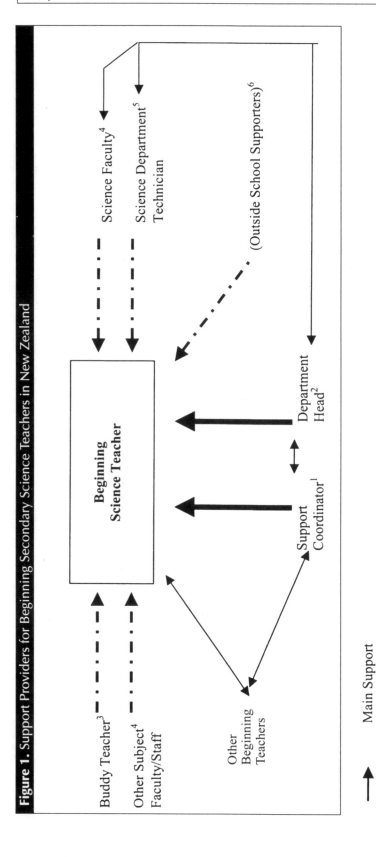

Figure 1. Support Providers for Beginning Secondary Science Teachers in New Zealand

Buddy Teacher[3]

Other Subject[4] Faculty/Staff

Science Faculty[4]

Science Department[5] Technician

(Outside School Supporters)[6]

Beginning Science Teacher

Department Head[2]

Support Coordinator[1]

Other Beginning Teachers

Common Interactions Between Support Providers

Main Support
Additional Support

REQUIRED
REQUIRED
OPTIONAL
UNOFFICIAL
UNOFFICIAL
OPTIONAL

[1] Usually a deputy principal.
[2] Sometimes an experienced teacher.
[3] Often an accomplished, early career teacher.
[4] Usually through faculty coffee breaks, department meetings, or impromptu interactions.
[5] Depends on disposition of science department lab technician.
[6] Science teachers in other schools, regional advisors, workshops, courses.

ning teachers in the school] were really valuable. Officially, Dorothy and Glenda were assigned to me by Mr. Hastings. But with Irene, it just turned out that she was a lot of help to me too.

One aspect of the New Zealand educational system that makes beginning teacher support programs effective is a commitment throughout the educational system to beginning teacher support. Players at all levels of the system assume that new teachers have particular needs and, therefore, that the system must pay explicit attention to addressing them. Many new teachers state that they feel free to approach most anyone in their department for advice. For example, new teachers feel they can ask other teachers to drop in to see how they teach some specific topic or activity. This strong culture of support makes it easier to implement beginning teacher support programs and activities.

In all five countries studied, induction programs coordinated support from multiple sources. Most support in New Zealand was within-schools because there are no school districts in the country; each school interacts directly with the national ministry of education. In other countries, school districts, district or regional professional development centers, and/or teacher preparation institutions also played a strong role in teacher induction. Such induction systems are organizationally complex, requiring coordination and articulation of induction activities across multiple levels of the education system.

Developing Science Courses, Lessons, and Hands-on Instruction

The general nature of the language of New Zealand's national science curriculum framework affords schools wide latitude in specifying the detailed topics to be taught and how to teach them. School science departments must devise their own agreements on the curriculum of each science course, particularly in the lower secondary grades (eight and nine). Departments, for each science unit, compile and continually update instructional ideas and resources, or even lesson plans. However, teachers have the freedom to choose among the available lessons and resources, and also to create their own. Textbooks generally play a very minor role in most New Zealand science classrooms, serving as an infrequently used class resource rather than daily medium of instruction.

The quality and amount of a department's course specifications and locally developed curricular resources are strong influences on all teachers—and particularly on the new teacher. A strong syllabus and ample resources lay out an instructional course of action for beginning teachers and equip them to deliver it. In other schools, the yearlong course specifications are less detailed, necessitating that new teachers work on their own or in collaboration with others to flesh them out. Departments also vary in the extent to which details are on hand for how to teach the topics (e.g., what activities to use, what resources are available). Smaller science departments found in smaller schools, particularly rural schools, find it more challenging to marshal such specific curricular guides. Any new teacher entering a school as its lone science teacher would be extremely hard-pressed to create a strong science course if his or her predecessor did not leave one behind.

The New Zealand science curriculum emphasizes investigation through hands-on experiences, referred to as "practicals." Hands-on science is emphasized particularly in the integrated science courses of grades eight to ten. Over 80 percent of the lessons we observed engaged pupils in activities during 70–95 percent of the class period. Coping with active learning in hands-on science adds layers of complexity to the general learning challenge of a beginning teacher. For example, it requires learning how to effectively use science supplies and apparatus with pupils, which is quite different from how teachers used them in their college science courses. Fortunately, the existence of science laboratory technicians in New Zealand schools reduces the need to learn how to acquire and assemble supplies and to spend time doing this. Even so, the following comments by a deputy principal express a common perception that beginning science teachers have a lot to learn about teaching science:

> It's important to remember that the universal experience of new teachers of needing more time is compounded for new science teachers. They have to become familiar with new materials, equipment, facilities, etc., needed for the practicals. Teachers need to run experiments themselves beforehand if they aren't familiar with them in order to see what happens.

Implications for Supporting U.S. Science Teachers

1. *Help beginners with planning science courses and lessons.* Planning one or a few sample science units during even an excellent preservice program cannot fully prepare beginning science teachers for the entirety of planning science courses and lessons. Remember that beginners are asking the following questions for the first time: Exactly what science topics will I teach tomorrow, next week, and next month, and how will I teach them? On my first day of teaching (Britton), I asked my principal just what science topics to teach for each of the five science courses that he had assigned to me. His only answer was to hand me a pile of textbooks. None of the other four science teachers offered any guidance.

   Support providers need to help novices determine the details of the science curriculum for a semester or yearlong course (or, worse yet, several courses), the lessons that would best fulfill unit goals, what school resources are available for them, and the strengths and weaknesses of the students they are teaching. Induction programs sometimes fail to include such teacher learning, incorrectly assuming that when it comes to a secondary teacher's subject, no help is needed.

   Beginners' needs for help in developing their science curriculum may be particularly acute in these types of schools: (a) small schools where they are one of a few science teachers or the only one; (b) larger schools where the science departments leave almost all curriculum and lesson planning to individual teachers;

(c) schools with poorly prepared students; and (d) textbook-oriented schools where dependence on texts can deter implementation of inquiry-oriented teaching.

2. *Help beginners learn about instructional resources and methods for inquiry-based teaching.* If U.S. science education is ever to fulfill the vision of inquiry teaching called for by the National Science Education Standards, induction programs will need to help new science teachers get started. If class time is to be spent on *doing* science in addition to knowing science facts, more time and effort will have to be spent on how to prepare, execute, and follow up inquiry-based lessons. That's a tremendous challenge for a new science teacher. Since U.S. schools do not have science department laboratory technicians like those in New Zealand (and other countries such as Australia and the U.K.), who is going to help novice science teachers accomplish this?

3. *Avoid being the lone support provider.* If you participate in an induction program that formally assigns the entire responsibility for mentoring a beginning teacher to you, recognize that you inherently have been charged with something that is rarely attainable. Given the very wide range of beginning teachers' needs, why would one expect a single individual to have the background, experiences, and personality that can be effective for addressing them all? Make a list of all your novice's needs, including subject-specific issues, and decide which ones you have the background or circumstances to address. Try to enlist, informally if need be, additional faculty or administrators who can better address the other needs in coordination with you.

   If the design of the induction program in your school or district makes it difficult to enlist others, at least strike a balance among your expectations of what you are likely and unlikely to achieve. Take encouragement from knowing that whatever you are able to do will help novices' early career learning much better than if they had to go it alone. Don't avoid the charge because the scope of it seems overwhelming. Identify the most important, doable strategies, and dive in.

4. *Promote a faculty culture of supporting beginning teachers.* Related to the previous suggestion, while the strong colleague culture among faculty in New Zealand schools is rather rare in U.S. schools, consider prodding your peers toward such a mindset and environment. Do not view this suggestion as adding yet one more item to the already long list of support provider activities. Whatever successes you have in promoting a supportive culture will only benefit your ability to carry out your own work in supporting novices, since more colleagues will be inclined to help you.

5. *Don't overlook the role of peer support.* Facilitated peer support activities strongly meet some beginners' needs that cannot be addressed well by mentors. Among the many types of support activities we encountered in New Zealand, we were struck by the importance of "facilitated peer support." We use this term for the frequent meetings when administrators convene all the beginning teachers in the school or the special day(s) when the regional advisory service convenes beginning teachers from many schools.

In our study of Swiss science teacher induction, we encountered another version of facilitated peer support (Raizen, Huntley, and Britton 2002). School districts organized regular "practice groups" of beginning teachers from different schools, where counselors facilitated the novices' problem solving around substantive teaching issues they were encountering. The counselors are carefully selected and extensively trained; providing professional development for support providers is an aspect of the induction system that was surprisingly weak in New Zealand and some other countries' induction systems. In the Swiss approach, novices also visited each other's schools to observe and provide feedback on their peers' teaching, as did their experienced teacher-mentors.

The U.S. field of teacher induction often places an emphasis on providing support through experienced teachers who use mentoring or other induction activities. However, the facilitated peer support activities in New Zealand and Switzerland address important needs that those other induction strategies are less able to fulfill—providing opportunities for beginners to more candidly express their needs and describe their experiences. Further, meeting with peers in other subjects enriches novices' perspectives about several aspects of teaching. Meetings in which teachers come from different schools provide even more safety for disclosure than the within-school meetings. The exchanges about induction experiences also diversify the participants' expectations of the kinds of support they might request or expect from their other support providers.

References

Britton, E., L. Paine, D. Pimm, and S. Raizen. 2002. *Comprehensive teacher induction: Systems for early career learning.* Dordrecht, Netherlands and San Francisco: Kluwer Academic Publishers and WestEd.

Britton, E., L. Paine, S. Raizen, and M. Huntley. 2000. *More swimming, less sinking.* Paper prepared for the National Commission on Mathematics and Science Teaching for the 21st Century. San Francisco: WestEd.

Britton, E., S. Raizen, and M. Huntley. 2002. Help in every direction: Supporting beginning science teachers in New Zealand. In *Comprehensive teacher induction: Systems for early career learning.* Dordrecht, Netherlands and San Francisco: Kluwer Academic Publishers and WestEd.

Moskowitz, J., and S. Kennedy. 1997. Teacher induction in an era of educational reform: the case of New Zealand. In *From students of teaching to teachers of induction around the Pacific Rim*, eds. J. Moskowitz and S. Kennedy, 131–68. Washington, DC: Department of Education.

Raizen, S., M. Huntley, and E. Britton. 2002. Collegial cooperation and reflective practice: Swiss induction programs. In *Comprehensive teacher induction: Systems for early career learning.* Dordrecht, Netherlands and San Francisco: Kluwer Academic Publishers and WestEd.

Teacher Registration Board. 1993. *Advice and guidance programmes for teachers.* Wellington, New Zealand: Teacher Registration Board.

———. 1997. *Information for newly registered teachers.* Wellington, New Zealand: Teacher Registration Board.

A Review of Literature on the Mentoring and Induction of Beginning Teachers with an Emphasis on the Retention and Renewal of Science Teachers

Brenda S. Wojnowski, Mary Louise Bellamy, and Sharon Cooke

Brenda S. Wojnowski is the associate director of The Science House at North Carolina State University. The Science House is the educational outreach arm of the College of Physical and Mathematical Sciences at North Carolina State University. The mission of The Science House is to build partnerships between the University and K–12 schools and school systems. Dr. Wojnowski is a former award-winning teacher who has conducted numerous professional development experiences for teachers, administrators, and university faculty. She has received funding from a variety of sources, including the National Science Foundation and the U.S. Department of Education, and has given many presentations at professional meetings and conferences on topics ranging from science education, to equity issues, to partnership building. Her doctoral dissertation concerned the mentoring of beginning teachers.

Mary Louise Bellamy is the K–12 educational outreach coordinator for the National Science Foundation's Science and Technology Center for the Study of Environmentally Responsible Solvents and Processes, The Science House, North Carolina State University. She is a former teacher and former education director of the National Association of Biology Teachers. Bellamy has authored and edited numerous articles and books.

Sharon Cooke is a retired high school teacher and a graduate research assistant for the National Science Foundation's Science and Technology Center for the Study of Environmentally Responsible Solvents and Processes, The Science House, North Carolina State University.

The growing number of teachers leaving the profession before retirement is a significant cause of teacher turnover and subsequent teacher vacancies. Compounding this situation is the fact that top undergraduates … who become teachers are more likely than their peers to leave teaching in three to five years. In addition, analysis of data … indicates that teachers who have not participated in induction or mentoring programs during their first few years of teaching, are twice as likely as those who have participated to leave after their first three years of teaching. The shortage of [science] teachers is more severe than it is in other areas, making [science] teacher retention a national priority.

(National Science Foundation 2001, 33–34)

This work was supported in part by the STC Program and the Division of Biological Infrastructure of the National Science Foundation under Agreement No. CHE-9876674 and Award No. DBI-0115642. Any opinions, findings, and conclusions or recommendations expressed in this material are those of the authors and do not necessarily reflect the views of the National Science Foundation.

A number of recent reports point to the lack of achievement and understanding in science among pre-college students in the United States. Two of the most notable, *What Matters Most: Teaching for America's Future* (National Commission on Teaching and America's Future 1996) and *Before It's Too Late: A Report to the Nation from the National Commission on Mathematics and Science Teaching for the 21st Century* (National Commission on Mathematics and Science Teaching 2000) reach the same conclusion: The only way to combat the problem of low student achievement is to improve the quality of science teaching in America's schools.

The report *What Matters Most* explicitly states: "Student learning in this country will improve only when we focus our efforts on improved teaching" (6). In *Before It's Too Late,* the problem is described as follows: "In an age now driven by the relentless necessity of scientific and technological advance, the preparation our students receive in … science is, in a word, unacceptable" (10). The report goes on to call for changes in science teaching in order to address the problems of student achievement in this critical area. It concludes that the "need for high-quality teaching … demands a vigorous, national response that unifies the efforts of all stakeholders in … science education" (24).

Mentoring and Induction Programs as a Means of Improving Teaching

In *Local Leadership for Science Education Reform,* Anderson and Pratt (1995) describe the problem of teacher isolation as it relates to school reform and, hence, student achievement. They feel that the customary isolation among teachers found in most school cultures acts to inhibit the change process. The effects of isolation are well documented in mentoring and induction educational literature. (See, in chronological order, Lortie 1975; Grant and Zeichner 1981; Pataniczek and Isaacson 1981; Egan 1986a; Huffman and Leak 1986; Huling-Austin 1986; Zaharias and Frew 1987.)

In his landmark study described in *A Place Called School,* Goodlad (1984), like Anderson and Pratt, described the isolation in which teachers work and their lack of opportunity for collaborative efforts with their peers. He felt that America's schools must endeavor to improve the conditions under which teachers labor if the nation is to upgrade its schools.

Many current references call for effective mentoring and induction programs for beginning teachers as a way to improve teacher-teacher interaction and reduce isolation, especially among early career teachers. The report *Building a Profession: Strengthening Teacher Preparation and Induction* by the American Federation of Teachers (2000) cites the need for induction programs "for all beginning teachers" (10). Plummer and Barrow (1998) and the National Commission on Mathematics and Science Teaching for the 21st Century (2000) agree that beginning teachers are especially in need of the support that can be provided through a formal induction program. *Before It's Too Late* (National Commission on Mathematics and Science Teaching 2000) goes on to advocate "formal mentoring relationships" as part of these programs (33). Likewise, in order for positive change in teacher preparation and professional development to occur, *What Matters Most* (National Commission on Teaching and America's Future 1996) calls for the creation of "mentoring programs for beginning teachers that provide support and evaluate teaching skills" (20).

In the current U.S. education climate, it is especially important to support teachers who are new to a school and those new to the profession because they will represent such a large percentage of the overall teaching force. "Over the next decade [1999-2009], America will need to hire some 200,000 K–12 teachers annually, a staggering hiring demand" (Fideler and Haselkorn 1999, 4). According to Darling-Hammond (1997), "the nation has never before hired as many teachers in a decade as it will between [1997] and the year 2007. The demand for teachers will continue to grow sharply as student enrollments reach their highest level ever, and teacher retirements and attrition create large numbers of vacancies" (15).

Difficulties Associated with the Early Years of Teaching

The first year of teaching is widely recognized as an extremely difficult and traumatizing experience for many beginning teachers (Grant and Zeichner 1981; Hawley 1986; Hoffman et al. 1986). Gold (1996) describes the critical nature of the first year of teaching: "Few experiences in life have such a tremendous impact on the personal and professional life of a teacher as does the first year of teaching" (548). The initial year in the profession can be a time of intense distress during which neophytes face harsh situations and potentially overwhelming problems while functioning in a state of isolation (Pataniczek and Isaacson 1981).

Too often beginning teachers are expected to enter the teaching profession with a complete repertoire of teaching skills (Fagan and Walter 1982). "Fully responsible for the instruction of his students from his first working day, the beginning teacher performs the same tasks as the twenty-five year veteran. Tasks are not added sequentially to allow for gradual increase in skill and knowledge.... If it is true that too much anxiety retards learning, some beginning teachers will have difficulty making accurate perceptions and thoughtful decisions" (Lortie 1975, 72) during the critical induction period when they will be shaping the attitudes, skills, and strategies that will govern their entire teaching careers (Egan 1986b; Grant and Zeichner 1981).

What Matters Most (National Commission on Teaching and America's Future 1996) defines the problems beginning teachers face in this way: "Beginning teachers ... are typically given the most difficult assignments and left to flounder on their own, without the kind of help provided by internships in other professions. Isolated behind classroom doors with little feedback or help, as many as 30% leave in the first few years, while others learn merely to cope rather than to teach well" (14). Berliner (1988) describes how teachers become better at their profession the longer they teach. He details five stages of teacher career development: novice, advanced beginner, competent teacher, proficient teacher, and expert. According to Berliner, a teacher is not likely to reach the level of competence until the third year of teaching. If a teacher does not stay with the profession long enough to achieve this level of competence, then students are constantly being taught by individuals in the early stages of career development. The logical outcome is that, over time, the achievement and understanding of students taught by these early career teachers will suffer.

Plummer and Barrow (1998) report an escalating continuum of attrition from 1965 through 1998 associated with the difficult circumstances of the early years of teaching. Middle and high school teachers need special support during their early years of teaching (Fideler and Haselkorn 1999; Gold 1996). According to Fideler and Haselkorn (1999), "Teachers new to working with high school and inner-city students in schools with large numbers of minority and lower income students are especially prone to attrition. This effectively ensures that students in the nation's most challenging classrooms will continue to get its least qualified teachers" (4).

Veenman (1984) compiled a comprehensive review of literature detailing the needs of beginning teachers. These needs include generic pedagogical knowledge and skills, such as classroom discipline and management. Gold (1996) goes on to say that although beginning teachers need help in developing these essential early career survival skills, they also need help in developing pedagogical content knowledge (PCK). The term *pedagogical content knowledge* was originally defined by L. Shulman (1986) as "the most useful forms of representation (of ideas in a discipline), the most powerful analogies, illustrations, examples, explanations, and demonstrations—in a word, the ways of representing and formulating the subject that makes it comprehensible to others" (9). (The definition of PCK has since been broadened to include other aspects of teacher knowledge; see Cochran, DeRuiter, and King 1993.)

Gold (1996) explicitly concludes, "To limit the majority of the instructional support to these [early survival] needs fails to provide the beginning teacher with an understanding of the more complex nature of the structure of knowledge and the process of acquiring pedagogical content knowledge that is needed" (562).

Types of Educational Mentoring

According to Loucks-Horsley et al. (1998), "reflection by an individual on his or her own practice can be enhanced by another's observations and perceptions.... [B]y simply holding up a mirror, a coach or mentor can bring to consciousness some useful information for teachers with regard to their practice" (127).

Traditional Mentoring

Mentoring is certainly not a new idea. In Homer's *Odyssey*, Odysseus assigned the care of his young son, Telemachus, to his friend, Mentor. The recent revival of interest in mentoring can be traced to the work of Erickson (1950) and Levinson et al. (1978) in their classic studies, *Childhood and Society* and *The Seasons of a Man's Life,* respectively.

Mentoring is currently making significant inroads in many areas of education in large part because of the need to reduce teacher isolation and retain new teachers. Mentoring relationships often develop informally. However, because "we need mentors throughout our lifelong journey" (Darling 1989, 12), institutions sometimes initiate formal planned mentoring programs to fill the void often left by informal unplanned mentoring. According to Ganser (1996), "Mentor relationships can emerge naturally, but teacher isolation makes this unlikely for many new teachers. Mentor programs must assure that mentoring is not left to chance" (9).

According to Guskey (2000) and Loucks-Horsley et al. (1998), a mentoring relationship typically involves matching an experienced teacher with a less experienced one. Loucks-Horsley et al. (1998) specifically refer to the mentoring relationship of beginning science teachers in this way: "Mentors in science ... programs are typically teachers with more content knowledge or experience in using a particular program or practice who work with those less experienced" (127).

Collegial Mentoring

Collegial mentoring, often referred to as peer coaching, consists of pairs of teachers who work together toward a common goal: improving their educational practices. Collegial mentoring differs from other forms of mentoring in that it exists between equals (Anderson and Pratt 1995). Collegial mentoring can be invaluable when an experienced teacher changes jobs or grade levels (Egan 1986a; Recruiting New Teachers, Inc. 2000; Shulman, J. 1988).

Each member of the coaching pair has the benefit of a colleague to provide reflective feedback on his or her progress and to offer positive support for his or her efforts (George 1989; Joyce and Showers 1982; Krajewski and McCumsey 1984). At the same time, "opportunities provided for professional teacher growth by means of collegial support alleviate classroom isolation, which can be detrimental to teacher satisfaction and development" (Taylor 1987, 27).

Professional Development Mentoring

Training for academic mentoring usually takes the form of professional development. To be effective, professional development activities must be targeted to the needs and concerns of the participants, as well as to the innovation under discussion—in this case, mentoring (Hall and Loucks 1978). According to Guskey (2000), "the mentoring model of professional development typically involves pairing an experienced and highly successful educator with a less experienced colleague" (28). The National Research Council's *National Science Education Standards* (1996) discusses the need for such interactions among science teachers in particular: "Professional development activities must: Support the sharing of teacher expertise by preparing and using mentors ... to provide professional development opportunities" (68).

Characteristics of Good Mentoring/Induction Programs

How should mentoring and induction programs be structured to provide the most valuable support for new teachers? Based on research and the expertise of those working in this field, characteristics of effective mentoring and induction programs have been identified.

- An induction program should span more than one year and address the changing needs of teachers as they grow professionally (Fideler and Haselkorn 1999; Recruiting New Teachers, Inc. 2000).
- "Beginning teachers should be placed in situations that are appropriate to their novice status so they will have the opportunity to develop fully as teaching professionals," according to the California Commission on Teacher Credentialing (1997, 10).
  - Beginning teachers should be given reasonable teaching schedules and should not be assigned the hardest students to teach (National Commission on Mathematics and Science Teaching 2000).
  - Beginning teachers should be given fewer extracurricular duties than are assigned to experienced teachers (National Commission on Mathematics and Science Teaching 2000).
- Effective mentoring should be an integral part of any induction program (Fideler and Haselkorn 1999). The mentoring program should include the following elements:
  - Mentors should be identified carefully (American Federation of Teachers 2000; Recruiting New Teachers, Inc. 2000) and should be able to interact effectively with other teachers (Recruiting New Teachers, Inc. 2000). Guskey (2000) indicates that mentors need to be experienced and excellent teachers. "The best mentors have great credibility among their colleagues and are recognized for their ability to initiate curriculum and school change. They are also highly competent in their subject area and respected by students" (28).
  - Mentors should receive appropriate and sufficient training in order to be effective in supporting new teachers (American Federation of Teachers 2000; Fideler and Haselkorn 1999; Recruiting New Teachers, Inc. 2000; Loucks-Horsley et al. 1998). According to the California Commission on Teacher Credentialing (1997), "excellent teachers are not necessarily prepared to help others develop professionally" (15). Consequently, Ganser (1996) describes knowledge and skills that mentors need to learn during training in order to be effective. The areas of *knowledge* include (1) concerns of beginning teachers; (2) stages of teacher career development; (3) how adults learn; (4) how beginning teachers have been prepared in preservice programs; and (5) innovative curriculum and teaching strategies. The *skills* mentors need to learn, according to Ganser, include (1) conferencing skills, (2) observation skills, and (3) problem-solving skills. (See also *A Guide to Developing Teacher Induction Programs* [Recruiting New Teachers, Inc. 2000, 25] for knowledge and skills mentors need.)
  - The mentoring process should begin before school starts, with mentors and mentees meeting before the beginning teachers are actually responsible for their own classrooms (Ganser 1996; Recruiting New Teachers, Inc. 2000).

- Loucks-Horsley et al. (1998) maintain that "For coaching and mentoring to succeed as strategies for professional development, several key elements must be in place ... A Focus for Learning or Improvement ... Mechanisms for Sharing and Feedback... [and] ... Opportunities for Interaction" (128). Mentors (American Federation of Teachers 2000; Fideler and Haselkorn 1999; Recruiting New Teachers, Inc. 2000) and early career teachers (California Commission on Teacher Credentialing 1997) should be given adequate time to meet with each other and observe each other teaching. According to the California Commission on Teacher Credentialing (1997), "support providers/assessors and beginning teachers [should be] given dedicated time in the form of released time, reduced teaching load, and/or joint planning periods to work together" (20).
  - Mentors should be compensated for their work with beginning teachers (American Federation of Teachers 2000; Recruiting New Teachers, Inc. 2000).
- Teachers should have access to and support in computer technologies, including communication resources such as e-mail (Fideler and Haselkorn 1999; Recruiting New Teachers, Inc. 2000). They should be given needed instruction in the use of these resources in their classrooms (National Commission on Mathematics and Science Teaching 2000).

The importance of these elements of mentoring and induction is summarized in *Building a Profession: Strengthening Teacher Preparation and Induction* (American Federation of Teachers 2000): "No package of teacher education reforms can be expected to ensure a continuing supply of qualified teachers unless it is coupled with high-caliber induction programs, better salaries and improved working conditions" (15).

Barriers to Successful Mentoring/Induction Programs

Although mentoring and induction programs have become widespread in the United States in recent years, significant barriers to their effectiveness exist and often prevent such programs from being as successful as they could be. While it is beyond the scope of this article to provide an exhaustive review of the literature, some of these barriers include:

- Lack of mentors, time, and professional development (Phillips-Jones 1989; Woodruff 1990);
- Inadequate and unpredictable funding (Fideler and Haselkorn 1999; Recruiting New Teachers, Inc. 2000); and
- The traditional culture of most schools. "Norms of isolation and privacy work against many teachers' willingness to open their classrooms and their teaching to observation and scrutiny" (Loucks-Horsley et al. 1998, 131).

Positive Outcomes of Mentoring/Induction Programs

Research evidence shows three important positive outcomes associated with mentoring and/or induction programs:

- Improvement of the teaching practices of new teachers
- Benefits to the mentor as well as to the beginning teacher
- Lowering of attrition rates for new teachers

Research data provide evidence that mentoring experiences can help early career teachers improve their teaching practices. Citing Giebelhaus and Bowman (2000), Holloway (2001) states: "Data analysis indicated that prospective teachers who were assigned mentors trained in using [a] discussion framework demonstrated more complete and effective planning, more effective classroom instruction, and a higher level of reflection on practice than did new teachers whose mentors had received only an orientation program. The researchers concluded that formal induction program models … provide a framework for discussion, reflection, and goal setting and lead to more effective teaching by novices" (8).

Gold's 1996 article on beginning teacher support programs reported that the attrition rate of beginning teachers who were mentored was appreciably lower than the rate for their nonmentored peers. Loucks-Horsley (1999) stated, "[R]esearch indicates that effective mentoring programs can lower the attrition rate of new teachers, significantly decreasing the length and trauma of their induction period into the profession" (26).

Guskey (2000) maintains that the mentoring experience benefits both the mentor and the protégé. Research evidence from studies reported by Scott (1999), Hegstad (1999), and Holloway (2001) supports Guskey's assertion. "A focused, systematic mentoring program has a positive influence on the performance of new teachers—and is advantageous to mentors as well. Above all, this support for new teachers benefits their students" (Holloway 2001, 9).

How Mentoring/Induction Experiences Can Meet the Needs of Science Teachers

The characteristics of effective mentoring and induction programs described earlier are important to all early career teachers, including science teachers, as they learn to teach in reform-based ways. As discussed earlier, Gold (1996) states that beginning teachers need help not only with survival skills that include classroom management, but also with increasing their pedagogical content knowledge (PCK). Mentors are an important source of this knowledge (Loucks-Horsley et al. 1998).

Characteristics and development of PCK are described by Cochran (1997): "[P]edagogical content knowledge is highly specific to the concepts being taught, is much more than just subject matter knowledge alone, and develops over time as a result of teaching experience" (2). Loucks-Horsley et al. (1998) describe the importance of PCK in the teaching mentoring relationship in this way: "The critical and specialized knowledge that experienced teachers have—pedagogical content knowledge—is [the very knowledge] that helps teachers understand what their students need, how they come to understand certain concepts and principles of the content, and what they need to increase that understanding. Sharing this kind of expertise is at the core of coaching and mentoring" (128).

The importance of the PCK of the mentor strongly suggests that the mentor and the early career teacher should teach the same content area. Loucks-Horsley et al. (1998) support this suggestion: "[T]he more a coach or mentor understands about the content being taught and knows from experience how students learn it (and how to teach it), the better. Although good coaches and mentors can help teachers become more reflective in their practice, and better inquirers into problems and dilemmas of teaching, they can be of much greater assistance if they know the specific content being taught by the teachers with whom they are working" (129). Beginning science teachers, therefore, benefit the most by being paired with excellent mentors who are also science teachers.

References

American Federation of Teachers. 2000. *Building a profession: Strengthening teacher preparation and induction.* Report of the K–16 Teacher Education Task Force. Washington, DC: American Federation of Teachers.

Anderson, R. D., and H. Pratt. 1995. *Local leadership for science education reform.* Dubuque, IA: Kendall/Hunt.

Berliner, D. C. 1988. *Implications of studies of expertise in pedagogy for teacher education and evaluation.* Paper presented at the 1988 Educational Testing Service Invitational Conference on New Directions for Teacher Assessment, New York City.

California Commission on Teacher Credentialing. 1997. *Standards of quality and effectiveness for beginning teacher support and assessment programs: A description of professional induction for beginning teachers.* Sacramento, CA: State of California.

Cochran, K. F. 1997. *Pedagogical content knowledge: Teachers' integration of subject matter, pedagogy, students, and learning environments.* Research Matters—to the Science Teacher No. 9702. National Association of Research in Science Teaching (NARST) publication.

Cochran, K. F., J. A. DeRuiter, and R. A. King. 1993. Pedagogical content knowing: An integrative model for teacher preparation. *Journal of Teacher Education* 44: 263–72.

Darling, L. W. 1989. The mentoring discovery process: Helping people manage their mentoring. *Mentoring International* 3(2): 12–16.

Darling-Hammond, L. 1997. *Doing what matters most: Investing in quality teaching.* Kutztown, PA: National Commission on Teaching and America's Future.

Egan, J. B. 1986a. Characteristics of classroom teachers' mentor-protégé relationships. In *Proceedings of the First International Conference on Mentoring* (Vol. 1), eds. M. M. Gray and W. A. Gray, 55–62. Vancouver, B.C., Canada: International Centre for Mentoring.

———. 1986b. *Induction the natural way: Informal mentoring.* Paper presented at the Eleventh Annual National Council of States on Inservice Education, Nashville, Tennessee, November 21–25, 1986. (ERIC Document Reproduction Service No. ED 275656.)

Erickson, E. 1950. *Childhood and society.* New York: Norton.

Fagan, M. M., and G. Walter. 1982. Mentoring among teachers. *Journal of Educational Research* 76(2): 113–18.

Fideler, E., and D. Haselkorn. 1999. *Learning the ropes: Urban teacher induction programs and practices in the United States.* Retrieved January 16, 2002, from Belmont, MA: Recruiting New Teachers, Inc. website: *http://www.mt.org/publications/ropes.html*

Ganser, T. 1996. Preparing mentors of beginning teachers: An overview for staff developers [Electronic version]. *Journal of Staff Development* 17: 8–11.

George, M. 1989. Maximizing the experience of mentor teachers: An evolving process. *Mentoring International* 3(2): 21–24.

Gold, Y. 1996. Beginning teacher support: Attrition, mentoring, and induction. In *Handbook of research on teacher education* (2nd ed.), eds. J. Sikula, T. J. Buttery and E. Guyton, 548–94. New York: Macmillan.

Goodlad, J. I. 1984. *A place called school*. New York: McGraw-Hill.

Grant, C. A., and K. M. Zeichner. 1981. Inservice support for first year teachers: The state of the scene. *Journal of Research and Development in Education* 14(2): 99–110.

Guskey, T. R. 2000. *Evaluating professional development*. Thousand Oaks, CA: Corwin Press.

Hall, G., and S. Loucks. 1978. Teacher concerns as a basis for facilitating and personalizing staff development. *Teachers College Record* 80(1): 36–53.

Hawley, W. D. 1986. Toward a comprehensive strategy for addressing the teacher shortage. *Phi Delta Kappan* 67(10): 712–18.

Hegstad, C. 1999. Formal mentoring as a strategy for human resource development: A review of research. *Human Resource Development Quarterly* 10(4): 383–90.

Hoffman, J. V., S. A. Edwards, S. O'Neal, S. Barnes, and M. Paulessen. 1986. A study of state-mandated beginning teacher programs. *Journal of Teacher Education* 37(1): 16–21.

Holloway, J. H. 2001. Research Link/The benefits of mentoring [Electronic version]. *Educational Leadership* 58(8).

Huffman, G., and Leak, S. 1986. Beginning teachers' perceptions of mentors. *Journal of Teacher Education* 37(1): 22–25.

Huling-Austin, L. 1986. What can and cannot reasonably be expected from teacher induction programs. *Journal of Teacher Education* 37(1): 2–5.

Joyce, B., and B. Showers. 1982. The coaching of teaching. *Educational Leadership* 40(1): 4–9.

Krajewski, R. J., and N. L. McCumsey. 1984. How to help beginning teachers. *Streamlined Seminar* 2(6): 1–6.

Levinson, D. J., C. N. Darrow, E. B. Klein, M. A. Levinson, and B. McGee. 1978. *The seasons of a man's life*. New York: Ballentine Books.

Lortie, D. C. 1975. *School teacher*. Chicago: University of Chicago Press.

Loucks-Horsley, S. 1999. *Ideas that work: Science professional development* (GPO Publication No. ENC 99-004). Washington, DC: U.S. Department of Education.

Loucks-Horsley, S., P. W. Hewson, N. Love, and K. E. Stiles. 1998. *Designing professional development for teachers of science and mathematics*. Thousand Oaks, CA: Corwin Press.

National Commission on Mathematics and Science Teaching for the 21st Century. 2000. *Before it's too late: A report to the nation from the National Commission on Mathematics and Science Teaching for the 21st Century*. Washington, DC: U.S. Department of Education.

National Commission on Teaching and America's Future. 1996. *What matters most: Teaching for America's future*. New York: Teachers College, Columbia University.

National Research Council. 1996. *National science education standards*. Washington, DC: National Academy Press.

National Science Foundation. 2001. *Elementary, secondary, and informal education program solicitation and guidelines* (GPO Publication No. NSF 01-060). Washington, DC: U.S. Government Printing Office.

Pataniczek, D., and N. S. Isaacson. 1981. The relationship of socialization and the concerns of beginning secondary teachers. *Journal of Teacher Education* 32(3): 14–17.

Phillips-Jones, L. 1989. Common problems in planned mentoring programs. *Mentoring International* 1: 36–40.

Plummer, D. M., and L. H. Barrow. 1998. Ways to support beginning science teachers. *Journal of Science Teacher Education* 9(4): 293–301.

Recruiting New Teachers, Inc. 2000. *A guide to developing teacher induction programs.* Belmont, MA: Recruiting New Teachers, Inc.

Scott, N. H. 1999. *Supporting new teachers: A report on the 1998-99 beginning teacher induction program in New Brunswick.* New Brunswick: University of New Brunswick. (ERIC Document Reproduction Service No. ED437347)

Shulman, J. 1988. Look to a colleague. *Instructor and teacher* 97(5): 32–34.

Shulman, L. S. 1986. Those who understand: Knowledge growth in teaching. *Educational Researcher* 15(2): 4–14.

Taylor, S. E. 1987. The California mentor teacher program: A preliminary evaluation of one district's program. *International Journal of Mentoring* 1(1): 27–30.

Veenman, S. 1984. Perceived problems of beginning teachers. *Review of Educational Research* 54(2): 143–78.

Woodruff, B. S. 1990. *The mentoring of beginning teachers: A program review.* Doctoral diss., University of North Carolina at Greensboro.

Zaharias, J. A., and T. W. Frew. 1987. Teacher induction: An analysis of one successful program. *Action in Teacher Education* 9(1): 49–55.

Induction Programs for Science Teachers: What the Research Says

Julie A. Luft

Julie A. Luft is an associate professor of science education in the Department of Curriculum and Instruction and the Center for Science Education at the University of Texas at Austin. She is a director-at-large for the Association for the Education of Teachers of Science and an associate editor of the *Journal of Research in Science Teaching*. Her current research interests include beginning secondary science teachers, multicultural science education, and undergraduate science education. Prior to obtaining her Ph.D. in science education at the University of Iowa in 1994 she was a high school science teacher for five years—and "did not swim, but sank" as a first-year science teacher.

The dialogue surrounding teacher induction has increased substantially in the last 20 years (Huling-Austin 1990). Contributors to this discussion include educational researchers who are exploring induction programs and beginning teacher development, policy makers who are calling for the development of induction programs, and professional development specialists who are creating and disseminating programs for beginning teachers. However, this conversation is not new; educators were discussing the induction process and possible programs in the early 1900s. John Hall (1913), for example, authored a paper in *The Twelfth Yearbook of the National Society for the Study of Education* about a University of Cincinnati program in which teachers were supervised during their teacher education program and throughout their first years of service. The program was administered by the College of Teachers and entailed cooperation between the city's public school system and the local university. While current conversations about beginning teachers are similar to those of over 80 years ago, they are also proposing new directions for induction programs.

The recently released Glenn Commission Report, *Before It's Too Late: A Report to the Nation from the National Commission on Mathematics and Science Teaching for the 21st Century* (National Commission on Mathematics and Science Teaching for the 21st Century 2000), emphasizes the importance of fostering the development of beginning mathematics and science teachers. In Goal 3 of the report, the authors call for the establishment of focused induction programs for mathematics and science teachers that acclimate the teachers to the profession, create formal mentoring relationships, and introduce teachers to inquiry groups. The intention of this goal is to improve the environment in which beginning teachers work, thereby retaining teachers and promoting teaching as an attractive career choice. Ingersoll (2001), in a comprehensive review of data on teachers, echoes this progressive stance by concluding that more attention should be given to decreasing the demand for teachers than to increasing the supply of teachers.

As university educators and district staff development specialists develop alternatives for beginning science teachers in response to national directives, they will consult relevant educational research in the area of induction. The intention of this chapter is to share important studies in this domain. It begins by summarizing research relevant to beginning science teachers, with a focus on their cognitive and behavioral development. After this overview, implications are drawn regarding the development and enactment of induction programs for science teachers. The chapter concludes with comments about the potential and importance of science-based induction programs.

Beginning Science Teachers

As teacher educators develop programs for beginning teachers, they will consult the literature in order to understand this unique phase in the teacher development process. Some educators will explore literature that describes teacher development stages, and others will review research that discusses the behavioral and cognitive development of beginning teachers. While these literature bases offer different perspectives regarding new teachers, they ultimately give direction in the design of induction programs. Specifically, they direct the framework of the program by revealing essential knowledge that supports the process, appropriate strategies to use, and interpretations of the context in which beginning teachers work. Loucks-Horsley et al. (1998) note that these elements are vital in planning effective professional development programs.

Research discussing the development of science teachers has traditionally fallen into the domains of preservice or inservice education. This has not gone unnoticed in the science education community. During the last decade, science educators have acknowledged the lack of research in the area of induction and have called for additional studies in this domain (Anderson and Mitchener 1994; Adams and Krockover 1997). While the education community addresses this void, there are still informative studies that can guide educators' understanding of beginning science teachers. Fuller and Brown (1975), for example, describe the process of teacher development in stages. In the first stage, teachers have concerns for themselves, which entails a focus on adequacy and survival in the classroom. As they progress to the task stage, they attend to the methods, materials, and skills that they use in their classes. In the final stage, they have concerns about the impact of their instruction on students. In contrast, Bell and Gilbert (1996) describe science teacher development as consisting of social, personal, and professional aspects. Social development involves progressing from individual to collaborative studies of instructional practice. Personal development entails moving from accepting problems with one's teaching situation toward feeling empowered to rectify those problems. Professional development encompasses learning and incorporating new instructional practices in the classroom. While these studies are two among many, they clearly provide models that can be used to guide the development of induction programs.

Research regarding the problems of beginning science teachers is, to a great extent, in agreement. Issues related to classroom management and distinct qualities inherent in science instruction are salient among several studies. Adams and Krockover (1997), for example, report that beginning science and mathematics teachers have concerns about classroom management, classroom assignments, curriculum development, time management, and the presentation of content. Their non–subject-related findings were similar to those of Veenman (1984), who conducted a comprehensive review of studies about beginning teachers and found that classroom discipline, motivating students, and dealing with individual differences in the classroom were new teachers' most pressing concerns. Emmer (1986), in a study of the practices of first-year teachers, concluded that beginning science teachers adhered to traditional practices because of the nature of science teaching, the variety of tasks they encountered, the large number of preparations, and the scarcity of established curriculum guides.

Researchers note that the unique constraints experienced by beginning science teachers are often a result of the disparity that exists between their teacher-training programs and the reality of the classroom (Loughran 1994; Wubbels et al. 1982; Veenman 1984). Proposed solutions to this experienced disparity have focused on increased independent instruction during student teaching (Koestsier and Wubbels 1995) or extended and more meaningful field experiences (McIntyre, Byrd, and Foxx 1996).

Research on the beliefs and practices of beginning science teachers has revealed the developing nature of their practices. It is acknowledged that teaching beliefs directly influence a teacher's classroom instruction (Richardson 1996). This implies that beginning science teachers need teaching beliefs that are conducive to inquiry instruction. Unfortunately, the teaching beliefs of beginning science teachers are not stable or well defined (Brickhouse and Bodner 1992; Simmons et al. 1999); as a result, these teachers often fluctuate between using student- and teacher-centered approaches. Simmons et al. (1999), through interviews and videotape analyses, found that science and mathematics teachers in their first and second years were likely to demonstrate a disparity between their beliefs and practice. By the third year, however, beginning science teachers demonstrated more alignment between their beliefs and practices toward either student- or teacher-centered approaches. Kagan (1992), in a review of studies on preservice and beginning teachers, found that beliefs did not significantly change during preservice programs. It was not until students experienced the reality of the classroom in their first years that their beliefs changed. It has been suggested that support programs may assist beginning science teachers in modifying their beliefs in ways that reinforce the use of student-centered practices (Luft 2001), which leads to the next topic.

Support programs are important for beginning teachers (Huling-Austin 1990, 1992; Huling-Austin and Murphy 1987; Gold 1996; Griffin 1985). Huling-Austin (1990), for example, concluded that support programs can improve the teaching performance of beginning teachers, increase the retention of beginning teachers, promote the personal and professional well-being of beginning teachers, and transmit the culture of the system to beginning teachers. In addition, she suggested that such programs can help beginning teachers to satisfy induction and certification requirements. In a later review of studies on beginning teachers, Huling-Austin (1992) noted a number of factors that corresponded with their success in the classroom. Two salient factors were collegial support and mentoring, which are key components of induction programs.

Although these studies have contributed significantly to the dialogue about the potential of induction programs, they have overlooked the critical aspect of subject-specific support. Luft et al. (2001), in a small study, demonstrated that a science-focused induction program had a greater impact on the practices and beliefs of beginning science teachers than did general induction programs. Specifically, the secondary science teachers in the university–school district support program implemented more student-centered inquiry lessons, held beliefs aligned with student-centered practices, and felt fewer constraints in their teaching than did teachers with no support or those in a general induction program. Collectively, these studies and reviews reinforce the importance of induction programs that are developed in response to the specific needs of teachers, which includes discipline-focused support.

Crafting Induction Programs for Science Teachers

The discussion in the previous section conveyed the complex process of beginning teacher development and suggested areas that should be part of induction programs for science teachers. The following discussion builds on the above-mentioned research by including additional studies that are relevant to the development of induction programs. Specific areas to consider in the development of induction programs are discussed, and guiding questions (Figure 1) are offered to assist those charged with developing induction programs for science teachers.

Program Format

Induction programs for science teachers should be consistent with effective professional development practices. Loucks-Horsley et al. (1998) and Rhoton and Bowers (2001) provide guidance for those charged with planning and designing such programs. Their collective suggestions are grounded in research and practice, and they offer a vision for progressive professional development programs. However, their recommendations should be carefully reviewed and modified appropriately to meet the unique needs of beginning science teachers. This would result, for example, in the design of programs that focus on new teachers' fluctuating beliefs and limited

Figure 1. Guiding Questions in the Development of an Induction Program for Beginning Science Teachers

Component	Questions
1. Program format	Who will oversee and direct the program? What will be the duration of the program (1, 2, or 3 years)? How will the program interface with other efforts to support beginning science teachers? How will teachers learn about the program? What will be their incentive for participating? How will the program be institutionalized? How will ongoing support be provided to the beginning teachers throughout the school year? What will be the specific components of the program (e.g., monthly meetings, electronic communications, new teacher tool kit, observations of beginning teachers)? How do these components support the program goals?
2. Mentor teachers	How will mentor teachers be recruited and selected? What will be the roles and responsibilities of the mentor teachers? How will the roles and responsibilities interface with the various constituents represented in the program? How will mentor teachers participate in their own professional development? How will mentor teachers be compensated for their participation?
3. Linkages	How will collaborative linkages be formed between important constituents? What will be the needed knowledge that each constituent will bring to the program? What will be the incentives for constituents to participate? What feedback will participating constituents receive from the induction program that is relevant to their position in the teacher development process?
4. Program content	What will be the goals of the program? How will the state and national standards be incorporated into the induction program? How will the program content align with the content required in schools? How will the content of the program align with the concerns and development of the beginning teachers? How will the content of the program interface with the entire process of science teacher development?
5. Evaluation	How will the goals of the program be evaluated? How will data be collected and analyzed regarding the different parties in, and affected by, the program? Who will conduct the evaluation? What opportunities will exist during the program to adjust the program? How will feedback be given to those involved in the program?

classroom experience and that address both the characteristic short-term needs of beginning teachers (e.g., What will I teach tomorrow? Where do I get the tennis balls for my experiment?) and long-term goals for science teacher development (e.g., How well did my students learn that concept? How do I participate in this profession?).

Mentor Teachers

The plethora of literature regarding mentor teachers (e.g., Huling-Austin 1990, 1992; Gold 1996; Capel 1998) attests to the importance of mentors to beginning teachers. Their contributions are complex. Such contributions include providing the new teacher with a colleague to talk or listen to, a source for suggestions on classroom management, a counterpart who assists in planning lessons and locating materials, an experienced educator who helps navigate school policies or procedures, and a facilitator of reflective practice (Abell et al. 1995; Huling-Austin and Murphy 1987; Luft and Cox 2001; Wildman et al. 1992). To carry out these roles effectively, mentor teachers should not be involved in the evaluation of a beginning teacher. When mentor teachers serve as evaluators, they are no longer colleagues who give assistance, but reviewers who are making summative and retention decisions. Ultimately, mentor teachers can play a critical role in purposefully crafted induction programs by facilitating the socialization process of beginning science teachers into their schools and the profession of science education.

Linkages

Induction programs need to create seamless transitions for beginning science teachers as they leave teacher preparation programs and enter the classroom. To ease the disconnect that is often experienced by beginning teachers, induction programs should link faculty and staff from teacher preparation programs with faculty and staff from local school districts. According to Brockmeyer (1998), school district staff can help beginning secondary science teachers with issues such as organization, discipline, classroom routine, local supplies and resources, and school procedures. University faculty and staff, on the other hand, provide beginning teachers with the current research and standards background and with instructional support regarding pedagogy and the enactment of lessons. Such collaborations are important and have been shown to be beneficial to all involved (Gold 1996; Henry 1989; Luft and Patterson, in press; Stroot et al. 1999; Varah, Theune, and Parker 1986). As teacher preparation and school district faculty and staff participate in such programs,

- beginning teachers see the importance and connection of theory and practice,
- faculty of teacher preparation programs receive feedback on their programs and information about current issues in schools, and
- school district participants acquire current information regarding science education reform.

Program Content

While all teachers would benefit by participating in an induction program, beginning science teachers need specialized support that addresses their unique pedagogical and content needs as described by various researchers (e.g., Adams and Krockover 1997; Emmer 1986; Roehrig and Luft, in review; Sanford 1988). This support includes traditional areas that are of frequent concern to all beginning teachers (e.g., classroom management, lesson planning) (Veenman 1984), and it extends to support in planning and managing laboratory instruction, implementing inquiry- and standards-based lessons, and fostering an understanding of the nature of science among students. Furthermore, such support is appropriate for the increasing number of secondary science teachers who do not have adequate science or pedagogical knowledge (Ingersoll 2001). Providing appropriate subject-specific support for science teachers throughout their entire professional development process ensures their ongoing learning and helps them to acquire local, state, or national certification. Our current system, which primarily gives subject-specific support during preservice and inservice years, overlooks a unique opportunity to advance the knowledge of science education in science teachers when it is most critical and in a format that bridges preservice and inservice education.

Evaluation

Effective program evaluation is critical in facilitating the growth of participants. Such efforts need to extend beyond the traditional use of Likert assessments, in which participating teachers indicate their degree of satisfaction with an event on a one to five scale. At the least, the following information should be collected and analyzed during a professional development program: beginning teachers' beliefs about teaching and their behaviors in the classroom, their students' work in the classroom, the instructors' perceptions and experiences, administrators' understanding and participation in the program, and documents regarding the participation and activity of the beginning teachers. This information is then used to provide direction for modification of the professional development program while informing program coordinators, directors, and administrators about the impact of the program. Loucks-Horsley et al. (1998), in their model of professional development design for science and mathematics teachers, stressed the importance of monitoring practitioners throughout a professional development event in order to modify the program to meet participants' changing needs. This process—"set goals, plan, do, and reflect"—should be included in every teacher education program.

Conclusions and Implications

As induction programs are designed and implemented, it is important to consider their limitations as well as their benefits. In this chapter quite a bit has been discussed regarding their potential, which includes providing teachers with subject-specific content and pedagogical support, assistance with the modification of curriculum, emotional support and logistical assistance, and opportunities to reflect on their practice. These benefits contribute to the professional development of a science teacher, and often when the teacher needs it most. However, it is easy for those developing induction programs to envision a greater impact than is realistic. For example, while induction programs can assist beginning teachers in shaping their beliefs and practices, they cannot create significant changes in beliefs, practices, or knowledge. In addition, they cannot directly improve school working conditions, nor are they the panacea for the retention of beginning teachers.

Induction programs are an important component in the professional development of a science teacher. They reinforce practices learned in preservice education and prepare teachers for forthcoming professional development experiences. Furthermore, they have the potential to involve school district and university personnel in the socialization of beginning teachers, which also has an impact on the instructional environment of schools and teacher preparation programs. Ultimately, induction programs are an important and worthwhile investment in our science teaching force.

References

Abell, S. K., D. R. Dillion, C. J. Hopkins, W. D. McInerney, and D. C. O'Brien. 1995. Somebody to count on: Mentor/intern relationships in a beginning teacher internship program. *Teaching and Teacher Education* 11(2): 172–88.

Adams, P. E., and G. H. Krockover. 1997. Concerns and perceptions of beginning secondary science and mathematics teachers. *Science Education* 81: 29–50.

Anderson, R. D., and C. P. Mitchener. 1994. Research on science teacher education. In *Handbook of research on science teaching and learning*, ed. D. L. Gabel, 31–44. New York: Macmillan.

Bell, B., and J. Gilbert. 1996. *Teacher development: A model from science education.* London: Falmer Press.

Brickhouse, N., and G. Bodner. 1992. The beginning science teacher: Classroom narratives of convictions and constraints. *Journal of Research in Science Teaching* 29(9): 471–85.

Brockmeyer, M. A. 1998. *The impact of an extended inquiry-based in-service program on the beliefs and practices of beginning secondary science teachers.* Unpublished doctoral diss., University of Iowa, Iowa City.

Capel, S. 1998. The transition from student teacher to newly qualified teacher: Some findings. *Journal of In-service Education* 24(3): 393–409.

Emmer, D. T. 1986. Academic activities and tasks in first-year teachers' classes. *Teaching and Teacher Education* 2: 299–44.

Fuller, F. F., and O. H. Brown. 1975. Becoming a teacher. In *Teacher education (74th yearbook of the National Society for the Study of Education, Part II)*, ed. K. Ryan, 25–52. Chicago: University of Chicago Press.

Gold, Y. 1996. Beginning teacher support: Attrition, mentoring, and induction. In *Handbook of research on teacher education*, ed. J. Sikula, 548–94. New York: Macmillan.

Griffin, G. A. 1985. Teacher induction: Research issues. *Journal of Teacher Education* 36: 42–46.

Hall, J. W. 1913. Supervision of beginning teaching in Cincinnati. In *The Twelfth Yearbook of the National Society for the Study of Education,* 97–109. Chicago: University of Chicago Press.

Henry, M. A. 1989. Multiple support: A promising strategy for effective teacher induction. In *Teacher induction,* ed. J. Reinhartz, 74–80. Washington, DC: National Education Association.

Huling-Austin, L. 1990. Teacher induction programs and internships. In *Handbook of teacher education*, ed. W. Houston, 535–48. New York: Macmillan.

———. 1992. Research on learning to teach: Implications for teacher induction and mentoring programs. *Journal of Teacher Education* 43: 173–80.

Huling-Austin, L., and S. C. Murphy. 1987. *Assessing the impact of teacher induction programs: Implications for program development*. Paper presented at the annual meeting of the American Educational Research Association, Washington, DC. ED 283 779.

Ingersoll, R. M. 2001. Teacher turnover and teacher shortages: An organizational analysis. *American Educational Research Journal* 38(3): 499–534.

Kagan, D. M. 1992. Professional growth among preservice and beginning teachers. *Review of Educational Research* 62: 129–69.

Koestsier, C. P., and J. T. Wubbels. 1995. Bridging the gap between initial teacher training and teacher induction. *Journal of Education for Teaching* 21(3): 333–45.

Loucks-Horsley, S., P. Hewson, N. Love, and K. E. Stiles. 1998. *Designing professional development for teachers of science and mathematics*. Thousand Oaks, CA: Corwin Press.

Loughran, J. 1994. Bridging the gap: An analysis of the needs of second-year science teachers. *Science Education* 78: 365–86.

Luft, J. A. 2001. Changing inquiry practice and beliefs? The impact of a one-year inquiry-based professional development program on the beliefs and practices of secondary science teachers. *International Journal of Science Education* 23(5): 517–34.

Luft, J. A., and W. E. Cox. 2001. Investing in our future: A survey of support offered to beginning secondary mathematics and science teachers. *Science Educator* 10(1): 1–9.

Luft, J. A., and N. C. Patterson. In press. Supporting beginning science teachers. *Journal of Science Teacher Education*.

Luft, J. A., G. Roehrig, N. C. Patterson, and S. M. Uyeda. 2001. *Contrasting induction programs: A comparison of different support programs for beginning science teachers*. Paper presented at the meeting of the American Educational Research Association, Seattle, WA (April).

McIntyre, D. J., D. M. Byrd, and S. M. Foxx. 1996. Field and laboratory experiences. In *The handbook of research in teacher education* (2nd ed.), ed. J. Sikula, 171–91. New York: Macmillan.

National Commission on Mathematics and Science Teaching for the 21st Century. 2000. *Before it's too late: A report to the nation from the National Commission on Mathematics and Science Teaching for the 21st Century*. Washington, DC: U.S. Department of Education.

Richardson, V. 1996. The role of attitudes and beliefs in learning to teach. In *The handbook of research in teacher education* (2nd ed.), ed. J. Sikula, 102–19. New York: Macmillan.

Rhoton, J., and P. Bowers, eds. 2001. *Issues in science education: Professional development planning and design*. Arlington, VA: NSTA Press.

Roehrig, G. H., and J. A. Luft. In review. Constraints and experiences of beginning secondary science teachers. *International Journal of Science Education*.

Sanford, J. P. 1988. Learning on the job: Conditions for professional development of beginning science teachers. *Science Education* 72: 615–24.

Simmons, P. E., A. Emory, T. Carter, T. Coker, B. Finnegan, D. Crockett, L. Richardson, R. Yager, J. Craven, J. Tillotson, H. Brunkhorst, M. Twiest, K. Hossain, J. Gallager, D. Duggan-Haas, J. Parker, F. Cajas, Q. Alshannag, S. McGlamery, G. Krockover, P. Adams, B. Spector, T. La Porta, B. James, K. Rearden, and K. Labuda. 1999. Beginning teachers: Beliefs and classroom actions. *Journal of Research in Science Teaching* 36: 930–54.

Stroot, S. A., J. Fowlkes, J. Langholz, S. Paxton, P. Stedman, L. Steffes, and A. Valtman. 1999. Impact of a collaborative peer assistance and review model on entry-year teachers in a large urban school setting. *Journal of Teacher Education* 50(1): 27–41.

Varah, L., W. S. Theune, and L. Parker. 1986. Beginning teachers: Sink or swim? *Journal of Teacher Education* 37(1): 30–34.

Veenman, S. 1984. Perceived problems of beginning teachers. *Review of Educational Research* 54(2): 145–78.

Wildman, T., S. Magliaro, R. Niles, and J. Niles. 1992. Teacher mentoring: An analysis of roles, activities, and conditions. *Journal of Teacher Education* 43(3): 205–13.

Wubbels, T., H. A. Creton, H. P. Hooymayer, and A. J. Holvast. 1982. Training teachers to cope with the "reality shock." *Studies in Science Education* 9: 147–60.

Needs Assessment for Beginning Teacher Assistance Programs

Stephen P. Gordon and Jane Butters

Stephen P. Gordon is an associate professor of educational administration at Southwest Texas State University in San Marcos, Texas. He is the co-author of two best-selling books, *How to Help Beginning Teachers Succeed* (ASCD 2000) and *SuperVision and Instructional Leadership: A Developmental Approach* (Allyn and Bacon 2001). Dr. Gordon has written numerous articles on instructional supervision, professional development, and support for beginning teachers. He has chaired a state task force on standards for entry-year support and has consulted for numerous school districts on developing beginning teacher support programs.

Jane Butters is an assistant principal of curriculum and instruction and lead mentor at a middle school in Austin, Texas. She has taught seventh-grade mathematics and was voted as her campus's teacher of the year and nominated for the Presidential Award for Excellence in Mathematics and Science Teaching. She has given numerous presentations on professional development and mentoring new teachers. Currently, she is a doctoral student majoring in school improvement at Southwest Texas State University in San Marcos, Texas.

Beginning teachers face enormous challenges during their first years of teaching, yet they tend to receive little assistance for surviving in the educational system. Schools that truly support beginning teachers would be wise to establish comprehensive beginning teacher assistance programs (BTAPs).

Effective BTAP needs assessment addresses four areas. The first area is the school environment in which the novice works. Environmental conditions go beyond the beginner's knowledge and skill development needs. They involve such things as work assignments, clarity of expectations, available resources, and whether the school culture is isolated or collegial. Needs in this area can be met only by improving aspects of the school environment that inhibit beginners' growth and development.

A second needs assessment area, the most obvious, is concerned with specific needs of beginning teachers, including cognitive, affective, and pedagogical needs. In this area, needs assessment can get complicated. For example, if a school hires several new teachers, these teachers will no doubt have some needs in common, but as individuals they also will have unique needs. Also, beginners' needs change over time. This month's needs assessment may not be relevant next month!

Most BTAPs assign experienced teachers as mentors to beginning teachers. In fact, mentoring often is the most important component of a BTAP (Gordon and Maxey 2000). Effective mentoring is a difficult task. Success as a classroom teacher is not sufficient preparation for being a mentor; mentors require training as well as ongoing assistance and support. Thus, a third area of BTAP needs assessment is determining the needs of mentors.

Finally, once the first three areas of needs assessment (environmental, beginning teacher, and mentor) have been completed, the BTAP planning team must determine resource needs. What resources will be necessary to carry out support activities and to determine the effects of these activities? If a resource needs assessment is completed effectively, needs, support activities, and resources will be aligned.

Before looking more closely at the four areas of BTAP needs assessment, we present several recommendations regarding effective needs assessment.

1. The school should assemble a BTAP development team to assess needs and to develop other components of the BTAP. The team should include an administrator, staff developer, and a majority of teachers.
2. The school should request assistance from a "critical friend," someone from outside the school with expertise in needs assessment and BTAP development. The critical friend can be a university professor, a retired practitioner, or a leader from another school district. The critical friend works with the school throughout the needs assessment process, sharing objective feedback, providing technical assistance with data gathering and analysis, and facilitating team decision-making.
3. Members of the BTAP development team and other members of the school community should read and reflect on the literature concerning problems and needs that BTAPs are created to address. One format for reviewing literature is the study group, which allows for collaborative review and dialogue. Of course, reviewing the literature by itself is insufficient for identifying needs within a particular school, but it is a starting point, a way to gather background information and to develop support for an effective BTAP.
4. Multiple data sources and multiple data gathering methods should be used during needs assessment. Examples of data sources are students, beginning teachers, mentors, other teachers, administrators, archival records, classrooms, and student work. Examples of data gathering methods are questionnaires, interviews, classroom observations, videotaping, and systematic review of archival records. Using multiple data sources and multiple data gathering methods is likely to result in an accurate identification and understanding of needs.The use of multiple sources and methods, however, does not mean that a needs assessment must be overly complex or require assistance from a team of university researchers. Needs can be identified through fairly simple data gathering and analysis techniques (as illustrated in Figures 1, 2, and 3), and the BTAP team, with assistance from other members of the school community and its critical friend, should be able to con-

duct all aspects of the needs assessment.

In the remainder of this chapter we will examine more closely each of the four areas of comprehensive BTAP needs assessment (environmental, beginning teacher, mentor, and resource), discuss analysis of needs assessment data, and describe how needs assessment is connected to other aspects of continuous BTAP development.

Environmental Needs Assessment

A school's environment—its degree of collegiality, collaboration, access to resources, conflict, and workload—plays a significant role in the success of the beginning teacher. All parts of the system must create an environment that provides new teachers with a smooth transition to the classroom.

Most effective needs assessments begin with a review of literature. Following that, it is important to review archival records to gain insight into the school's past and current "way of doing things." The review can include previous professional development activities, attrition rates, exit surveys or interviews given to nonreturning teachers, surveys or questionnaires addressing anything from job satisfaction to campus decision-making, teacher attendance rates, and so on. Basically, the review should include any existing documents that help paint an accurate picture of where the school has been and what its current environment is.

Objective observations can also help to identify environmental needs. Because the school's critical friend comes from outside the organization, he or she is a good choice to make such observations. By conducting informal observations of teachers' interactions, conversations, job duties, general attitudes, and participation in schoolwide activities and decision-making, the observer can gain an overall impression about the climate of the campus.

Questionnaires are another method for gathering data on environmental needs. It is important to administer questionnaires to both beginning and experienced teachers, but responses from beginning teachers should be analyzed separately, in addition to being included in a schoolwide analysis. Figure 1 is an example of an environmental needs assessment questionnaire. Observations by the critical friend can be used to help create additional questions that address the school's unique climate.

Open-ended, oral feedback from a variety of groups also contributes to an understanding of the school environment. This type of data can be gathered through formal interviews or informal discussions. Interview questions about the school environment could include the following: Do teachers on our campus have equitable schedules and class loads? What is the quality of communication on our campus? How are decisions made on our campus? What is the level of collaboration on our campus? Information gathering from a group can also occur in department meetings. Consider the following scenario:

The school's lead mentor, Kelly, observes an after-school science department meeting, which is attended by all twelve science teachers, including a beginning

---

Figure 1. Environmental Needs Assessment Questionnaire

Part A. Please choose the response for each item that most nearly indicates your opinion on the level of need for improvement in the area described in the item.

Possible Responses:
A.   **Little or no need** for improvement in this area
B.   **Some need** for improvement in this area
C.   **Moderate need** for improvement in this area
D.   **High need** for improvement in this area
E.   **Very high need** for improvement in this area

1.   ____Equitable class sizes
2.   ____Effective scheduling of courses
3.   ____Effective scheduling of students
4.   ____Adequate time for planning instruction
5.   ____Clearly defined schoolwide procedures
6.   ____Clearly defined expectations of teachers
7.   ____Teachers' understanding of their professional roles
8.   ____Communication among teachers
9.   ____Communication between teachers and administrators
10. ____Communication between teachers and parents
11. ____Clearly defined schoolwide expectations of students
12. ____Easily accessible resources
13. ____Clearly defined procedures for ordering resources
14. ____Collaboration among departments
15. ____Collaboration among grade levels
16. ____Collaboration within grade-level teams
17. ____Trust among adult members of the school community
18. ____Effective support systems for beginning teachers
19. ____Professional dialogue among faculty members
20. ____Opportunities for professional dialogue among faculty members
21. ____Opportunities for collaboration among faculty members
22. ____Collegiality among faculty members
23. ____Opportunities for teacher leadership
24. ____Opportunities for teacher input in schoolwide decision-making
25. ____Effective campuswide communication
26. ____Administrative support of teachers

Part B. Please respond to the following items.
27. What are some additional areas that you feel need to be improved in our school?

28. What do you view as our school's most significant impediment(s) to improvement?

---

sixth-grade teacher, Chris, and a beginning eighth-grade teacher, Maria. During the meeting, Maria asks, "I have been buying a lot of my own materials. How do I go about getting materials?" Most of the veteran teachers respond that they have accumulated materials over many years and have learned "shortcuts" for requesting and acquiring additional resources. As a science department, they do not agree on a clearly defined procedure for procuring materials and resources. Later in the discussion, Chris shakes his head and says, "Five of my six periods have well over 35 students in them. Whenever we attempt a lab, the class is too disruptive, and we have to stop. I worry about safety issues." Betty, a veteran sixth-grade science teacher, responds by saying, "I had no idea that your classes were larger than mine. We can talk to the counselor tomorrow about leveling our class sizes." At the end of the meeting, Mary, the science department chairperson, asks the entire group, "Have you all attended the follow-up training to the integrative science seminar?" Everyone nods, except the two beginning teachers. Maria and Chris's confused expressions seem to ask, "What integrative science follow-up training?"

By observing the department meeting, Kelly is aware of three possible environmental needs: (a) the need for clear procedures to request and attain materials and resources, (b) the need for reasonable class loads, especially for new teachers, and (c) the need for effective communication about professional development opportunities.

A thorough environmental needs assessment can lay a solid foundation for the creation of a BTAP that meets both school and beginner needs. A school's culture or environment consists of communication patterns, levels of collaboration, relationships, roles, and attitudes, all of which can profoundly affect new teachers. The nature of the school environment also increases or decreases the level of resistance to, or acceptance of, change. All these factors must be considered when developing a BTAP.

Beginning Teacher Needs Assessment

A preliminary plan for providing direct assistance to beginning teachers should be designed before the school year starts. This plan can be based on the research literature on beginners' needs, needs reported by the school's beginning teachers in recent years, and experienced teachers' perceptions of beginners' needs. It is critical, however, that the preliminary plan be tentative and sufficiently flexible so that it can change based on direct assessment of beginners' needs once the school year has begun.

It is important to begin assessing beginners' specific needs as soon as they become members of the school community. New teachers likely will have some common needs that can be identified through common assessment methods. The BTAP development team can design and administer to beginning teachers questionnaires like the one in Figure 2.

The BTAP development team can conduct group or individual interviews after they analyze the questionnaire data in order to gather more in-depth data on general needs identified by the questionnaire. For example, if analysis of questionnaire data has identified "Evaluating student progress" as a need, the team can ask probing and clarifying questions about that need as part of a group interview.

Once mentors have worked with new teachers for a few weeks, they also become sources of information concerning new teachers' needs. Mentors too can complete questionnaires and participate in group or individual interviews in which they share

---

Figure 2. Needs Assessment Questionnaire for Beginning Teachers

Part A. Please choose the response for each item that most nearly indicates your level of need for assistance in the area described in the item.

Possible Responses:

A.   **Little or no need** for assistance in this area
B.   **Some need** for assistance in this area
C.   **Moderate need** for assistance in this area
D.   **High need** for assistance in this area
E.   **Very high need** for assistance in this area

1.   ____Finding out what is expected of me as a teacher
2.   ____Communicating with the principal
3.   ____Communicating with other teachers
4.   ____Communicating with parents
5.   ____Organizing instructional resources and materials
6.   ____Maintaining student discipline
7.   ____Obtaining instructional resources and materials
8.   ____Planning for instruction
9.   ____Managing my time and work
10. ____Diagnosing student needs
11. ____Evaluating student progress
12. ____Motivating students
13. ____Assisting students with special needs
14. ____Dealing with individual differences among students
15. ____Understanding the curriculum
16. ____Completing administrative paperwork
17. ____Using a variety of teaching methods
18. ____Facilitating group discussion
19. ____Grouping for effective instruction
20. ____Administering standardized achievement tests
21. ____Understanding the school system's teacher evaluation process
22. ____Understanding my legal rights and responsibilities as a teacher
23. ____Dealing with stress
24. ____Dealing with union-related issues
25. ____Becoming aware of special services provided by the school district

Part B. Please respond to the following items.
26. List any professional needs you have that are not addressed by the preceding items.

27. What types of support that are not currently available should the school district provide to you and other beginning teachers?

From *How to Help Beginning Teachers Succeed,* 2nd ed., by Stephen P. Gordon and Susan Maxey. Alexandria, VA: Association for Supervision and Curriculum Development. Copyright © 2000 ASCD. Reprinted by permission. All rights reserved.

their perceptions of beginners' cognitive, affective, and pedagogical needs. Beginning teacher and mentor perceptions then can be compared. We recommend that both beginning teachers and their mentors complete needs assessment questionnaires and participate in interviews near the beginning of the school year and about midway through the school year.

Up to this point, our discussion of beginning teacher needs assessment has focused on common needs of a group of new teachers. This type of assessment can result in common assistance activities such as study groups, workshops, and support seminars. BTAPs, however, also must address the specific needs assessment of individual teachers. In most BTAPs, the beginner's mentor will be in the best position to identify those needs. The mentor should become familiar with the new teacher's personal and academic history. In addition, many individual needs can be identified through informal conversations between the mentor and new teacher. It also is critical for the mentor to observe the beginner teaching on a regular basis, gathering nonevaluative data on the new teacher's instructional performance. The beginner's classroom is where the action is and where the mentor needs to be for effective needs assessment. The mentor can examine the new teacher's unit and lesson plans and student assessment methods as well as student products (daily assignments, projects, test results) that measure student growth. The mentor can encourage a beginner to engage in reflective writing on his or her teaching and other professional activities and to share those reflections with the mentor. Individual needs assessment by the mentor naturally will lead to individualized forms of mentoring, such as demonstration teaching, observation and feedback, co-teaching, and assistance with individual professional development plans.

Mentor Needs Assessment

If mentors are to successfully assist new teachers, their own needs as mentors must be understood and addressed. We recommend that an assessment to gauge the needs of mentors be conducted before new teachers arrive on the campus. Administering a questionnaire (see Figure 3) and then compiling and analyzing the data can generate a list of common mentor needs. Educational research has shown that the two predominant needs of mentors are adequate time and training for mentoring (Gordon and Maxey 2000).

Interviewing mentors as a group is another way to assess their needs. These interviews can be formal or informal. Questions to ask in an interview could include the following: Do you prefer your mentee to be in the same grade level or department as you? How important to you is the proximity of your classrooms? How will you determine the areas in which you will assist your mentee? In what areas do you not feel adequately prepared to assist beginning teachers?

As is the case with beginning teachers, individual mentors also have unique needs. Talking informally with mentors is an effective starting place to develop a sense of where a teacher is in his or her own professional development as a mentor. Informal discussions can be carried out by the critical friend, BTAP coordinator, lead mentor, or other school leader. Also, the questionnaire could be administered to all mentors, but analyzed on an individual as well as group level.

Another needs assessment method is observing mentor-mentee interactions. The observer can look for gaps in a mentor's training (e.g., effective questioning

Figure 3. Needs Assessment Questionnaire for Mentors

Part A. Please choose the response for each item that most nearly indicates your level of need for assistance in the area described in the item.

Possible Responses:

A. **Little or no need** for assistance in this area
B. **Some need** for assistance in this area
C. **Moderate need** for assistance in this area
D. **High need** for assistance in this area
E. **Very high need** for assistance in this area

1. ____Learning more about what is expected of me as a mentor
2. ____Collecting classroom observation data
3. ____Diagnosing needs of my mentee(s)
4. ____Interpersonal skills
5. ____Assisting my mentee(s) with classroom management
6. ____Helping my mentee(s) develop a variety of effective teaching strategies
7. ____Using principles of adult learning to facilitate the professional growth of my mentee(s)
8. ____Socializing my mentee(s) into the school culture
9. ____Helping my mentee(s) maintain student discipline
10. ____Helping my mentee(s) design a long-range professional development plan.
11. ____Finding resources and materials for my mentee(s)
12. ____Providing emotional support for my mentee(s)
13. ____Co-teaching with my mentee(s)
14. ____Managing my time and work
15. ____Problem-solving strategies
16. ____Helping my mentee(s) motivate students
17. ____Helping my mentee(s) assist students with special needs
18. ____Helping my mentee (s) diagnose student needs
19. ____Helping my mentee(s) deal with individual differences among students
20. ____Helping my mentee(s) evaluate student progress
21. ____Engaging in expert coaching of my mentee(s)

Part B. Please respond to the following items.

22. List any needs you have as a mentor that are not addressed by the preceding items.

23. What types of support that are not currently available should the school district provide to you and other mentors?

From *How to Help Beginning Teachers Succeed,* 2nd ed., by Stephen P. Gordon and Susan Maxey. Alexandria, VA: Association for Supervision and Curriculum Development. Copyright © 2000 ASCD. Reprinted by permission. All rights reserved.

techniques). The mentee's concerns give further insight into the mentor's training needs. The observer should look for evidence of collaboration, trust, and compatibility among new teachers and their mentors. In considering the needs of mentors, it is helpful to review existing data such as prior training, records of the mentor's performance with previous mentees, mentors' and beginning teachers' journals, and beginning teachers' performance data and attrition rates.

Data Analysis

Because environmental, beginning teacher, and mentor needs assessments use many of the same types of data gathering methods (e.g., questionnaires, interviews, observations, review of archival data), data analysis is similar across these three types of assessments. Whether the data is quantitative (e.g., a multiple-choice questionnaire) or qualitative (e.g., an open-ended interview), one goal is to reduce the data to displays that can be easily reviewed and compared. For example, Figure 4 is a portion of a display of quantitative data gathered using the Needs Assessment Questionnaire for Beginning Teachers (see Figure 2 for the entire questionnaire). This data display

Figure 4. Questionnaire Data Display

Number of beginners who responded: 12

Item	Little or No Need (1)	Some Need (2)	Moderate Need (3)	High Need (4)	Very High Need (5)	Group Mean
Finding out what is expected of me			2	1	9	4.6
Communicating with principal		1	3	4	4	3.9
Communicating with teachers		2	1	5	4	3.9
Communicating with parents		1	3	2	6	4.1
Organizing and managing classroom	1	3	2	1	5	3.5
Student discipline				1	11	4.9
Instructional resources and materials	1	1	1	6	3	3.8
Planning instruction		3	4	2	3	3.4
Managing time and work			1	3	8	4.6
Diagnosing student needs	1	2	1	5	3	3.6

Note: Figure 4 is only a portion of the original data display.

indicates that most of the beginners who completed the questionnaire perceived that assistance with finding out what was expected of them, handling student discipline, and managing time and work were critical needs.

For an example of summarizing qualitative data, let's assume that beginning teachers have been interviewed by members of the BTAP development team. As BTAP members review interview transcripts, they make notes of various responses to each interview question, and then compare notes to determine the most common responses. Figure 5 includes brief summaries of the three most common responses to each of five interview questions.

Once the different types of data have been summarized as data displays, the team needs to compare different types of data for consistency. In case of inconsistency across different types of data, the team may need to return to its sources to gather additional information. Once the team is confident that it has accurately identified

Figure 5. Responses to Oral Interview

Question	Most Common Response	Second Most Common Response	Third Most Common Response
Please describe three things about which you are excited.	Working with students	Getting to know other teachers	Having a classroom
Please describe three things about which you are nervous.	Discipline and classroom management	My ability to teach my subject effectively	School policies and procedures
What types of things would you like to see in an orientation?	Strategies for effective classroom management	Role-playing activities	Sample lesson plans
In what areas do you feel you would like guidance?	Classroom management	Staying on top of everything	How to plan lessons
Describe to me your "fantasy first year" as a teacher.	Small classrooms, no traveling	Well-behaved students	Students perform at a high academic level

environmental, beginning teacher, and mentor needs, it is necessary to prioritize the needs so that the BTAP can address the highest priority needs first.

So far we have discussed analysis of data for the purpose of planning schoolwide assistance. Analysis of data on the needs of an individual beginning teacher or mentor is simpler, but still should be done in a systematic manner. For example, a mentor might analyze data from several classroom observations of a new teacher to determine patterns of classroom behavior that indicate beginning teacher needs. For another example, the mentor might review his or her notes from an ongoing review of student performance in the new teacher's classroom to identify recurring themes that indicate beginner needs.

One thing to remember regarding individual needs assessment—whether it be the assessment of a beginner's needs by a mentor or of a mentor's needs by a BTAP leader—is that the person doing the assessing should not assume the role of an evaluator or an all-knowing expert. Rather, the assessor should establish a collaborative relationship with the beginner or mentor. Collaboration often should extend even to the involvement of the beginner or mentor in the analysis of his or her own needs assessment data.

Resource Needs Assessment

Needs assessment is the basis for BTAP planning. Although program planning is beyond the scope of this chapter, planning leads to resource needs assessment, which cuts across the three types of needs assessment discussed previously. Resource needs assessment consists of doing task analyses of planned support and program assessment activities and identifying resources needed to implement each activity. If the BTAP is properly designed, needs statements (often converted to program

Figure 6. Needed Resources Aligned with Needs, Support, and Program Assessment

Related Needs	Activities	Needed Resources
Environmental Need: • Improved collegiality and collaboration	**Support Activity:** • Collegial support groups focused on improved instruction **Program Assessment Activities:** • Logs of support group activities • Teachers surveys	• Refreshments at collegial and support group meetings • Training of collegial support group facilitators • Release time for evaluation team
Beginning Teacher Needs: • Effective use of varied instructional strategies • Improved collegiality and collaboration	**Support Activities:** • Four instructional strategies workshops attended by beginners and mentors • Ongoing classroom coaching by mentors • Mentor and beginner participation in same collegial support group **Program Assessment Activities:** • Beginner surveys on effectiveness of workshops, coaching, and collegial support groups • Mentors' observations of beginners' teaching • Mentors' ongoing review of student achievement data	• Cost of instructional strategies workshops • Release time for beginners to attend instructional strategies workshops • See above, resources for collegial support groups • See above, release time for evaluation team
Mentor Needs: • Review of varied instructional strategies • Peer coaching skills • Collegial support	**Support Activities:** • Four instructional strategies workshops attended by mentors and beginning teachers • Workshops on coaching skills • Mentor and beginner participation in same collegial support group **Program Assessment Activity:** • Survey on effectiveness of instructional strategies workshops, coaching workshops, and collegial support groups	• See above, cost of instructional strategies workshops • Cost of coaching workshops • Release time to attend instructional strategies and coaching workshops • Release time for classroom coaching of beginners • See above, resources for collegial support groups • See above, release time for evaluation team

objectives), support activities, program assessment activities, and resources will be aligned. Figure 6, a portion of a BTAP plan that addresses one set of related needs, provides an example of the alignment to which we refer.

In Figure 6, a need of beginning teachers identified by the BTAP team is effective use of varied instructional strategies. The team also has concluded that a broader problem within the school environment—a lack of collegiality and collaboration— means that beginning teachers do not learn the variety of instructional strategies used by many of the school's experienced teachers. To meet the environmental need of improved collegiality and collaboration, the BTAP team has planned for schoolwide collegial support groups that will include beginning as well as experienced teachers. The collegial groups will focus on teachers sharing instructional strategies and providing support to colleagues who wish to try out the strategies. The collegial support groups, thus, will assist not only beginning teachers, but also experienced teachers. Other planned support activities focus directly on meeting beginning teachers' needs for varied instructional strategies. Beginners will attend workshops on instructional strategies and receive coaching from their mentors as they implement the new strategies. To provide optimal support to the new teachers, mentors will need to "refresh" themselves on varied instructional strategies, develop classroom coaching skills, and receive collegial support. These mentor needs will be met through participation in the same instructional strategies workshops and collegial support groups that their mentees will attend, as well as participation in peer coaching workshops.

Environmental, beginning teacher, and mentor support activities in Figure 6 each are followed by program assessment activities intended to measure the effects of the support activities. Finally, the right-hand column of Figure 6 lists resources needed to carry out both the support activities and program assessment. Needed resources, thus, are aligned with needs, support activities, and program assessment activities. (Keep in mind that Figure 6 shows only one of several sets of support activities, program assessment activities, and needed resources.)

Needs Assessment and Continuous BTAP Development

The initial BTAP needs assessment should be considered as the first phase of ongoing needs assessment, which in turn is part of ongoing program development. Needs assessment, planning, implementation, and program assessment should be viewed as parts of a continuous cycle of program development rather than as linear steps. Figure 7 depicts needs assessment as part of a continuous cycle of BTAP development.

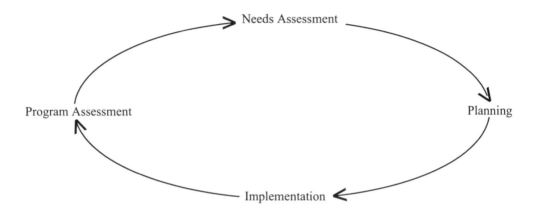

Figure 7. Needs Assessment as Part of the Beginning Teacher Assistance Program (BTAP) Development Cycle

Ongoing needs assessment should lead to revised planning and improved support activities throughout the school year. Often, needs assessment data also can be used for program assessment data, and vice versa. Eventually, needs assessment and program assessment will begin to merge, since they both involve gathering and using data for a more effective BTAP. Thus, needs assessment can both initiate and improve beginning teacher assistance programs.

Reference

Gordon, S. P., and S. Maxey. 2000. *How to help beginning teachers succeed,* 2nd ed. Alexandria, VA: Association for Supervision and Curriculum Development.

A Systemic Approach to Support Teacher Retention and Renewal

Michael P. Klentschy and Elizabeth Molina-De La Torre

Michael P. Klentschy is the superintendent of schools of the El Centro School District in El Centro, California. He is also the principal investigator for the National Science Foundation–funded Valle Imperial Project in Science (VIPS), co-director of the California Science Subject Matter Project Regional Center, Imperial Valley, and the National Science Resources Center—California LASER Project. Dr. Klentschy is also an instructor at San Diego State University where he conducts research on the longitudinal effects of inquiry-based science programs on student achievement. His present work also includes collaboration with James Stigler from the University of California, Los Angeles in the development of video-based technology for lesson study applications.

Elizabeth Molina-De La Torre is the coordinator of the nationally recognized National Science Foundation's Valle Imperial Project in Science (VIPS), a consortium of 14 school districts in Imperial Valley, California. Ms. Molina-De La Torre has also served as development associate on several science initiatives with the California Institute of Technology and the National Science Resources Center—California LASER Project. She is an instructor at San Diego State University, teaching science methods courses to preservice teachers. Ms. Molina-De La Torre has served as a consultant to school districts and systemic reform projects in 14 states and Mexico.

Teacher retention and renewal are critical issues facing school districts across the United States. It is imperative that school districts use systemic approaches to address these issues, especially in light of the projected increasing demand for teachers—an increase of 1.1 percent annually for the next decade (Yasin 2000). It is widely accepted that the projected increase in the need for teachers is a function of enrollment growth, teacher retirement, and a lack of systemic approaches to retain current teachers. This need is especially true for—and potentially even greater in—the critical shortage area of science (National Center for Education Statistics 1997). The need for teacher retention comes at a time when school districts are also facing a need for teacher renewal due to the increasing challenge of standards, assessment, and accountability; thus, school districts across the United States must redefine expectations for teaching and learning in their classrooms.

The lack of systemic approaches to retain and renew our nation's science teachers is not a new problem. Several studies (Darling-Hammond 1984; Boe and Guilford 1992; National Academy of Sciences 1987) predicted a dramatic rise in the demand for new teachers due to an increase in the retirement rate of teachers and an increase in student enrollment. Despite these reports of predicted shortages, only about 60 percent of newly prepared teachers enter teaching jobs upon graduation. The American Association for Employment in Education (1998) reported that the greatest shortages are geographically linked to the West and the South and nationally to academic fields like mathematics and science. Ingersoll (2001) conducted an analysis investigating the possibility that other factors having an impact on teacher retention levels were rooted in the organizational characteristics and conditions of schools. His analysis of the data indicated that while teacher retirement is increasing, the overall amount of turnover accounted for by retirement is relatively minor when compared to that resulting from other causes, such as teacher job dissatisfaction and teachers pursuing other careers.

Over the past two decades, substantial research has been conducted to determine which kinds of teachers are more prone to leaving teaching and why (Bobbitt et al. 1994; Chapman and Green 1986; Grissmer and Kirby 1992, 1997; Murnane 1987; Schlecty and Vance 1983; Weiss and Boyd 1990). Among the most important findings has been that teacher turnover is strongly affected by academic field and age. Mathematics and science are typically found to have the highest turnover, with 30 percent of new teachers leaving the profession within five years of entry. In addition, almost half of the teacher turnover rate can be attributed to the migration of teachers from one school to another (Ingersoll 1995).

Very few studies have examined the effects of organizational and staffing problems embedded in the schools themselves. Schools have been traditionally characterized as organizations dependent on commitment and cohesion among their members (Bidwell 1965; Lortie 1975). Without these elements, schools are vulnerable to employee turnover. From this viewpoint, high rates of teacher turnover are of concern because they may be an indicator not only of underlying problems in how schools are functioning but also of poor quality of school performance.

Rosenholtz (1989) and Bryk, Lee, and Smith (1990) have outlined seven symptoms of problematic school organization: (1) a disconnection between preservice programs and actual teaching, (2) science teachers teaching out of subject majors, (3) teacher isolation in individual schools and in rural districts, (4) lack of opportunities for teacher collaboration in schools and within systems, (5) lack of ample time for professional development, (6) lack of teacher-centered subject area networks, and (7) lack of teacher empowerment. Many of these symptoms are interrelated and are indicators of a much deeper problem, the lack of a systemic plan of action to address teacher retention and renewal. These symptoms are most acute in rural areas.

Tabulations conducted by Ingersoll (1999) for the National Commission on Teaching and America's Future, from data contained in the National Center for Education Statistics's Schools and Staffing Surveys for 1990–1991 and 1993–1994 (NCES 1991, 1994) indicated that approximately 30 percent of newly hired teachers held substandard teaching certification or no licensure at all. The distribution and placement of these teachers was highest in schools with large low-income and minority student populations. Darling-Hammond (2000) found that a strong negative predictor of student achievement was the proportion of teachers on emergency certificates; she found this particularly true in urban areas and poor rural areas where a large number of teachers on emergency certification were hired. Thus, student learning was compromised due to inappropriate teacher hiring. Effective long-term solutions to the problems of teacher retention and renewal rest on systemic approaches that prepare teachers for the tasks they face.

The Valle Imperial Project in Science and the Imperial Valley

The Valle Imperial Project in Science (VIPS) has recognized the need to provide systemic approaches for teacher retention and renewal for 14 school districts in Imperial County, California. Rural and isolated in the extreme southeastern corner of the state, this county is one of the largest (4,597 sq. mi.) and most sparsely populated (142,361) counties in California (U. S. Census Bureau 2000). Residents live in extreme poverty, with household incomes having declined in real dollars over the last decade. The IRS reported a 1998 mean per capita income of $17,550 (U. S. Department of Commerce 1999), the lowest of all California counties. Unemployment rates increased from 17.1 percent in 1991 to 26.3 percent in 2000 (California Employment Development 2000), while statewide rates remained lower than 4.9 percent.

Most Imperial Valley residents have strong cultural and linguistic ties to Mexico. Of 32,898 K–12 students in Imperial Valley, 81.5 percent are Hispanic (California Department of Education 1998–99). Caucasians (13.4 percent), African Americans (2.0 percent), Asians (1.0 percent), and Native Americans (1.6 percent) make up the rest of the population; 46.7 percent of the students in the county are Limited English Proficient; 10 percent are children of migrant farm workers. Nearly all of the county's schools qualify for Title I, with 65.8 percent of the students eligible for free and reduced lunches. The need for a systemic approach to teacher retention and renewal is acute in this region.

VIPS has served as a catalyst to develop a strong partnership among the 14 participating school districts and the local university, San Diego State University–Imperial Valley Campus (SDSU-IVC), modeled after the partner schools associated with the National Network for Education Renewal (Clark 1995). The partnership created a plan of action to address teacher retention and renewal based on a professional development model designed by Loucks-Horsley et al. (1998). The VIPS action plan views teacher retention and renewal as multidimensional and provides science teachers with the following ten elements: (1) a link between preservice and actual classroom practice, (2) institutes to deepen their content understanding, (3) opportunities to strengthen their pedagogical skills, (4) in-classroom support from science resource teachers, (5) leadership development, (6) materials support, (7) time for collaboration and networking within and between schools, (8) applications of technology, (9) workshops focusing on student work as the centerpiece of standards-based performance assessment, and (10) opportunities to refine instructional delivery through reflection and lesson study groups. Each of these ten elements is discussed below.

1. *Link between preservice and actual classroom practice.* Recognizing that knowledge of subject matter and knowledge of teaching and learning acquired in teacher education are strongly correlated with teacher performance in the classroom (Guyton and Farokhi 1987; Southern Regional Education Board 1998), the action plan established a partnership for preservice between SDSU-IVC and the 14 VIPS school districts in Imperial County. More than 90 percent of new teachers hired in Imperial County receive preservice training from SDSU-IVC. The science coordinator for VIPS was hired by the university and teaches the science methods course there; thus preservice methods classes are linked to practices expected at the time of employment. The preservice methods course focuses on inquiry-as-a-process, content, pedagogy, and student assessment strategies.

   Not all teachers enter the work force through traditional pathways. Ingersoll (1999) notes that about 30 percent of newly hired teachers enter the work force with substandard certification. Recognizing that this situation represents a challenge to the overall quality of science teaching in Imperial Valley schools, the action plan assigns teachers with substandard certification to the California Intern Program. Jointly conducted by VIPS and SDSU-IVC, this program provides a means for teachers to reach full certification; the teachers take science content courses designed to prepare them to successfully complete the California requirements for alternative certification. Participating teachers receive weekly support from one of the VIPS science resource teachers.

2. *Institutes to deepen teacher content understanding.* There is a growing recognition that enhanced teacher knowledge is among the most productive means for increasing student learning. Research indicates that for every $500 spent on increasing teacher education there is a 0.22 standard deviation increase in student achievement on standardized achievement tests (Greenwald, Hedges, and Laine 1996). The VIPS action plan provides multiple entry points for teachers to participate in specialized content institutes. Annually, science teachers are surveyed regarding their needs and their desire to participate in content institutes. The survey gives teachers an opportunity to have a voice in the content training that is provided. Content choices are aligned to grade-level, specific California content standards.

   The survey data are tabulated and form the core of Summer Science Institute content courses. Teachers have the choice of taking the 45-hour content course for college credit, to be used for salary advancement and alternative certification credit, through SDSU-IVC, or of receiving a cash stipend provided by VIPS or CSP (the California Science Project). Thus, a reward incentive encourages teachers to participate in the Summer Science Institutes. Science department staff members from SDSU-IVC and the California Institute of Technology lead the Summer Science Institutes. Their goal is to deepen the content understanding of the teachers and to demonstrate how to align content to the California Science Content Standards.

Recognizing that teachers also need to expand their content knowledge with experiences that go beyond the offerings of the Summer Science Institutes, the action plan provides opportunities for Imperial Valley teachers to participate in national institutes. Middle school science teachers participate in field-study content institutes offered by the Lawrence Hall of Science, University of California, Berkeley; NASA-Houston, Texas; and the Smithsonian Institution, Washington, D.C. Teachers thus deepen their content understanding and network with their peers from across the nation. Several teachers who participated in national institutes now serve in peer leadership roles in Imperial Valley.

Among other opportunities, science teachers in Imperial Valley are now able to obtain advanced degrees through a local master's degree program in curriculum and instruction, with a specialization in science education. The program, established by SDSU-IVC, was designed to deepen content understanding in life, physical, and Earth sciences; provide a field experience related to the content strand; and relate it to California Science Content Standards. The first cohort of 24 Imperial Valley teachers received their master's degrees in June 2001; three of those teachers now serve as science resource teachers in VIPS. A new cohort of 25 teachers began the program in fall 2002.

3. *Opportunities for teachers to strengthen their pedagogical skills.* Opportunities for teachers to strengthen their pedagogical skills are important in any systemic reform effort aimed at improving science education (Clark 1995). Recognizing this key element, the VIPS preservice and professional development designs link content to research-based "best practices" for instructional delivery.

In the preservice program, pedagogical design issues are patterned after research-based practices described by Marzano, Pickering, and Pollock (2001). Prospective teachers in the preservice program also can participate in professional development sessions with practicing teachers. And because the VIPS coordinator teaches the science methods course, the content of the course is directly linked to actual classroom practices. Thus, each preservice teacher can practice "best practices" and receive appropriate formative feedback from the supervising teacher.

The professional development design of the VIPS action plan recognizes that strengthening pedagogical skills of teachers is important. Embedded in each training session related to content are pedagogical issues, with special emphasis placed on English language development. The goal of the design is to enhance content language acquisition without leaching away the science content itself. To achieve that goal, the training session developers have prepared a storyline representing the connection of the activities in each unit to a "big idea" in science. The storyline has been embedded into each of the initial professional development activities. Teachers are thus exposed both to the "big idea" of the unit, depicted in the storyline from a content perspective, and the best instructional methods for presenting that big idea.

4. *In-classroom support from science resource teachers.* We know that the contributions of science resource teachers promote the retention and renewal of teachers. Useem (1995), for example, describes the importance of resource teachers in teacher support and mentoring. Berlinger (2000) states that this type of support contributes significantly to the likelihood that teachers will choose to remain in the teaching profession. Hargreaves and Fullan (2000) see these activities as part of a school culture development process that can help teachers form strong relationships. In-classroom support is especially critical for novice teachers, who usually have little time to develop tools for succeeding and burn out early in their careers (Bernshausen and Cunningham 2001). The use of in-classroom support for novice teachers increases their likelihood for retention, especially when these programs are expanded over several years (Eberhard, Reinhardt-Mondragon, and Stottlemyer 2000).

The position of science resource teacher also represents a career pathway for experienced teachers and aids in their retention rate. Science resource teachers are experienced classroom teachers who have demonstrated an excellent understanding and delivery of the prescribed standards-based curriculum. The science resource teachers visit novice teachers weekly and assist them with pacing a lesson, planning the prescribed standards-based curriculum, and managing materials. They also co-teach lessons, model language acquisition strategies, provide formative feedback, conduct demonstration lessons, and facilitate large and small group discussions.

5. *Leadership development.* VIPS has devoted a considerable amount of time to developing teacher leaders. The designation "lead teacher" represents another career pathway for teachers; its primary goal is to provide a leadership development strand to the science systemic change program in Imperial Valley and to use the teachers as leaders in professional development activities. The lead teachers sign an agreement with the program to participate in 70 hours of professional development in the following capacities: (1) mentoring teachers in regard to curriculum implementation, inquiry strategies, materials management, and notebook integration; (2) leading or facilitating grade-level curricular and unit reflection sessions; (3) serving as site facilitator to assist new teachers; (4) recruiting and assisting trainers; (5) participating in a summer leadership institute; and (6) attending monthly lead teacher meetings. Lead teachers may select from this list of activities to fulfill the 70-hour requirement.

6. *Materials support.* The lack of materials, supplies, and a coherent curriculum are factors that mitigate against teacher retention, especially in urban secondary schools (Clark 1995). The VIPS action plan contains a very strong, standards-based curriculum and makes provisions for teachers to have all essential materials. VIPS operates a full-service materials center that acts as the materials center for the

entire county. The center ships all materials directly to teachers' classrooms every quarter. VIPS is based on a philosophy that teacher time is best spent in planning and teaching, not searching out materials. Through a cost-sharing agreement among the 14 participating school districts, the materials center orders, manufactures, inventories, refurbishes, and delivers all science materials. Classroom teachers are never expected to provide any of their own materials.

7. *Time for collaboration and networking within and between schools.* The report of the National Education Commission on Time and Learning (1994) offered a comprehensive review of the relationship between time and learning in our nation's schools. The commission concluded that there has been little attempt to restructure the use of time so that schools can focus on sustained professional development for teachers.

   The VIPS action plan recognizes that time must be provided for teachers to collaborate and network within and between schools, and especially within subject areas, as part of their professional development. Time is allocated through a variety of measures. Some schools use pupil-free days for professional development. Other schools use shortened days. Many schools add minutes to four days each week and release students early on the fifth day. Most schools use a combination of these strategies to provide time for teacher collaboration and planning.

   The VIPS senior staff meets with principals annually to offer a selection of site-based professional development activities for principals and teachers. These activities include program introduction; opportunities to revisit and reflect on units of study; integrating writing, literacy, English language development, and mathematics in science; inquiry as a process; and assessment strategies. This menu of services is not static; it continuously changes according to teacher needs and interests. Neighboring schools often meet together for these professional development activities.

8. *Applications of technology.* Teachers in the Imperial Valley have access to a countywide fiber-optic network. Numerous computers, each equipped with Internet access, are found in every classroom. The Imperial County Office of Education offers frequent workshops on technology applications for classroom teachers. The workshops focus on the use of technology for teacher and student Internet access, graphics, digital imaging, teacher and student word processing, PowerPoint, spreadsheets, and lesson plan preparation. Due to Imperial Valley's geographic isolation, professional development opportunities are conducted over the fiber-optic network, thus reducing travel time and distance for teachers. Regionalized centers conduct simultaneous professional development, assisted by teacher leader facilitators. Participants can interact and view the same content simultaneously.

   In early 2001, VIPS established a partnership with LessonLab Inc. through the California Science Subject Matter Project. Current work with LessonLab Inc. focuses on launching a comprehensive software platform to support the development and implementation of innovative, case-based professional learning programs over the World Wide Web. This technology incorporates a mix of streaming video, user discussions, supplemental materials, and personal learning tools to create an enriching professional development experience. The LessonLab platform allows teachers and preservice teachers to study and discuss VIPS-produced science videos and artifacts of best classroom practices face-to-face and over the Internet services provided on the countywide fiber-optic network. The VIPS senior staff are building a digital library of successful teaching practices, creating a tool to strengthen teaching in the district.

9. *Workshops focusing on student work as the centerpiece of standards-based performance assessment.* According to Marzano, Pickering, and Pollock (2001), the centerpiece for gauging the impact of any teacher professional development program is whether it results in high-quality student work. New teachers (those new to the district but not necessarily new to the profession) and beginning teachers (those just starting their careers) are afforded multiple professional development entry points to improve the quality of their students' work. VIPS has developed two pathways to assist all teachers in this regard: by increasing their understanding of (1) performance assessments and embedded science assessments and (2) the use of student science notebooks.

Each of the designed instructional science units has an end-of-unit performance assessment and embedded assessments. These formative assessments were developed by VIPS staff in collaboration with teachers. Teachers attend workshops to help them understand how to implement, score, and ensure the reliability of the assessments. In follow-up sessions, teachers bring samples of their students' work to discuss and they reflect on their own instructional practices.

Student science notebooks are an integral part of the VIPS instructional program. They are maintained by each student for each unit of study. In workshops, teachers study examples of student science notebooks, establishing and discussing common components of exemplary work and strategies for assessment, scoring, and reflecting on student work. Examples of exemplary student work for each of the instructional units have been collected over time, and a scoring rubric has also been developed. These form the key components of a teacher "tool kit," which is used during the teacher workshop to assist teachers in setting benchmarks for their own students' work.

10. *Opportunities to refine instructional delivery through reflection and lesson study groups.* "Lesson study" is a problem-solving process used by Japanese teachers for professional enhancement. It involves systematic examination of teaching-learning processes through initial planning, teaching, observation, and reflection. The process works like this. Four teachers work with a facilitator. Collectively they select one lesson for the lesson study process. Teacher 1 teaches the lesson as

designed in the teacher's guide with the facilitator, and the other three teachers observe and take notes on a template. Student work is collected. At the end of the day, all four teachers and the facilitator meet and discuss the student work and the lesson. The lesson is usually adjusted. The next day, Teacher 2 teaches the adjusted lesson with the other teachers and the facilitator observing and taking notes. Again, student work is collected and the teachers meet and discuss the student work and the lesson. The lesson is usually adjusted again. The next day, Teacher 3 teaches the refined lesson…and so on. The final step in lesson study is to share findings with colleagues.

The benefit of lesson study as a means for sustained teacher professional development is well documented by Stigler and Hiebert (1999). They state that "the power of lesson study is that it facilitates teachers' contribution to the field and to their own professional development. That is, when teachers are able to contribute to the field of education they are simultaneously developing their professional understandings" (176).

The lesson study normally occurs after teachers have participated in a sustained program of professional development that focuses on both deepening their science content knowledge and strengthening their pedagogical skills. As a more intellectually rigorous and self-reflective process it is the next step in professional development. The challenge is now a second-order task—that is, a task that requires the participants not only to be familiar with materials and best practices, but also to be reflective of their own practices. This task is one that has been deliberately addressed by VIPS and has resulted in substantial progress. During the 2000–2001 school year, VIPS offered teachers their first opportunity to participate in lesson study groups. Selected lessons were videotaped and discussed during the following meeting. These lessons also became a part of the LessonLab platform.

Conclusion

Teacher retention and renewal in science are critical issues facing our nations' schools. A clear commitment from schools and school districts is needed to face the challenge of professional support for new and beginning teachers during their first five years of teaching. VIPS has taken a significant step forward, with a cohesive professional development action plan that views teacher retention and renewal as a multi-dimensional challenge and provides science teachers with numerous opportunities and entry points designed to specifically address this issue. The program has created a strong partnership, based on commitment and support from the 14 school districts in Imperial County, California, SDSU-IVC, and the California Science Subject Matter Project. Implementation of the program's action plan has created a balanced and teacher-focused array of opportunities to grow professionally that are strongly supported by participating school districts, with a clear goal of teacher retention and renewal as well as a long-term goal of developing a broad countywide base of sustained teacher leadership.

References

American Association for Employment in Education. 1998. *Teacher supply and demand in the United States: 1997 report.* Evanston, IL: American Association for Employment in Education,

Berlinger, D. C. 2000. A personal response to those who bash teacher education. *Journal of Teacher Education* 51(5): 358–71.

Bernshausen, D., and C. Cunningham. 2001. The role of resiliency in teacher preparation and retention. Paper presented at the 53rd Annual Meeting of the American Association of Colleges for Teacher Education, Dallas, TX (March).

Bidwell, C. 1965. The school as a formal organization. In *Handbook of organizations*, ed. J. March, 973–1002. Chicago: Rand-McNally.

Bobbitt, S., M. Leich, S. Whitener, and H. Lynch. 1994. *Characteristics of stayers, movers, and leavers: Results from the teacher follow up survey, 1991-1992.* Washington, DC: National Center for Education Statistics.

Boe, E., and D. Guilford. 1992. *Teacher supply, demand, and quality.* Washington, DC: National Academy Press.

Bryk, A., V. Lee, and J. Smith. 1990. High school organization and its effects on teachers and students: An interpretive summary of the research. In *Choice and control in American education,* Vol. 1: *The theory of choice and control in education,* eds. W. H. Clune and J. F. Witte. New York: Falmer Press.

California Employment Development Department. 2000. *Unemployment rates.* Sacramento: California Economic Development Association.

Chapman, D., and M. Green. 1986. Teacher retention: A further examination. *Journal of Education Research* 79: 273–79.

Clark, R. 1995. *National network for education renewal: Partner schools.* Washington, DC: National Network for Education Renewal. (ERIC Document Reproduction Service No. ED 380 418.)

Darling-Hammond, L. 1984. *Beyond the commission reports: The coming crisis in teaching.* Santa Monica, CA: Rand Corporation.

———. 2000. *Teacher quality and student achievement.* Seattle, WA: Center for the Study of Teaching and Policy, University of Washington.

Eberhard, J., P. Reinhardt-Mondragon, and B. Stottlemyer. 2000. *Strategies for new teacher retention: Creating a climate for authentic professional development for teachers with three or less years of experience.* Corpus Christi, TX: South Texas Research and Development Center, Texas A&M University.

Feiman-Nemser, S. 1996. *Teacher mentoring: A critical review.* (ERIC Digest, Report No. EDO-SP-95-2.)

Gibbs, E. 1996. Networking—A path for teacher renewal. In *Critical issues in K–12 service learning: Case studies and reflection,* eds. G. Gulati-Partee and W.R. Finger. Indianapolis, IN: Pearson Publishing.

Greenwald, R., L. Hedges, and R. Laine. 1996. The effects of school resources on student achievement. *Review of Education Research* 66 (3): 361–96.

Grissmer, D., and S. Kirby. 1992. *Patterns of attrition among Indiana teachers, 1965–1987.* Santa Monica, CA: Rand Corporation.

———. 1997. Teacher turnover and teacher quality. *Teachers College Record* 99: 45–56.

Guyton, E., and E. Farokhi. 1987. Relationships among academic performance, basic skills, subject matter knowledge, and teaching skills of teacher education graduates. *Journal of Teacher Education* 38(5): 37–42.

Hargreaves, A., and M. Fullan. 2000. Mentoring in the new millennium. *Theory into Practice* 39(1): 143–55.

Ingersoll, R. 1995. *Teacher supply, teacher qualifications, and teacher turnover.* Washington, DC: National Center for Education Statistics.

———. 1999. The problem of underqualified teachers in American secondary schools. *Educational Researcher* 28(2): 26–37.

———. 2001. Teacher turnover, teacher shortages, and the organization of schools. Seattle, WA: Center for the Study of Teaching and Policy, University of Washington, Document R-01-1.

Lortie, D. 1975. *School teacher.* Chicago: University of Chicago Press.

Loucks-Horsley, S., P. Hewson, N. Love, and K. Stiles. 1998. *Designing professional development for teachers of science and mathematics.* Thousand Oaks, CA: Corwin.

Marzano, R., D. Pickering, and J. Pollock. 2001. *Classroom instruction that works: Research-based strategies for increasing student achievement.* Alexandria, VA: Association for Supervision and Curriculum Development.

Murnane, R. 1987. Understanding teacher attrition. *Harvard Education Review* 57(2): 177–82.

National Academy of Sciences. 1987. *Toward understanding teacher supply and demand.* Washington, DC: National Academy Press.

National Center for Education Statistics (NCES). 1991. *Schools and staffing surveys, public school teacher questionnaires.* Washington, DC: NCES.

———. 1994. *Schools and staffing surveys, public school teacher questionnaires.* Washington, DC: NCES.

———. 1997. *America's teachers: Profile of a profession, 1993-1994,* Tables A8, 11a-e. Washington, DC: NCES

National Education Commission on Time and Learning. 1994. *Prisoners of time: Schools and programs making time work for students and teachers.* Washington, DC: U.S. Government Printing Office.

Rosenholtz, S. 1989. *Teacher's workplace: The social organization of schools.* New York: Longmans.

Schlecty, P., and V. Vance. 1983. Recruitment, selection and retention: The shape of the teaching force. *Elementary School Journal* 83: 469–87.

Southern Regional Education Board (SREB). 1998. *Improving teaching in the middle grades: Higher standards for students are not enough.* Atlanta, GA: SREB. (ERIC Document No. ED428070.)

Stigler, J., and J. Hiebert. 1999. *The teaching gap.* New York: Free Press.

U.S. Census Bureau. 2000. *California census data.* Washington, DC: U.S. Government Printing Office.

U.S. Department of Commerce. 1999. *U.S. income statistics.* Washington, DC: U.S. Department of Commerce, Bureau of Economic Analysis.

Useem, E. 1995. Urban teacher curriculum networks and systemic change. Paper presented at the Annual Meeting of the American Educational Research Association, San Francisco, CA (April).

Weiss, I. R., and S. E. Boyd. 1990. *Where are they now? A follow-up study of the 1985-86 science and mathematics teaching force.* Chapel Hill, NC: Horizon Research.

Yasin, S. 2000. *The supply and demand of elementary and secondary teachers in the United States.* ERIC Digest, ERIC Clearinghouse on Teaching and Teacher Education. Report Number EDO-SP-1999-6.

Mentoring and Coaching for Teachers of Science: Enhancing Professional Culture

Kathy A. Dunne and Anne Newton

Kathy A. Dunne, director of professional development, has been with Learning Innovations at WestEd since 1996. She manages and coordinates large-scale professional development and technical assistance efforts. Dr. Dunne also serves as project director for Teachers as Learners: Professional Development in Science and Mathematics, a three-year project funded by the National Science Foundation. She has been a high school and middle school classroom teacher, a college instructor, and a curriculum supervisor for a state department of education.

Anne Newton is the lead author of *Mentoring: A Resource and Training Guide for Educators* (Regional Laboratory for Educational Improvement 1994). She has been a classroom teacher, reading specialist, staff developer, and mentor. Currently, she is a program director at Jobs for the Future in Boston, Massachusetts.

By the year 2007, over 2 million new teachers will be needed in our nation's schools (National Center for Education Statistics [NCES] 2002; National Commission on Teaching and America's Future [NCTAF] 1996). Currently, one of the critical teacher shortage areas is in science. In the face of that reality, over 20 percent of high school science teachers lack a minor in their main teaching field. Additionally, 56 percent of high school students taking physical science are taught by out-of-field teachers (National Commission on Mathematics and Science Teaching for the 21st Century 2000). This shortage of qualified science teachers amidst high demand is magnified by continued high rates of teacher attrition. Thirty to fifty percent of new teachers leave the profession during their first few years of service, with the highest attrition rates occurring in urban settings (NCTAF 1996). In spite of this crisis, there is good news. Mentoring and induction programs can and do make a difference in significantly reducing teacher attrition. The challenge, however, is twofold and framed by two key questions: How can we improve mentoring and induction programs for science teachers? What specific strategies for recruitment, preparation, and licensure will enhance the qualifications of science teachers in our nation's schools? This chapter does not explore the second question; however, it is an imperative for increasing the quality and the number of science teachers K–12. Responding to the first question, this chapter suggests key strategies, structures, policies, and practices that will contribute to quality mentoring and induction for our teachers of science.

Developing a Mentor Program for Science Teachers

Mentor programs for science teachers help to improve the teaching, learning, and assessing of science. Mentor programs enable teachers to (1) increase their knowledge of content, (2) improve their understanding of how to embed scientific inquiry into teaching, (3) increase their instructional competence by reflecting on and analyzing the impact of teaching practices on their students' learning, (4) share in a school's norms of collegiality and experimentation, and (5) enhance their ability to deal effectively with diversity (diverse groups of individuals, different learning styles, and various teaching styles). In turn, effective mentor programs offer a way to assist districts to retain highly qualified new and experienced teachers.

Keys to Effective Program Design and Sustainability

Designing and sustaining an effective mentor program depends on several conditions. The following key factors can mean the difference between a successful program and one that does not achieve desired results:

- *Key inputs (knowledge base, context, and critical issues) are essential to effective program design.* It is critical to gather and analyze data related to these inputs prior to or while designing a program. The knowledge base consists of research on teaching, learning, and assessing; the nature of the academic discipline; and knowledge of mentoring and professional development. The context includes information on the participants (e.g., who they are, what their needs are) and the history of mentoring and professional development in the district. Critical issues encompass equity, diversity, and time.
- *Supports and challenges in the system need to be considered before implementing a new program.*
  - Will the district's professional culture support a mentor program? For example, will administrators articulate the importance of mentoring? Will they nurture and support a learning community in their schools?
  - Are there policies, procedures, and schedules in place that will support the program, or is the climate conducive to these changes? For example, does the current schedule provide time for teachers to meet during the day? Will administrators allocate or reallocate time to enable mentors and new teachers to observe each other and work together to nurture their own development?
  - How will the mentor program for science teachers fit into the district's professional development system or with its current mentor program?
- *Continuous assessment maintains program integrity and aids in sustaining the program.* The intended results are most likely to be achieved if continuous assessment of a program's effectiveness—including its impact on students' learning and teachers' teaching, learning, and assessing practices—is ensured. Without assessment, the context can change, and the program can be unresponsive to those adjustments. Continuous assessment also provides data to aid in sustaining a program.

◆ *The building of a professional culture in a school or district matters.* Collaborative planning by a multi-representative planning group lays the groundwork for empowerment, ownership, shared leadership, and sustainability of the mentor program.

Designing a Mentor Program

Designing a program includes a series of critical tasks: establishing a diverse, multi-representative planning group, developing the program and the policies and procedures to maintain it, ensuring a supportive environment within the district, preparing and supporting mentors, supporting new teachers, and evaluating the mentor program. Each of these is briefly discussed below.

Establishing a Diverse, Multi-Representative Planning Group

To lay the groundwork for a collaborative design process, a diverse, multi-representative planning group needs to be established and charged with designing and evaluating the program. Its membership may consist of science teachers (potential mentors and second-year teachers); administrators, both central office and school-based; representatives of the teachers' association; school board members; parents and/or community members; and faculty from colleges and universities that prepare teachers (if geographically possible).

The importance of this group cannot be overstated. Without the support of those who affect or are affected by the program, it may fall short of its intended outcomes or even fail. Comprehensive representation also offers the potential of broad support when budgets need to be trimmed.

Developing the Program

The planning group needs to design a program that fits the needs of its specific population of teachers and students, that fully uses resources (people, practices, and funds) available within the district or community, and that accommodates organizational constraints. Several variables can influence the program's design, such as the number, background, and skills of new science teachers; the number, interest, and competence of potential mentors; the extent to which a district's norms and expectations encourage collegiality and experimentation; administrative support; current supervision and evaluation procedures; quality of functioning professional development programs; and available financial resources.

Thus, the multi-representative planning group may undertake a series of tasks as it designs the program. Among these are the following: reviewing current research and best practice; joining a professional organization's chat room or listserv; identifying the program's philosophy, mission, and goals; determining how the program for science teachers can be incorporated into the district's mentor program (if appropriate); defining roles and responsibilities of participants in the program; determining the criteria and procedures for selecting mentors and assigning them to new teachers; assessing the needs of new teachers and mentors in the district; providing options for finding time for mentors and new teachers to meet; determining the content and design of mentor training; developing a proposed budget; presenting a proposal to the school board; providing for the evaluation of the program; establishing a plan for piloting the program; and overseeing the implementation of the program.

Much emphasis is placed on the relationship between a mentor and a new teacher, but the success of a mentor program depends on many people and institutions. All of these critical players have particular roles and responsibilities to fulfill, as displayed in Table 1. The planning group has the responsibility of identifying and communicating these roles and responsibilities to key players.

Developing Policies and Procedures

Prior to implementation, the collaborative planning group should develop, articulate, and record policies and procedures for different aspects of the program—for example, selection criteria for mentors and processes for selecting mentors, matching mentors and new teachers, and reassigning pairs. In establishing selection criteria for mentors, it might be helpful to review the qualities of mentors offered by the literature (Odell 1989; Ohio Department of Education 1990; Oregon Department of Education 1990; Zimpher and Rieger 1988). In choosing those that are relevant, the planning group needs to apply its knowledge of the local district and the purpose of the district's program. In selecting mentors, the planning group can assess an applicant's qualities in several ways: through application forms, interviews, letters of recommendation, informal conversations, records of continuing professional development, observations, or videotapes.

Experience has shown that several factors should be taken into account when assigning mentors to new teachers and that procedures must be in place to enable reassignments when necessary. There is general agreement that it is important to assign mentors to new teachers who teach the same subject and grade level and have ready access to each other (e.g., in adjoining classrooms, on the same floor, in the same building). In addition, it has been found that mentoring relationships form best when teaching style and ideology mesh.

These conditions are ideal, of course, and cannot always be met. Occasionally, mentoring relationships will not work. Procedures need to be in place that enable the mentor or the new teacher to express his or her concerns to a third party for resolution. Some districts have discovered that training a "pool" of mentors each year allows them flexibility to reassign mentors to new teachers when a relationship falters or to match a mentor to a new teacher who is hired in the middle of the school year. A mentoring relationship that does not work need not be seen as failure, but rather as a difference in style.

Table 1. Roles and Responsibilities of Participants in a Mentor Program

Mentor	New Teacher	Administrators	Other Faculty	School Board	Teacher-Preparation Institutions	State Education Agency
Orients new teachers to school, district, and community	Plans, teaches, facilitates, and evaluates progress of students in own classroom	Supervise and evaluate new teachers (building)	Serve on planning group	Establishes policy to make mentoring of new teachers one of the district's priorities	Focus on content and reflection on practice in preservice training	Works with interested parties to establish program guidelines
Links new teachers to resources	Attains higher instructional competence by reflecting on and analyzing the impact of teaching practices on students' learning	Facilitate faculty and community awareness and support for mentor program (e.g., personnel, resources, programs, and organizational structure) (building, district)	Serve on mentor selection committee	Ensures support for mentor program (e.g., personnel, resources, programs)	Serve as member of multi-representative planning group, if proximity permits	Provides technical assistance to local districts
Provides continuing systematic support to new teachers			Support mentor program			Coordinates and establishes communication networks among districts
Enables new teachers to increase their knowledge of the content and process for embedding scientific inquiry into teaching	Enhances ability to deal effectively with diversity in students, learning styles, and teaching styles	Serve on planning group and on mentor selection committee (B, D)	Assist in creating a supportive teaching environment in the school, encourage collegiality	Establishes planning group	Contract with district to provide training to mentors, new teachers, and/or administrators; evaluate the program; facilitate group seminars for mentors and new teachers; or coordinate action research	Shares information with and links districts to resources
				Serves on planning group		Conducts regional meetings for mentors and new teachers
Enables new teachers to analyze their teaching practice in terms of its impact on student learning	Participates in needs assessments	Participate in orientation and training sessions (B, D)	Provide direct assistance to new teachers as arranged through mentors	Approves a district position, full- or part-time, to coordinate a mentor program	Serve as member of a mentor team for new teachers	Consults with colleagues in state education agencies in the region
	Develops own professional development plan for year	Develop schedules for release time or common planning, observation, or conferencing time (B)	Participate in evaluation of mentor program	Reviews evaluation of mentor program	Function as substitute to release new teacher for conferencing, planning, professional development, or cross-visitations	
Facilitates or assists in professional development of new teachers	Meets and conferences with mentor (or mentoring team) on a regular basis	Recognize and plan for changes in interpersonal and interorganizational relationships (B, D)				
Attends all mentor training programs						

(Continued on p. 76)

Table 1. Roles and Responsibilities of Participants in a Mentor Program (continued)

Mentor	New Teacher	Administrators
Models continual professional development and assists new teachers in designing their own professional development plans	Participates in variety of professional development activities (e.g., training activities for new teachers, cross-visitations with mentors and other faculty)	Meet with mentors and new teachers at least two to three times per year (B, D)
		Coordinate programs throughout the district (D)
Participates in evaluation of mentor program	Participates in evaluation of mentor program	Provide professional development activities for program participants (D)
Assists in revision of program for next year	Assists in revision of mentor program for next year	Ensure and participate in program evaluation as well as revision (B)
		Establish collaborative relationships with local colleges and universities

Source: Newton, A., K Bergstrom, N. Brennan, C. Gilbert, N. Ibarguen, M. Perez-Selles, and E. Thomas. 1994. *Mentoring: A Resource and Training Guide for Educators.* Andover, MA: The Regional Laboratory for Educational Improvement of the Northeast and Islands.

Ensuring a Supportive Environment within the District

The most difficult task of implementing a mentor program is scheduling time for mentors to meet informally or for observations and conferences. Teachers or administrators who are involved in mentor programs offer the following solutions:

- release mentors and new teachers from noninstructional duties;
- schedule common preparation times once or twice a week for mentors and new teachers to discuss issues of concern to the new teachers;
- arrange for mentors and new teachers to share a common break time or lunch period for informal interaction;
- employ a roving substitute one or two days each month;
- use volunteer substitute teachers, employ retired teachers, or use visiting teachers (e.g., experts from museums or industry who come to teach a class);
- have veteran teachers present a lesson to two classes; and/or
- provide opportunities for team teaching, demonstration lessons, and observations that benefit students in both teachers' classrooms.

Preparing and Supporting Mentors

Preparation and follow-up support offered to mentors are critical elements of a mentor program. Thrust into this new role, mentors will question their skills, the processes they use, and their impact on new teachers throughout the mentoring experience. Answers provided through training and networking with other mentors, colleagues, administrators, and faculty from teacher preparation programs will allay fears and strengthen programs.

The skills and knowledge needed to begin the mentoring process are often provided during a two- to five-day summer institute for mentors. During the school year, follow-up support in the form of regularly scheduled study groups, seminars, or sharing sessions offers opportunities for new mentors to address the issues they are facing.

The preparation and ongoing support of mentors should address the following:

- the roles, responsibilities, and expectations of being a mentor;
- the goals of the program;
- the concerns and needs of beginning teachers;
- the impact of cultural differences among teachers, students, and parents;
- adult development;
- the change process;
- coaching and mentoring skills (communication, observation, and conferencing);
- effective teaching, learning, and assessment practices (e.g., content expertise in science, reflection on the influence of teachers' behavior on students, different assessment strategies, how to co-plan and co-teach a lesson); and
- curriculum development strategies and resources.

It is critically important to give teachers time to use and reflect on the knowledge and expertise they are gaining. They can practice techniques among themselves or with new teachers, reflect on the impact of these strategies, and be an integral part of the continuous improvement of the program.

Supporting New Teachers

The relationship a new teacher has with a mentor enables her or him to try new instructional strategies, interact with parents, or co-design a new lesson with a trusted colleague. Targeted professional development opportunities can complement this mentoring relationship. These might include the following: (1) a formal, facilitated meeting with other new teachers on a monthly basis to discuss what they are learning about teaching and learning; (2) a new teacher's attendance at a professional conference with his or her mentor, time to process what they have learned together, and an opportunity to share their learning with the faculty; and (3) the co-development and implementation of lessons and units with follow-up reflection on what was done, why, and with what impact on students. All of these experiences assist new teachers on their journey to becoming exceptional teachers.

Evaluating the Mentor Program

Any new intervention requires ongoing evaluation of its effectiveness. A mentor program may be assessed through surveys, interviews, and quantitative data on new teachers' attendance, involvement in school and professional activities, and retention over time. Provisions for an evaluation should be established early in the design by the multi-representative planning group or an evaluation team it appoints. Decisions need to be made about the focus of the evaluation, what baseline data will be gathered, how the evaluation will be conducted, when, and by whom. As the program is being developed, a rubric can be used to assess the relative effectiveness and focus of the development process itself. What are the key pieces of infrastructure of effective programs? Is improved instructional practice a goal? What student outcomes can be anticipated? (See Table 2.) Long-term evaluation of the program's effectiveness should address the following:

- effectiveness of the program in meeting its organizational and individual goals;
- changes in new teachers' ability to process classroom experience and modify their behavior;
- benefits and challenges identified by mentors and new teachers;
- new teachers' perceptions of their mentor's impact on them;
- mentors' views of their new teachers' impact on them;
- new teachers' impact on their own classes, staff members, and parents;
- the program's impact on students by race and ethnicity;
- the program's impact on the entire school;
- retention of new teachers and mentors; and

Table 2. Developing an Effective Mentor Program

Task: To design and implement a mentor program in which experienced teachers serve as new teachers' mentors for one year.

Criteria for Success	1 Unacceptable	2 Basic	3 Proficient	4 Exemplary
Involvement of Key Stakeholders	Mentor program is designed and planned by a few individuals. Could be "top down" or "bottom up."	Teachers and administrators work together to design the mentor program.	Teachers and administrators representing all grade levels, school committee members, parents, and students are involved in designing and planning the mentor program.	There is a multi-representative design team that continually assesses the program, identifies what is working and not working, and makes changes along the way.
Selection Criteria and Process for Mentor Teachers	No criteria exist. Building principal "hand picks" the mentor teachers.	Mentors volunteer and are selected by a mentor program committee. No criteria exist.	Criteria for selecting mentor teachers are identified, and a mentor program committee selects mentors with input from the building principal.	Potential mentors complete an application, which includes recommendations from colleagues.
Mentor and New Teacher Matches	Mentors and new teachers are matched without consideration of grade level, content area, or geographic location.	Mentors and new teachers are matched (to the degree possible) according to grade level and content area.	Building principals contribute to the matching process by considering the compatibility of individual styles of the mentors and new teachers.	A procedure exists whereby, in the event of unworkable matches, both parties are "held harmless" and a new match is made.
Training and Support	Training consists of disseminating and "walking through" the new teacher handbook.	An orientation session is held for mentors outlining roles and responsibilities.	Three to four days of mentor training is provided to all mentor teachers. Training includes qualities of effective mentors, needs of new teachers, active listening and questioning skills, cognitive coaching, and data collection techniques.	Mentor and new teacher pairs are provided with on-site coaching and support throughout the year.

(Continued on p. 80)

Table 2. Continued

Criteria for Success	1 Unacceptable	2 Basic	3 Proficient	4 Exemplary
Supporting Policies and Procedures	There are no policies in place to support the mentor program. However, the district has decided to implement a mentor program.	A set of guidelines is developed to support the mentor program. Incentives are provided for mentor teachers. Training dates are set. Mentors and new teachers have to "catch as catch can" to find time to meet.	Structures are in place to provide mentors and new teachers with time during the day to meet and visit each other's classroom.	The school schedule provides regular professional development time during the school day for all teachers allowing new teachers to link with and learn from other colleagues.
Mentor Program Evaluation	There is no evaluation of the mentor program.	Evaluation of the mentor program focuses only on participant satisfaction and enjoyment.	The impact of mentor training on supporting mentors to successfully fill their roles is evaluated. A survey of new teachers' needs is conducted and used to evaluate how well the mentor program serves those needs.	Mentor teachers do a self-assessment around their performance as a mentor teacher. New teachers conduct a self-assessment of their teaching against clearly defined teaching competencies. Quantitative data are collected and analyzed on the new teachers' and mentors' involvement in school, district, and professional activities and their retention. A rubric identifying criteria for success of a mentor program is developed and used to assess its efficacy.

Source: Learning Innovations, a division of WestEd, 91 Montvale Avenue, Stoneham, MA 02180.

◆ involvement of new teachers and mentors in school and professional activities.

The collaborative planning group or the evaluation team should obtain, in a structured manner, feedback on these concerns from any individual who has been involved in the program. These data should be analyzed and shared with program planners and participants to revise the program prior to the next year's implementation.

Mentoring Teachers of Science: A Learner-Centered Construct

Regardless of the model of mentoring and induction, a learner-centered approach is essential. Deborah Ball's (1999) framework describes the relationship among student learning, teacher learning, and professional developer or leader learning. Figure 1 illustrates the intersecting content of math and science content, student thinking, and teaching strategies. That intersect becomes the content anchor for mathematics and science teaching. That anchor in turn intersects with teacher thinking and professional development strategies. The combining intersect becomes the content anchor for leadership development, which intersects with professional developer thinking and strategies for developing professional developers.

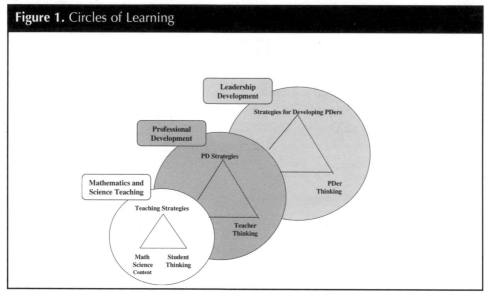

Figure 1. Circles of Learning

Source: Adapted from D. Ball. 1999. Presentation to the National Commission on Mathematics and Science Teaching for the 21st Century, Washington, DC.

Models of Mentoring: Moving beyond the One-on-One Approach

Historically, the primary model of mentoring has taken the form of a one-on-one approach. An experienced science teacher, for example, is selected and trained to serve as a mentor for a new science educator. During the first year of the new teacher's career, the mentor assists with the "nuts and bolts," providing classroom coaching and observation to support the new teacher in reflecting on his or her practice. This approach is powerful and focused, encouraging relationships and therefore reducing isolation, one of the top reasons new teachers leave the profession. (See the "Belmont, Massachusetts" text box.)

With a significant increase in the number of new teachers in our schools, however, the one-on-one model is not possible, particularly in larger schools. Lessons learned from several countries, including the United States, point to the need to expand the concept of mentoring and coaching (Britton et al. 2001). Other professional development strategies, such as the ones discussed below, can be effective in the right context, with the right processes, and given the required resources.

Study Groups/Team Mentoring

The value of study groups includes collegial interaction, teacher-selected areas of study, and the benefit of expert content knowledge on the part of the facilitator. Teachers participating in study groups often examine student work and reasoning, as well as curriculum and assessment. The focus on the teacher's actual work and the culture of collaboration are among the greatest benefits of this strategy. (See "Lansing, Michigan" text box.)

Mentor Teacher-Leader Model

Teacher leadership is often cited as a key aspect of school improvement and school reform. That said, all too often teachers are not afforded opportunities to assume leadership roles (unless they take on formal administrative roles). There are several examples of how well-designed teacher leadership programs can support science teachers who are leaders in their fields. The National Institute of Science Leadership Academy, now in its fourth year, supports professional developers in enhancing their leadership skills by providing professional development for science and mathematics teachers in their home states. Maine's A.A.R.B.E.C. program focuses on developing

Belmont, Massachusetts
Liz Sorrell, K–12 science coordinator for the Belmont, Massachusetts, school district, serves as a mentor and coach to science teachers in her district. While she has a supervisory responsibility, the one-on-one strategy of mentoring a new teacher includes a content-based approach that includes planning conferences, classroom observation and data gathering, and reflective conferences.

A videotape of this process is part of the video library *Teachers as Learners: Professional Development for Science and Mathematics*, available through Learning Innovations at WestEd. *www.wested.org/li*

Lansing, Michigan
Deb Smith, former professor at Michigan State University and now science teacher coordinator in the Lansing Public Schools, has designed and led several teacher study groups for science educators. Some of the implementation requirements for study groups include: time for teacher groups to meet; support from administrators; substantive topics to study and discuss; study group processes that allow for a variety of activities and access to human, electronic, and print resources; self-direction and self-governance on the part of the teachers; opportunities to enhance group interaction skills; and a facilitator with deep content knowledge.

For more information contact Deborah Smith, Lansing Public Schools *www.lsd.k12.mi.us*

teachers as leaders and professional developers. (See the A.A.R.B.E.C. text box.)

Collaborative Mentor Networks
Collaborative networks not only have an impact on local implementation of quality mentor programs, they also enhance the ability of the members of the network to collaborate. Collaborative networks are distinct from other networks in some fundamental ways. First, shared leadership among the coordinators and the network members tends to be the norm. Second, collaborative networks tap into the wisdom of experience and practice of their members and work to enhance the knowledge and skills of the members. Finally, collaborative networks often reinvent themselves and become a force of greater service than was the initial intent. (See the N.N.E.C.N. text box.)

In Conclusion
The need for qualified science teachers has never been greater. Mentoring programs that specifically respond to their preparation are necessary for retaining the teachers of science who will best serve our youth.

References

Ball, D. 1999. Paper presented to the National Commission on Mathematics and Science Teaching for the 21st Century. Washington, DC.

Britton, E., S. Raizen, L. Paine, and M. A. Huntley. 2001. *More swimming, less sinking: Perspectives on teacher induction in the U.S. and abroad.* Paper presented to the National Commission on Mathematics and Science Teaching for the 21st Century. Washington, DC.

National Center for Education Statistics (NCES). 2002. *Predicting the need for newly hired teachers in the U.S., to 2008-09.* Washington, DC: NCES.

National Commission on Mathematics and Science Teaching for the 21st Century. 2000. *Before it's too late: A report to the nation from the National Commission on Mathematics and Science Teaching for the 21st Century.* Washington, DC: U.S. Department of Education.

Advancing the Agenda for Results-Based Certification in Maine (A.A.R.B.E.C. Maine)
The Maine Department of Education is spearheading the A.A.R.B.E.C. project, the centerpiece of which is a regional mentor teacher leader model primarily supporting new teachers of science and mathematics. Eight teachers (each serving one of eight regions) are released from their regular teaching duties to serve as a regional mentor teacher leader for the school year. The primary role of these teacher leaders is to provide professional development and site-based support to schools and districts within their respective regions around the development and implementation of effective mentor and induction programs. Some of the essential elements for implementing this model include release time for teacher leaders, professional development for teacher leaders, administrative support, and resources (financial, time, and materials) for regional teacher leaders and local mentors.

For more information contact Judith Cox, Maine Department of Education *www.state.me.us/education*

The Northern New England Co-Mentoring Network (N.N.E.C.N.)
Under the leadership of Page Keeley of the Maine Mathematics and Science Alliance, the National Science Foundation–funded N.N.E.C.N. project will provide trained mentor teachers to work with new science and mathematics teachers who are seeking traditional and alternative certification in the northern New England states. This collaborative network will provide for tri-state professional learning opportunities and mentor training, sharing of key learnings and challenges within each state, and an overall evaluation of program impacts.

For more information contact Page Keeley, The Maine Mathematics and Science Alliance *www.mmsa.org*

National Commission on Teaching and America's Future (NCTAF). 1996. *What matters most: Teaching for America's future.* New York: Teachers College, Columbia University.

Newton, A., K. Bergstrom, N. Brennan, C. Gilbert, N. Ibarguen, M. Perez-Selles, and E. Thomas. 1994. *Mentoring: A resource and training guide for educators.* Andover, MA: The Regional Laboratory for Educational Improvement of the Northeast and Islands.

Odell, S. J. 1989. Developing support programs for beginning teachers. In *Assisting the beginning teacher*, eds. L. Huling-Austin, S. J. Odell, P. Ishler, R. S. Kay, and R. A. Edelfelt, 19–38. Reston, VA: Association of Teacher Educators.

Ohio Department of Education. 1990. *Assisting the entry-year teacher: A leadership resource.* Columbus, OH: Ohio Department of Education.

Oregon Department of Education. 1990. *Promoting collaboration and collegiality: A handbook for mentors in the Oregon beginning teacher support program.* Salem, OR: Oregon Department of Education.

Zimpher, N., and S. Rieger. 1988. Mentoring teachers: What are the issues? *Theory into Practice* 27: 175–82.

Personal Histories Supporting Retention of Beginning Science Teachers

Charles J. Eick

Charles J. Eick is an assistant professor of science education at Auburn University. He is a former middle and high school science teacher with research interests in preservice and beginning teachers' development. Listening to teachers' voices and studying teachers' lives is a focus for much of his current research. He is a long-standing member of the National Science Teachers Association (NSTA), former president of the Southeastern Association for the Education of Teachers of Science (SAETS), and southeastern regional director for the Association for the Education of Teachers in Science (AETS).

Why do some people choose to teach science? Even more importantly, why do some people remain science teachers after the difficult first years? Statistics on beginning teacher attrition reveal that as many as 40 percent (on average) leave within their first five years in the classroom (Darling-Hammond and Sclan 1996). Furthermore, the number of teacher retirements is increasing at a time when student population is rising. When faced with these demographics, policy makers see an urgent need to reduce attrition among beginning teachers. This need is even greater in science education where chronic teacher shortages have existed for some time.

Reducing attrition levels of beginning science teachers is not a simple task to accomplish. Beginning science teachers face numerous "survival issues" while making long-term decisions about staying in teaching. They face the shock of unexpected working conditions and difficulties with teaching and managing adolescent students (Adams and Krockover 1997a, 1997b). Also, they are especially vulnerable to attrition because of the number of higher paying jobs in their field (Shen 1997). As they struggle through the realities of the classroom, many of them choose to leave.

Nevertheless, many science teachers remain in their jobs past the "survival" years. Working conditions and collegial support have a great influence on their retention, as do past learning experiences and beliefs that form a beginning teacher's professional role identity (Schempp, Sparkes, and Templin 1999). For new science teachers, these professional identities are based on past experiences with science, learning experiences in science education, and science-related work experiences that inform belief systems and practice (Greenwood et al. 2002; Volkmann and Anderson 1998). A beginning teacher's ability to form his or her identity across classroom contexts depends on the strength of these related experiences (Knowles 1992). Rich past experiences in learning science, working in a science-related career, or teaching science can strengthen professional role identities and success early in a teacher's career.

In the preservice preparation of science teachers at our university, we seek to recruit and develop teachers with rich backgrounds in science education experiences that will support their personal choices as beginning science teachers. Early in our program, we focus on the prior educational experiences, backgrounds, beliefs, and values that our students bring to science teacher education and ultimately to their first jobs. We use this knowledge to determine factors that will help them to be successful. For example, personal histories that especially support inquiry-orienta-tions will allow beginning teachers to implement inquiry-based teaching in the class-room (Eick, in press). In studying the personal histories of our preservice teachers, we try to understand those supportive aspects of their lives and thinking, so that we can optimize our limited time in preparing them for beginning science teaching. A recent study of graduates who remain teaching after five years suggests that address-ing personal histories in our program can be a valuable tool in the recruitment, de-velopment, and retention of new science teachers (Eick 2002). Exemplary alterna-tive certification programs have also discovered the importance of studying applicants' background experiences to improve retention of graduates (Milner, Edelfelt, and Wilbur 2001).

Supportive Personal Histories for Beginning Teachers
Personal Histories Supporting Initial and Ongoing Career Choice
Beginning science teachers have deeply personal reasons for selecting science teaching as a career. Reasons for becoming a teacher are especially important to beginning teachers as they constantly reevaluate their initial career decisions (Kelchtermans and Vandenberghe 1994). Deep interest in science often precedes the decision to become a teacher of science. Personal reasons for remaining in this career include a long-term interest in science and in teaching others about it (Espinet, Simmons, and Atwater 1992; Jenkins 1998). Teachers who remain in their careers (in all fields) typically perceive that they have a great impact on students and student learning (Shen 1997; Weiss 1999). They find great job satisfaction in the affective rewards of teaching, such as shaping their students' lives through teaching and caring. Having strong feelings about wanting to teach science and work with adolescents may sus-tain beginning science teachers through the difficulties of their early years in the classroom.

Personal Histories Supporting Developing Pedagogical Content Knowledge
One of the National Science Education Standards for all science teachers is to teach science through inquiry (National Research Council [NRC] 1996). Beginning sci-ence teachers bring life experiences from their own learning and prior careers that can help them be successful as inquiry-oriented teachers (Crawford 1999; Green-wood et al. 2002; Helms 1998; Volkmann and Anderson 1998). These supportive

backgrounds include work experiences, broad content knowledge, teaching experience, and success in managing adolescents. Such background experiences enhance teachers' developing pedagogical content knowledge and student management skills (Adams and Krockover 1997a, 1997b). Past work experience in laboratory or research settings helps entering science teachers in planning and implementing laboratory-based lessons. Similarly, past work experience in engineering can help in teaching technological applications of science. Past teaching experience in science, such as in universities or museums, helps in developing a deeper understanding of content and how to teach it. Entering the classroom with a deeper pedagogical content knowledge in science helps beginning teachers in the successful implementation of their lessons. Teaching experience with adolescents develops greater disciplinary and management skills for the classroom. All of these experiences help beginning science teachers teach for scientific understanding and manage students in inquiry settings with much less frustration and failure.

Personal Histories Supporting Belief in Use of Inquiry
Beginning science teachers bring personal beliefs about teaching and learning science from past educational and work histories (Geddis and Roberts 1998; Greenwood et al. 2002). Beginning science teachers rely on memories of positive and negative science learning experiences as they formulate how they want to teach. Many recall motivational teachers or settings that inspired their love of science or successful work settings in prior science-related careers. These experiences influence their professional identities as science teachers and subsequent thoughts and actions as beginning science teachers (Eick, in press). For example, they often rely on how they learned science best to plan and implement lessons for their own students (Eick, in press; Geddis and Roberts 1998). These beliefs can aid or hinder the planning and implementation of inquiry approaches and student learning in the science classroom. Successful implementation of inquiry-based approaches aids student motivation and learning in science. Meeting students' learning needs and expectations of science helps to create a positive classroom climate that can support beginning teachers.

Building on Personal Histories in Science Teacher Preparation
Students who initially major in secondary science education at our university enter through traditional undergraduate or alternative fifth-year graduate programs. Early in the program they compose autobiographical papers focusing on their personal experiences and values that support their choice of science teaching as a career (Cole and Knowles 2000). The Appendix is an example of one assignment given to students early in our program. The study of beginning teachers through personal biographical accounts is one way to examine the life experiences that shape their knowledge, thinking, and early practice (Butt, Raymond, and Yamagishi 1988). Although great variation exists in each student's life story about wanting to become a science

teacher, Table 1 describes some general and common themes among students.

Table 1. General Personal Histories Supporting Career Choice of Science Education Students		
Science Histories	**Education Histories**	**Value Histories**
• Family members spark curiosity in science • Innovative school programming (e.g., Voyage of the Mimi curriculum, science fair) • Work with scientist • Positive outdoor and nature experiences • Positive tinkering experiences • Dislike for isolated, repetitive lab research • School science as fun or interesting • Love of discovery and exploration • Curious nature • Science television programming (e.g., Discovery Channel) • Scientist role models	• Dynamic and hands-on science teacher(s) • Informal teaching experiences (e.g., Sunday school, scouts, camps, wildlife programs, sports) • Formal teaching experiences (e.g., substitute teaching, tutoring, university teaching) • Family member(s) in education • School leadership roles • Enjoyment of school environment • Participation in school sports • Caring and inspirational teacher(s) • Love of learning	• Religious conviction to teach • Desire to teach others • Positive influence on kids • Care and love for children

Students share aspects of past histories that can be grouped into three general categories: (a) science histories, (b) education histories, and (c) value histories. Students share stories about their past involvement and interest in science, how education influenced this interest and their desire to teach, and other reasons for wanting to become science teachers. The common themes in each category create a composite profile of life experiences that inform the thinking, beliefs, and values of our students and their career choices. The profile points to those background experiences that eventually can support individuals on the job.

Sometimes, however, supportive life experiences and personal reasons for science teaching are lacking in an autobiographical paper. We use this lack of information in follow-up interviews with our students to probe an individual's background experience and personal reasons for wanting to become a science teacher. In these interviews, we also suggest appropriate experience(s) needed as they progress through our program and as they continually reevaluate their decision to become a science teacher. This process helps our students clarify their reasons for wanting to become a science teacher, and for those who continue in the program, it provides a means of tailored pre-professional development. For example, a student who lacks experience doing scientific inquiry is counseled to obtain this experience in a structured experience working with a university scientist. Students who show a unidimensional interest in a more didactic approach to learning science are asked to develop and teach lessons in other modes of learning. Students who lack actual teaching experience (formal or informal) are provided early teaching opportunities in local schools. We believe that providing these experiences early and throughout our program will give our students the tailored experiences that can support and sustain them in their professional roles as beginning science teachers.

Conclusion

Teacher preparation programs, whether alternative or traditional, with limited time and resources must carefully prepare beginning teachers for the difficulties that they will face in the classroom (Tusin 1999). Beginning science teachers will find it challenging to successfully carry out their chosen professional identities as science teachers as well as inquiry approaches in the science classroom (Adams and Krockover 1997a, 1997b; Flick et al. 1997). They need to have knowledge from past work experiences and as students in science to help guide and sustain their vision of teaching through early career challenges. Also, beginning science teachers need to have deeply personal reasons and values for wanting to become teachers of science; those reasons and values can help them to stay in the classroom despite any challenges they face as beginning teachers (Espinet, Simmons, and Atwater 1992; Jenkins 1998). Science teacher preparation programs can use various biographical approaches (résumés, interviews, autobiographical papers) to understand students who make initial choices to become science teachers. These approaches help in the selection and development of preservice teachers and in the retention of beginning teachers (Milner, Edelfelt, and Wilbur 2001). Counseling students based on this information can lead to deeper reflection on their career choice. In some cases, students may see that they lack compelling reasons and experiential backgrounds to support this choice. These students may self-select out or be shown that science teaching may not be the appropriate choice for their career. Counseling students can prompt the tailoring of experiences in science and teaching that develops their beginning pedagogical content knowledge and expands their conception of and ability to teach science through inquiry. Science education programs that address students' personal histories will be more effective in selecting and supporting beginning teachers who stay in the classroom and choose to make science teaching a lifetime career.

Appendix
Autobiography in Science and Education Writing Assignment

Who are you as a preservice teacher at this moment in time? What experiences and contexts in life have brought you to this methods course, to your decision to become a science teacher? Life histories and life experiences are powerful shapers of our lives and our ongoing career decisions. These experiences add meaning to our lives. Everyone has been provided with unique gifts, talents, or strengths through their life experiences. Sometimes life itself nurtures these gifts and we are made aware of them. How will these gifts serve you and others as a science teacher in the classroom? Everyone also has been shaped by life's experiences and events to form unique beliefs and values. These beliefs and values can be religious ones, but also can be beliefs about almost anything, including teaching and learning (and schooling). As science education majors, you also have unique beliefs and values about science. What unique beliefs and values do you have about teaching, learning, schooling, and science? How will these values and beliefs benefit you and your students as a science teacher in the classroom?

In this course, you will have the opportunity to confront and reflect on your life experiences, values, and beliefs, especially those regarding teaching science. You will have the opportunity to examine who you are in light of what other experts (scientists, science educators, classroom teachers) expect you to be as a science teacher. The classroom itself (students, administrators, parents) will place demands on you that will challenge your prior beliefs and expectations about teaching, learning, and schooling—beliefs based in *your* personal history and not that of your students. Some of others' expectations of you are based on research that supports science learning through certain approaches or methods (e.g., inquiry, constructivism, cooperative learning). Some of these expectations are culturally based and vary among countries, states, school districts, and science teachers. Will who you are as a science teacher be different from others' expectations? Can you justify *who you are* and *what you do* as a science teacher? This is a very important question that only you will be able to answer for yourself. *Self-reflection* and *change* are the keys to successful science teaching, regardless of who you are and what you do.

Write a brief (3–5 pages typed, double-spaced) but informative autobiographical story of *who you are* as a student in science education. [I do not ask you to discuss who you will be as a science teacher and what you will do as one because such an exercise is purely speculative at best, and, at worst, leads you to write what your instructor wants to hear.] In order to do this assignment, you will need to remember the contexts of your life and your life experiences that have shaped you and brought you to this point in time. In a simple way, you are writing about two key questions: (1) Why become a teacher? and (2) Why teach science? Think back in your life history to stories that you believe have shaped these two decisions.

The following questions may help you write your autobiography assignment. Choose those that are most pertinent to your story. Feel free to discuss other issues not mentioned here:

1. What memories are *vivid* for me, especially those memories that I believe help shape my ongoing life decisions, not just my choice to teach? Describe them.

2. How have family members and experiences influenced who I am and possibly shaped my decisions?

3. What gifts, talents, or strengths am I aware of that I bring to my vocation? How may these help me as a teacher? As a teacher of science?

4. What experiences in education as a student have shaped my career decisions? Describe them in detail.

5. What was learning like in those classrooms that I fondly remember? How were lessons taught? How was the classroom set up? What kinds of classrooms do I remember negatively and want to avoid in my teaching? Why were they negative experiences for me?

6. How has experience tutoring or teaching influenced my choice? Describe any teaching experience that you have had either in a formal classroom or with children outside of school. Describe your role as teacher in these instances.

7. What experiences with science have I had that have shaped who I am and my career decisions?

8. What beliefs or values do I hold strongly? Where do they come from? How might they serve me as a teacher of science and my future students? Where might they need to be open to change?

9. Who stands out in my past as being a *major* influence in my life (who I am) and/or on my decision to teach science? What qualities did that person have? If a teacher, how did he or she teach in their classroom?

10. What kinds of teaching or learning situations have the most impact on me? Why? How do I learn best?

Be creative and self-reflective in your writing. Don't just write about events and people without *describing the contexts* behind those situations and their *impact on you*. Write what *you* want to describe/discuss and not what will sound good to others, especially the instructor. Remember, this is a pass or fail assignment (i.e., full or no credit).

References

Adams, P. E., and G. H. Krockover. 1997a. Beginning science teacher cognition and its origins in the preservice secondary science teacher program. *Journal of Research in Science Teaching* 34: 633–53.

———. 1997b. Concerns and perceptions of beginning secondary science and mathematics teachers. *Science Education* 81: 29–50.

Butt, R., D. Raymond, and L. Yamagishi. 1988. Autobiographical praxis: Studying the formation of teachers' knowledge. *Journal of Curriculum Theorizing* 7: 87–164.

Cole, A. L., and J. G. Knowles. 2000. *Researching teaching: Exploring teacher development through reflexive inquiry.* Boston: Allyn and Bacon.

Crawford, B. A. 1999. Is it realistic to expect a preservice teacher to create an inquiry-based classroom? *Journal of Science Teacher Education* 10: 175–94.

Darling-Hammond, L., and E. M. Sclan. 1996. Who teaches and why: Dilemmas of building a profession for twenty-first century schools. In *Handbook of research on teacher education*, ed. J. Sikula, 67–101. New York: Association of Teacher Educators.

Eick, C. 2002. *Why I want to be a teacher: Longitudinal case studies of the personal histories supporting career science teachers.* Autobiographical paper presented at the annual meeting of the Association of Educators of Teachers in Science, Charlotte, North Carolina (Jan.).

———. In press. What makes an inquiry-oriented science teacher? The influence of learning histories on student teacher role identity and practice. *Science Education.*

Espinet, M., P. Simmons, and M. A. Atwater. 1992. Career decisions of K–12 science teachers: Factors influencing their decisions and perceptions toward science teaching. *School Science and Mathematics* 92(2): 84–91.

Flick, L. B., C. W. Keys, S. L. Westbrook, B. A. Crawford, and N. G. Carnes.1997. *Perspectives on inquiry-oriented teaching practice: Conflict and clarification.* Panel discussion presented at the meeting of the National Association for Research in Science Teaching, Oak Brook, Illinois.

Geddis, A. N., and D. A. Roberts. 1998. As science students become science teachers: A perspective on learning orientation. *Journal of Science Teacher Education* 9: 271–92.

Greenwood, A., M. Scribner-MacLean, R. Ravgiala, and K. Shea. 2002. *A panel symposium on science teacher education: Alternative and traditional routes to certification challenge science educators to determine what is "essential."* Papers presented at the annual meeting of the Association of Educators of Teachers in Science, Charlotte, North Carolina (Jan.).

Helms, J. V. 1998. Science—and me: Subject matter identity in secondary school science teachers. *Journal of Research in Science Teaching* 35: 811–34.

Jenkins, E. W. 1998. On becoming a secondary science teacher in England: A pilot study. *International Journal of Science Education* 20: 873–81.

Kagan, D. M. 1992. Professional growth among preservice and beginning teachers. *Review of Educational Research* 62: 129–69.

Kelchtermans, G., and R.Vandenberghe. 1994. Teachers' professional development: A biographical perspective. *Journal of Curriculum Studies* 26(1): 45–62.

Knowles, J. G. 1992. Models for understanding pre-service and beginning teachers' biographies. In *Studying teachers' lives,* ed. I. F. Goodson, 99–152. New York: Teachers College Press.

Milner, J. O., R. Edelfelt, and P. T. Wilbur, eds. 2001. *Developing teachers: Fifth year programs for outstanding students.* Lanham, MD: University Press of America.

National Research Council (NRC). 1996. *National science education standards.* Washington, DC: National Academy Press.

Schempp, P. G., A. C. Sparkes, and T. J. Templin. 1999. Identity and induction: Establishing the self in the first years of teaching. In *The role of self in teacher development*, eds. R. P. Lipka and T. M. Brinthaupt, 142–61. Albany, NY: SUNY Press.

Shen, J. 1997. Teacher retention and attrition in public schools: Evidence from SASS91. *Journal of Educational Research* 91(2): 81–88.

Tusin, L. F. 1999. Deciding to teach. In *The role of self in teacher development,* eds. R. P. Lipka and T. M. Brinthaupt, 11–35. Albany, NY: SUNY Press.

Volkmann, M. J., and M. A. Anderson. 1998. Creating professional identity: Dilemmas and metaphors of a first-year chemistry teacher. *Science Education* 82: 293–310.

Weiss, E. M. 1999. Perceived workplace conditions and first-year teachers' morale, career choice commitment, and planned retention: A secondary analysis. *Teaching and Teacher Education* 15(8): 861–79.

Wideen, M., J. Mayer-Smith, and B. Moon. 1998. A critical analysis of the research on learning to teach: Making the case for an ecological perspective on inquiry. *Review of Educational Research* 68(2): 130–78.

The Reemerging Cycle of Teacher Supply and Demand: North Carolina Takes Action

Gerry M. Madrazo, Jr.

Gerry M. Madrazo, Jr. has been a science teacher, science curriculum specialist, school administrator, and director of a science and mathematics education network. He is a clinical professor of science education at the University of North Carolina, where he obtained his Ph.D. in curriculum and instruction. He has been president of the National Science Teachers Association, the North Carolina Science Leadership Association, and the North Carolina Science Teachers Association. Dr. Madrazo has published extensively and has presented at national and international conferences on subjects from "science for all cultures" to "teacher professional development."

The U.S. Department of Education estimated that the United States will need two million new K–12 teachers by the year 2006 (Whithrow and Long 1999). According to U.S. Census projections, between 1990 and 2005, a 12 percent growth is expected in the elementary school population and a 28 percent growth is expected in the high school age population (*Network News* 1999). These factors, combined with an annual attrition rate of about 7 percent for public school teachers—to be intensified as "baby boomers" reach retirement age—present a dismal forecast of the teacher supply and demand in the United States (*Network News* 1999).

Brief History of Shortages in Mathematics and Science

Teacher shortages in the fields of science and mathematics education have been an ongoing problem. A study by Hudson (1996) assessed the change in science teacher supply over a period of 10 years. Comparing data to previous studies on the supply of science teachers, Hudson indicated that surveys conducted by the National Education Association from 1948 to 1982 consistently showed a shortage in science teachers, particularly in the physical sciences.

Findings by Watson and Anderson (as summarized in the *Greensboro, North Carolina, Daily News* in 1980) specifically addressed the science teacher shortage in that state. According to the statistical summary, 200 mathematics and science teachers graduated from North Carolina colleges and universities during the 1978–1979 school year, including all graduates of public and private universities who were eligible for teaching certification in math or sciences in grades 7–12. Of these graduates, only about half entered the teaching profession. In 1979 there were over 300 percent *fewer* mathematics teachers and over 300 percent *fewer* science teachers certified in North Carolina compared to the supply in 1974 (Figure 1.)

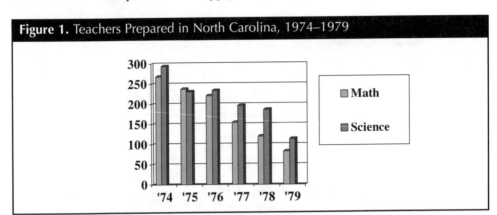

Figure 1. Teachers Prepared in North Carolina, 1974–1979

Source: Watson, L. W., and N. D. Anderson. 1980. A surplus of N.C. teachers? Not in sciences. *Greensboro, North Carolina, Daily News,* 20 July.

Research attempting to establish the determinants of this problem was conducted by Hounshell and Griffin (1989), whose report examined the reasons why science education graduates either chose not to enter the teaching profession or entered the teaching profession and then left. Of 89 science education majors contacted, 71.9 percent responded to the study, and subsequent contacts obtained information on the current occupational status of 86.5 percent of the science education majors. Of those who responded, 48.1 percent said they were not currently teaching. Of those, 32.4 percent had never entered the teaching profession. When asked the main reason they were attracted to another profession, 31 percent of the respondents cited the low salary of teaching. Low professional prestige was cited as the reason for leaving by 16 percent of the respondents, and 21 percent cited lack of professional freedom. Thirty-six percent of the respondents said that higher salaries might increase their satisfaction with teaching and prompt them to reenter the profession. The study indicated that certified science teachers who left did so after an average of 1½ years, with salary being a foremost concern *at that time.* Other serious determinants causing the participants in the study to leave the profession were social attitudes of teachers and "professionalism" within the profession. As Hounshell and Griffin (1989) conclude,

> *Salary, respect, and professionalism are all areas that policy makers* can *deal with, and while data from the study provide no surprises they do confirm what many people have been saying for a long time. Teachers* do *leave because of concerns in these areas and their concerns should be addressed!* (442)

Henry M. Levin of Stanford University (1985) pinpointed the cause of the teacher shortage of mathematics and science teachers: "Just as school salary policy, with its reliance on the single salary schedule, has not provided competitive salaries for mathematics and science specialists in the past, it continues to create a shortfall in the number of qualified mathematics and science personnel willing to take teacher training and offer their services to schools" (381). Although Levin mentioned other possible solutions to the teacher shortages—such as job sharing by teachers seeking only part-time work, retraining of teachers from other specializations, and increased use of educational technology to replace teachers—he also viewed increasing teacher salaries as a key to alleviating the shortage: "It is only by offering special increments to attract mathematics and science specialists that a long term solution can be effected" (381). This sentiment has been echoed in the literature and reports on science and math teacher supply.

North Carolina Takes Action

In response to dismal forecasts that have been presented since the early 1980s, North Carolina sought to take preventative measures to counteract such a crisis. The North Carolina legislature established various programs not only to *recruit* individuals into the teaching profession, but to also *retain* and *renew* teachers already in the profession. These initiatives were made possible because of the foresight of the governor, higher education executives, business leaders, and policy makers, as well as teachers themselves.

Recruitment Efforts

One such program, North Carolina Teaching Fellows (*http://teachingfellows.org*), is a component of a ten-point teacher recruitment proposal entitled *Who Will Teach Our Children?* developed by the Public School Forum of North Carolina. It offers a four-year college scholarship to selected high school students who plan to teach. The students are required to teach for four years in North Carolina after college graduation.

A federally funded program, North Carolina Teachers of Excellence for All Children (NC TEACH) (*http://ncteach.ga.unc.edu*), resulted from the state legislature's call for the State Board of Education and the Board of Governors of the University of North Carolina to submit a proposal aimed at recruiting mid-career college graduates into the teaching profession. Interested individuals may apply for the program if they have (1) obtained a baccalaureate degree, (2) achieved a 3.0 grade point average (GPA) in their major course of undergraduate study and an overall 2.5 GPA, (3) at least three years of professional experience, and (4) met score requirements on either the GRE or an equivalent MAT score. NC TEACH is working with host site universities to prepare new teachers to join the teaching force each year. Professionals participating in NC TEACH complete a six-week intensive residential course of study at one of the host sites and then receive assistance in obtaining a teaching position in a North Carolina public school. During their first year of teaching, the teachers attend weekly seminars and participate in a mentoring program with experienced teachers. After the successful completion of the first year of teaching, participants are assisted in obtaining an initial teaching license, but they are also required to complete all university level courses at their university before receiving full licensure. NC TEACH focuses on providing opportunities to prepare teachers for secondary math, science, special education, and second language classes and middle grades math, science, language arts, and social studies classes.

Likewise, the North Carolina Model Teacher Education Consortium (*www.ncmtec.com*), a collaborative partnership of select school systems, colleges and universities, and community colleges, assists individuals, such as teacher assistants, who are working toward teaching licensure. The partnership's mission is to increase the quantity of highly qualified educators by providing affordable, accessible, and high-quality education and training to both aspiring and practicing educators in North Carolina.

Learn NC—The North Carolina Teachers' Network (*http://www.learnnc.org*) has a variety of professional development resources. One such program is Carolina OnLine Teacher (COLT). Provided by UNC-Chapel Hill's School of Education, COLT offers continuing education licensure for K–12 teachers, who are able to achieve advanced competencies in online teaching methodologies and technologies. For teachers who do not have access to such professional development opportunities, distance or online education can serve as a viable option.

Renewal and Retention Efforts

In addition to increasing recruiting efforts in North Carolina, the state has also placed great emphasis on retaining and sustaining teachers by providing professional development and assistance for those already in the teaching profession. The Mathematics and Science Education Network (MSEN) (*www.unc.edu/depts/msen*) is one organization that provides such professional development and assistance. It does so by strengthening content and pedagogy in science and mathematics. An early report stated:

> *In 1980–81, North Carolina universities graduated only 167 mathematics teachers for 620 openings and only 218 science teachers for 310 openings. Nearly half the junior high school mathematics and science teachers, and fully one-third of the high school mathematics and science teachers, were not properly certified for the subjects they were teaching.* (MSEN 2001)

In response to statistics such as these, many state universities began to promote the education and reeducation of teachers in mathematics and science. MSEN annually offers about 300 professional development opportunities for teachers of mathematics and science, which are attended by approximately 5,000 teachers per year. The higher education component of the Eisenhower Professional Development Program, administered by MSEN, provides teachers and professional staff with inservice training in mathematics and science. The program provides participants with financial support and stipends, which it does competitively through grants, which are awarded to colleges and universities, as well as through nonprofit organizations, private universities, and community colleges. This ability to provide effective preparation of professional development for teachers in mathematics or science based subjects in grades K–12 has received favorable evaluation. It has had a major impact on classrooms and teacher behavior and attitudes (MSEN 2001).

Another professional development program offered to North Carolina teachers is the North Carolina Center for the Advancement of Teaching (NCCAT) (*http://www.nccat.org*), whose purpose is to restore teachers' enthusiasm for and commitment to teaching and learning. The program is unique. There is no comparable program or facility in the United States; in fact, educators from many states come to North Carolina to observe NCCAT. The center is open year-round and provides a full range of programs, from residential seminars and teacher-scholar residencies to collaborative professional development opportunities with school systems in the state. NCCAT was established in 1985 on the campus of Western Carolina University in Cullowhee, North Carolina. The idea came from the North Carolina Commission on Education for Economic Growth, a commission established by the governor in 1983 to develop plans to improve the state's schools. NCCAT was an idea ahead of its time. Pilot programs conducted in the summer of 1984 received positive feedback from teachers in the state. A year-round program of seminars was implemented, beginning in 1989. Currently, NCCAT conducts approximately 70 weeklong seminars a year, focusing on topics in the arts, sciences, and humanities and promoting conversation and intellectual development. Today, NCCAT is a model institution for the renewal of teachers and the teaching profession.

The North Carolina Teacher Academy (NCTA) (*http://www.ga.unc.edu/NCTA*) also offers professional development for teachers, in this case through a variety of summer programs. All North Carolina teachers are eligible to attend as part of a team, with priority given to teams that include a principal or assistant principal. NCTA modules are designed to encompass current theory with direct, hands-on activities. In 2001, NCTA offered a variety of sessions, ranging from Integrating Technology into Instruction to Implementing a Balanced Literacy Program.

A Reemerging Problem

Despite these steps toward improving teacher recruitment, retention, and renewal, North Carolina, like many other states, is still at risk for a drastic teacher shortage. According to a report published by the Public School Forum of North Carolina (1997), North Carolina is one of the ten states with the largest projected increases in enrollment over the next ten years for public elementary and secondary schools (Figure 2). The report states that "North Carolina's expected 110,000 students would be a nearly 10 percent jump in enrollment. North Carolina's high school population alone is expected to grow by 82,000 in the next ten years" (4). Yet, despite the great advancements made on behalf of teacher retention and renewal by North Carolina in the 1980s, the problem of teacher retention seems to have once again been placed on the back burner. As the Public School Forum report states, despite the state's early strides toward improving the teaching profession, "North Carolina has slipped to 42nd in beginning teacher salaries, and the Office of Teacher Recruiting has long since closed its doors" (4).

Figure 2. Expected Enrollment Growth (numbers in thousands)

State	Enrollment		Total Students
	1996	2006	
California	5,815	6,878	1,063
Texas	3,791	4,090	298
Washington	996	1,129	133
Georgia	1,324	1,436	113
Virginia	1,122	1,232	110
North Carolina	1,207	1,316	110
New Jersey	1,229	1,337	109
Florida	2,235	2,333	98
Maryland	838	931	92
Alabama	753	844	91

Source: Public School Forum of North Carolina. 1997. *A profession in jeopardy: Why teachers leave and what we can do about it.* Raleigh, NC: Public School Forum of North Carolina.

Teacher shortages still seem to be as much a looming crisis today as they were a decade ago. Recruiting New Teachers, Inc.'s (RNT) website (*www.rnt.org*), for example, points out in its "Field Facts" section that according to reports issued by the U.S. Department of Education, America will be educating more than 54 million students in 2006—three million more children than are currently enrolled in schools today. Morever, "across grade levels, most districts (97.5 percent) say they have an immediate demand for special education and 75 percent of districts say they have an immediate demand for teachers in three fields: science (97.5 percent), mathematics (95 percent), and bilingual education (72.5 percent)."

What Can Be Done?
Indeed, North Carolina has taken significant steps to alleviate present and future teacher shortages in all areas of specialization. Numerous preservice and inservice opportunities have been established, and North Carolina, having increased teacher

salaries, now ranks 21ˢᵗ in average teacher salaries across the nation (*NSTA Reports!* 2002). Teacher shortages, particularly in the fields of science and mathematics, continue to exist across the state and across the rest of the nation. So, what can be done to prevent these continuing shortages in the future? In *Preparing Schools and School Systems for the 21ˢᵗ Century*, published by the American Association of School Administrators (Whithrow and Long 1999), the authors assert that there must be "extensive preparation, professional development, and support for teachers, from preservice through lifelong education" (67). In addition, faculty must be well prepared in both content and learning theory.

North Carolina, as well as many other states, is trying various new programs to find out what works and what does not. One promising new program in North Carolina is The Collaborative Effort to Support New Professionals, a consortium of low-income counties, universities, and public agencies in northeastern North Carolina. With a focus on teamwork and networking, the collaborative provides opportunities for new teachers to develop individual leadership and initiative through orientation programs, mentoring, regional conferences, and various other meetings, collaborative teams, and support systems (Public School Forum of North Carolina 1997).

Other states, such as California, have established many new, innovative programs to address the issues of teacher recruitment and retention. California state funds supplement these activities to defray the costs of administration and evaluation in the school districts. One such initiative is the University of the Pacific/Lincoln Unified School District project, a preservice-inservice bridge program, using a supportive telecommunications network. This program provides each new teacher with a personal computer, two online mentors—a university professor and an experienced public school teacher—and the necessary telecommunications software and training to use the telecommunications network (Public School Forum of North Carolina 1997).

Across the nation, efforts have proven quite successful in attracting middle and high school students either to teaching or to choosing a career related to science and mathematics. As in California, where a pre-college program, Mathematics, Engineering, and Science Achievement (MESA), exists, the University of North Carolina's Mathematics and Science Education Network (MSEN) Pre-College Program is designed to recruit students and prepare them to pursue mathematics or science-related fields at the university level and in their professional careers. This program has an impressive track record. Almost 97 percent of MSEN pre-college graduates surveyed say they have gone on to college (MSEN 2001), and a majority say they intend to pursue careers related to math, science, or technology.

MSEN continues to offer numerous grants to support professional development for teachers in mathematics and science education. By improving teacher content and methodology, as well as the confidence to teach the content, MSEN hopes to provide support for individuals already in the field.

A policy group for the National Commission on Teaching and America's Future published a report entitled *Building on Our Investment: Teaching Policies in North*

Carolina (1997). This advisory group asserts that North Carolina has taken substantial steps to secure and retain quality teachers in all fields and suggests that the state build upon its investments. Recommendations from the advisory group include giving teachers a reduced teaching load during their first three years, allowing new teachers to observe a master teacher and have a mentor, providing quality professional development opportunities, and creating meaningful incentives to award good teaching and keep people in the profession.

Several states are now implementing alternative teacher licensure programs to meet the growing demand for teachers. Although there have been no complete assessments of these programs to determine the positive or negative aspects of alternative licensure, there is no question of the need to prepare more individuals for teaching careers. Florida is one state using such alternative licensure programs. The Florida Association of Colleges for Teacher Education issued *Alternative Teacher Certification: A Position Paper*, recommending the improvement of the alternative licensure programs in the state (Yarger and Kasten 2001). This paper recommends that the target for alternative licensure programs be critical-need areas only and that induction programs be developed to support all teachers in the first and second years on the job (Yarger and Kasten 2001). In 1988, Old Dominion University established a Military Career Transition Program to help active-duty and retired military personnel to become teachers. The program's courses build on the content knowledge of the military personnel while providing education experience. So far, the program has graduated 1,250 military personnel, who chose teaching as their career in 47 states (Yarger and Kasten 2001).

Despite these advancements and pioneering recruitment and professional development opportunities, there seems to be no end in sight when it comes to teacher shortage. Retaining teachers is often a neglected task. Without a definite and sustainable solution, this problem will only escalate. It is estimated that school districts in the United States will have two million teacher openings in the next decade (Yarger and Kasten 2001). Literature and data indicate that good teachers are the key to good schools, and good schools are imperative to provide quality education for all students; therefore, continuous professional development must be implemented to assist teachers in becoming and remaining knowledgeable in their content area.

Although specifically dealing with the issue of science education reform, Motz (1997) outlines some of the characteristics of quality professional and staff development programs that are applicable to all subjects. He states that the most effective staff development activities

- Are continuous and ongoing.
- Model the constructivist approach to teaching that teachers will use with their students.
- Provide opportunities for teachers to examine and reflect on their present practices and to work with colleagues to develop and practice new approaches.

◆ Provide good support structures for [teachers and administrators], among the [teachers and administrators] and the instructors, and from the school. (Motz 1997, 30)

Professional development activities must build on teachers' creativity and flexibility and renew their passion for teaching and learning. Moreover, inservice programs must help teachers develop new teaching and learning ideas through increased knowledge of content, educational research, and alternative methodologies. Additionally, teachers must be given the flexibility to transform their classrooms into "inviting environments for learning" (Purkey and Novak 1996). Above all, teachers must continuously receive administrative and system support and be given the resources to implement innovative ideas. Without these inservice opportunities and without infrastructural support, teachers will find it difficult to remain in the profession. If we are unable to sustain teachers once they have entered the profession, all recruitment efforts and policies will have been in vain. Policy makers, teacher educators, administrators, business leaders, and the community must do more to confront this problem head-on. The alternative is the reemergence of a vicious cycle of teacher supply and demand!

References

Hounshell, P. B., and S. S. Griffin. 1989. Science teachers who left: A survey report. *Science Education* 73(4): 433–43.

Hudson, S. P. 1996. Science teacher supply in the United States. *School Science and Mathematics* 96(3):133–39.

Learn NC—The North Carolina Teachers' Network. *http://www.learnnc.org*

Levin, H. M. 1985. Solving teacher shortages. *Educational Evaluation and Policy Analysis* 7(4): 371–82.

Mathematics and Science Education Network (MSEN). 2001. *www.unc.edu/depts/msen*

Motz, L. L. 1997. Infra-structural support needed to meet science education reform. *Science Educator* 6(1): 28–32.

National Commission on Teaching and America's Future. 1997. *Building on our investment: Teaching policies in North Carolina*. Raleigh, NC: North Carolina Policy Advisory Group.

Network News (A Quarterly Bulletin of the SHEEO/NCES Communication Network). 1999. Critical issues in teacher supply and demand. 18(1): 1–4.

North Carolina Center for the Advancement of Teaching (NCCAT). 2001. *http://www.nccat.org*

North Carolina Teacher Academy (NCTA). 2001. *http://www.ga.unc.edu/ncta*

North Carolina Teachers of Excellence for All Children. 2001. *http://ncteach.ga.unc.edu*

North Carolina Teaching Fellows. 2001. *http://www.teachingfellows.org*

NSTA Reports! 2002. Report shows teacher salaries not keeping pace with ed. expenditures (May/ June).

Public School Forum of North Carolina. 1997. *A profession in jeopardy: Why teachers leave and what we can do about it*. Raleigh, NC: Public School Forum of North Carolina.

Purkey, W. W., and J. M. Novak. 1996. *Inviting school success: A self-concept approach to teaching, learning, and democratic practice.* Belmont, CA: Wadsworth.

Recruiting New Teachers, Inc. *www.rnt.org*

Watson, L.W., and N. D. Anderson. 1980. A surplus of N.C. teachers? Not in sciences. *Greensboro, North Carolina, Daily News,* 20 July.

Whithrow, F., and H. Long. 1999. *Preparing schools and school systems for the 21st century.* Arlington, VA: American Association of School Administrators.

Yarger, S. J., and K. Kasten. 2001. *Alternative teacher certification: A position paper.* Boca Raton, FL: Florida Association of Colleges for Teacher Education, Florida Atlantic University.

Collaborative Efforts to Retain New Teachers: A University–School District Partnership

Denise K. Crockett, Geneal Cantrell, Shirley A. Ritter, and Michael Svec

Denise K. Crockett is an assistant professor of education at Furman University. She previously taught high school chemistry and physics in the public schools for 12 years. Dr. Crockett has published articles and book chapters in the areas of science, technology, diversity, and action research. Her Ph.D. is in science education from the University of Georgia with an emphasis in educational foundations and anthropology. She does qualitative evaluations, both internally and externally, with grants such as one from the Duke Endowment to evaluate the Northwest Crescent Child Development Center and St. Francis Hospital.

Geneal Cantrell is the Teacher in Residence at Furman University where she teaches both undergraduate and graduate courses. She is the trainer of mentor teachers in the Teacher to Teacher program. Her areas of interest include early childhood and elementary education teaching. Ms. Cantrell taught for over 21 years in the public schools. Her experience ranges from first through eighth grade, remedial through gifted, and self-contained to pullout in numerous content areas.

Shirley A. Ritter is a professor of special education at Furman University. She is a former teacher and the author of numerous journal articles. She is a past president of the Teacher Education Division of the Council for Exceptional Children and currently reviews manuscripts for several journals in the area of special education. Her research interests are collaboration; mild disabilities; and supporting novice teachers, particularly those whose students struggle academically in the general education setting.

Michael Svec is an associate professor of education at Furman University. His teaching responsibilities include elementary and high school science methods, educational technology, and supervision of teaching interns. He was the physics author for the ninth-grade Science Links textbook series and has served as evaluator for the Girl Scouts' Plugged In! project. He coordinated and taught summer workshops on constructing physics understanding in a computer-enriched environment in conjunction with San Diego State University. He holds a B.S. in physics from the University of Illinois-Urbana and a Ph.D. in curriculum and instruction from Indiana University-Bloomington.

The transition from student to professional is difficult for many beginning teachers. Feelings of isolation and uncertainty are all too common, as evidenced in the words of one first-year teacher:

> *I am so stressed. I just seem to be pulled in so many directions. I am trying so hard to be a good teacher but I don't think I am. I feel like I am so inefficient sometimes. I know that I am doing what I want to do. I love my kids. I just don't know if I can do it. Am I the only one who feels this way?* (Stonesifer 2001)

Unlike other professions in which newcomers receive a substantial period of training and a gradual increase in responsibility, new teachers must assume the full extent of their responsibilities from the very first day. First-year teachers are often expected to perform with the same level of expertise as seasoned teachers. In addition, many first-year teachers are assigned the most difficult students and have access to the fewest resources. Classrooms are usually equipped with minimal materials and, in many instances, the teachers feel they have no support from the administration and their colleagues. Research estimates that as many as 50 percent of new teachers leave the teaching profession within their first five years (Odell and Ferraro 1992). Science is a critical needs area, which compounds the problem. This shortage of qualified teachers results in non-licensed educators teaching science; therefore, it is especially important to retain the licensed teachers who teach science. One method for decreasing this first-year flight is through mentoring.

In 1997, Furman University in Greenville, South Carolina, received one of eight grants entitled "Recreating Colleges of Teacher Education," given by the BellSouth Foundation. This grant, in conjunction with seeking initial accreditation by the National Council for Accreditation of Teacher Education (NCATE) and Furman's affiliation with the National Network for Education Renewal (NNER), led to an inquiry into innovative and practical solutions to K–8 teacher preparation. The results of a self-study prompted university faculty to begin to transform the teacher education program into a tailor-made curriculum that fit the needs of local schools. A core component of this program involved training and using mentors with the first-year teachers.

Goodlad's National Network for Educational Renewal (1990, 1994) provided the impetus for programmatic changes in teacher education at Furman University. Goodlad's curriculum program initiatives include a post-baccalaureate sequence of well-supervised practice experiences in partner schools that have a commitment to prepare teachers, to create ongoing renewal, and to involve beginning teachers in inquiry.

The National Commission on Teaching and America's Future's (NCTAF) report *What Matters Most: Teaching for America's Future* (1996) provided a foundation for Furman's programmatic changes. The report concluded that current and appropriate knowledge about teaching and learning would not reach and benefit schools unless public schools and programs of teacher preparation at universities changed dramatically. Such changes could include developing extended teacher education programs that provide a yearlong internship in a professional development school and creating and funding mentor programs for beginning teachers.

Recognizing the importance of these issues and the need for teacher education reform, a partnership was created in the spring of 1999 between Furman University and a local rural school district. An important aspect of the partnership involved revamping the school district's existing mentor program. Stakeholders from the school district and the university collaborated in designing a new program, which began the following spring. With a common mission, the school district and the university embarked on a journey toward teacher preparation renewal. Together they created the Teacher to Teacher program to provide an avenue for improved teacher retention and mentoring. In the subsequent year, a second school district joined the collaborative partnership.

The National Science Education Standards (NRC 1996) point out that effective teachers have specialized knowledge that combines their understanding of science, learning, teaching, curriculum, and students. The standards state that this specialized knowledge is developed through experiences that deliberately connect science and pedagogy, model effective teaching practices, address the needs of teachers, take place in classrooms, and use inquiry, reflection, research, modeling, and guided practice. The Teacher to Teacher program provides those experiences throughout the course of two years.

The Teacher to Teacher Program

The Teacher to Teacher program has several unique features: (1) a senior year that includes an early, full-time experience of 15 days in the classroom and a spring-term senior block (explained below); (2) a yearlong paid internship for the induction year teacher; (3) a formal mentorship program whereby mentor teachers are released from all teaching responsibilities to supervise three to four teachers during their induction year; and (4) an action research course taken during the internship year. Table 1 presents an overall description and time line of the Teacher to Teacher program.

Table 1. Time Line for the Teacher to Teacher Program

Junior Year		Senior Year	Yearlong Induction Year

Winter term
- Group meeting to discuss Senior Block and Induction Year.

Spring term
- Meet to discuss starting dates and Early Experience Placements.

Fall and Winter Terms
- Early internship experience (August) provides valuable exposure to class procedures and a base for methods courses and internship.

- Seminars held most days after school during early experience. Van Manen training completed.[a] Format for interviewing individuals from the community introduced. Interviews conducted and tape recorded.

- Examination and adjustment of pedagogy according to individual learning preferences, culture, interest, and experiences started in early experience and continued throughout the academic year.

- Monthly meetings addressing course topics and field placement issues.

- Prejudice reduction workshop held.

- Field experiences for methods courses continue at same school.

- Interviewed by district personnel director.

Spring Term Senior Block
- Curriculum consists of assessment, technology integration, professional development, and multicultural pedagogy.

- Classes taught by three professors and a Teacher in Residence.

- Includes a minimum of 30 days of mentored teaching.

- Emphasis on critical thinking, reflection, and inquiry.

- Use of district and school community for building an understanding of the school population and its unique qualities.

- Students supported by Furman professors, mentor teachers, school, and district staff.

- Previous program graduates lead selected seminars during Senior Block.

- Development of participants from interns into teachers before their full-time teaching begins.

- Graduate!!

- Paid position at three-quarters salary, includes standard benefits and a tuition waiver for graduate courses.

- Inductees are supervised by Furman professors, the Teacher in Residence, mentor teacher/site coordinators, and school district personnel.

- Induction teachers are ideally placed at the schools they have worked in throughout the senior year, easing the transition and providing more nurturing support.

- Graduate credit earned during induction year can be applied to a master's degree.

- Induction Year incorporates the option for adding additional licensure in special education or early childhood education.

- Induction teachers use themselves and/or their students as a base for best practices experience and for inquiry and research projects as a component of the graduate studies.

[a]Presented as a reflective model to demonstrate a phenomenological approach (van Manen, M. 1986. *The tone of teaching*. Richmond Hill, Ontario, Canada: Scholastic).

This university–school district collaborative approach, which includes aspects of both the practical and theoretical worlds, was critical to the systemic change brought about through this program. Four educators—three Furman professors and one Teacher in Residence—struggled to create a 12-credit-hour instructional block, referred to as the "senior block." Three courses make up the elementary (currently grades 1–8) senior block: Assessment for Planning and Instruction; Diverse School Cultures: Teaching, Learning, and Management; and Integration of Curriculum and Technology; courses are planned and taught by a team of educators— three professors and one practitioner, the Teacher in Residence—and are woven into a single sequence of seminars and field experiences. Efforts are made to connect theory with practice.

Mentors

Mentoring is seen as a critical component in attracting new teachers into the profession, as well as supporting and retaining them (Lipton, Wellman, and Humbard 2001). Teachers are twice as likely to leave the profession where no mentoring programs are in place (Huling-Austin, Putnam, and Galvey-Hjornevik, 1986). These authors also suggest that mentoring is the most cost-effective means of nurturing novice teachers and keeping them in the teaching profession.

The Teacher to Teacher program employs mentoring as the cornerstone of its foundation and strength. Figure 1 depicts the layers of mentoring provided in the Furman model. The program also focuses on professional development of both the induction teacher and the formal mentor, by having them participate in action research projects and team meetings, where discussion and democratic decision-making take place.

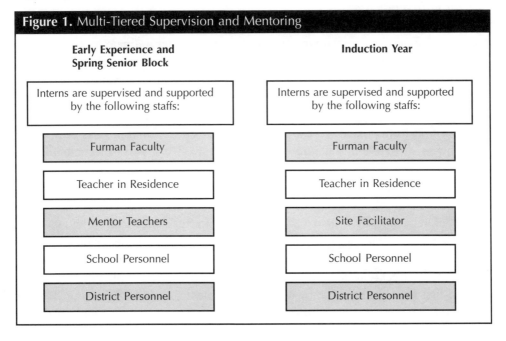

Figure 1. Multi-Tiered Supervision and Mentoring

Early Experience and Spring Senior Block	Induction Year
Interns are supervised and supported by the following staffs:	Interns are supervised and supported by the following staffs:
Furman Faculty	Furman Faculty
Teacher in Residence	Teacher in Residence
Mentor Teachers	Site Facilitator
School Personnel	School Personnel
District Personnel	District Personnel

Value of Mentor Teachers

A distinguishing feature of the Teacher to Teacher model is the amount and quality of mentoring provided to the induction teacher by the two partner school districts. The school districts provide the following human resources: on a rotational basis, one teacher released from one of the two districts, relieving her of her teaching responsibilities to become the university Teacher in Residence; mentor teachers released from teaching responsibilities to serve as on-site coordinators and supervisors of the induction teachers; and two district administrators to serve as liaisons. The Teacher in Residence provides the communication link among the district, the teachers, and the university. She provides a sounding board for induction teachers and their formal mentors, and also offers input and assistance in developing and implementing this new program. She teaches classes in the senior block and during the induction year, while also providing the mentors with consistency and insight into the entire program. The Teacher in Residence serves as a bridge between the practical and the theoretical worlds.

The key to providing effective mentors begins with the selection process and continues with providing training and support. The most successful model of mentor selection used in the Teacher to Teacher program involved an application process and an interview with both district and university representatives. The district and Furman's Department of Education then make a joint decision about whether to accept the recommendation. During the spring term, the teacher candidates are introduced to their mentors and assigned a supervising teacher educator who will support them during their field experiences.

Program Changes

Throughout the creation, implementation, and evaluation of this program, many program changes occurred at both the graduate and undergraduate levels. Needed changes became evident after a longitudinal examination of the pilot participants and continued evaluations of all participants at the district and university level. Through continued mentoring and support during the induction year, the Teacher to Teacher program has given the senior block faculty a deeper understanding of the transition from preservice experience into the educational profession. During this process, the university faculty's role evolved from a supervisor/evaluator role into a mentorship role.

Reflection of Interns

As part of her academic course load, the Teacher in Residence teaches an induction course to all first-year teachers in her district, including the teachers who are part of the Teacher to Teacher program. One of the requirements of the course is that the teachers write weekly reflections about their experiences. The following are reflections of first-year teachers, both with traditional mentors and the Teacher to Teacher mentors. The reflections demonstrate how powerful the mentoring relationship can be.

Shelly is a Furman graduate coming out of the traditional program and placed in the same school as one of the Teacher to Teacher mentors. She teaches third grade and had a traditional mentor teacher who was not affiliated with the Teacher to Teacher program. Shelly says of her mentor,

> I really feel like [mentor teacher affiliated with Teacher to Teacher] is my mentor because she is so accessible, and I see her all the time. She has helped me so much.

Shelly feels that a kinship has developed between her and the mentor of the Teacher to Teacher program. She initially felt dismissed, not supported by her assigned traditional mentor. Shelly talked of her frustration with her traditional mentor:

> The mentor ... and I never met officially in September. She was "winging" the form to just get it turned in—that was about three weeks late. I think we got off to a slow start. I did recently ask her to come in and observe [name of student] to give me some ideas—she was very helpful. I know she thinks that I am doing fine and all is well—not sure exactly where she gets her info, but I am glad she is so positive about me. However, as the mentee, it is sometimes hard to take the initiative for help. I am not complaining about [name of traditional mentor] because when I asked specifically for help with [name of student], I got it. I just wish she would take a little bit more initiative.

Shelly is frustrated. She feels that she must be resourceful and reach out to her mentor for help. As a novice teacher, the extra burden of being the one to ask constantly for help is troubling and overtaxing.

Cindy, another traditional first-year teacher, is taking the district-required induction course with the Teacher in Residence. She writes in one weekly reflection to her,

> I am a first-year teacher. I make mistakes. I desire criticism and advice from my mentor. She continues to tear me down in the eyes of the principal. The principal and my first mentor are friends. The principal has a tainted mindset of me by my first mentor teacher. As far as I can tell, the principal chooses to believe the teacher; it is obvious in our brief conversation on the switch in mentorship. They [the principal and now former mentor teacher] are forming a camaraderie.

Cindy experienced total disempowerment. She felt stripped of the essence of becoming a teacher. Cindy believed that instead of giving support, her mentor continually undermined her authority. Cindy was so distraught over the issue that she was reassigned to a new mentor. She says of her new mentor,

A mentor. I am so excited! What an incredible resource. We became friends quickly. My mentor confides personal information to me early, and this confidence I take very seriously. I always consider it a privilege when someone feels comfortable enough to confide in me. I feel at ease and fortunate to be getting along so well with my [new] mentor.

With the change in mentors, Cindy became validated again. She has reestablished a foundation where she can develop.

Jill, the Teacher in Residence, responds to an e-mail from one of the first-year teachers who does not have the advantage of a Teacher to Teacher mentor. She shares in her e-mail,

NEVER, NEVER question your ability as a teacher. You are doing a great job and I hear all sorts of wonderful things about you. As a parent, I know I would love for my child to be in your class. You are so organized and so "together." Things will be easier for you as time goes on. Research says it really takes five years of experience to become a teacher. So, be easy on yourself, and don't try to conquer the world in one day.

Jill understands the importance of relationship building for first-year teachers. She knows how to offer comforting words to a novice teacher; this is an affirmation of Jill's ability and choice as a teacher.

In contrast to the statements made by the traditional students, the comments of the teachers in the Teacher to Teacher program reveal the power of the program, with its strong mentor component. Heather is a first-year teacher who teaches fourth grade at a small rural school. She talks of her experiences with curriculum planning:

My mentor and I decided that was the way I needed to go. So, after making that decision, I faced the hard part—doing the planning. I was amazed at the support that was given to me during the days before I hoped to start my integrated teaching. [Teacher to Teacher mentor's name] was wonderful. My mentor group [mentor teacher and all mentees] met one Thursday night and pulled resources to help me plan. I could have not been more thankful for their help—or their time! We worked together, and by the end of the night I felt more comfortable with my next month of teaching.

Heather expresses her appreciation for the support she received from her mentor teacher. Heather, other interns, and their mentor teachers have created a support network that allows them not only to share content material but also to create professional networking.

Lori, a second-grade teacher involved in the program, shares her appreciation in a reflection to the Teacher in Residence,

The past few weeks have been exceptionally challenging. I did not fully appreciate the support this master's program offered until last week when I was feeling desperate and had no idea what to do. You and [name of Teacher to Teacher mentor] have been an amazing encouragement and support to me. Having outsiders observe and offer new ideas and opinions has been so helpful. I do not know how I would have gotten through the past few weeks without encouragement and support. [Teacher to Teacher mentor] and I talked for a long time last week about some new organizational strategies I need to use with the students. Thanks for all your help.

Lori shares that the networking of mentoring, both formally and informally, has encouraged her as a teacher. The strength of the scaffolding effect is especially significant early on in her professional development.

Lessons Learned from the Teacher to Teacher Program

Where do we go from here? How do we improve and maintain quality mentors? The following is a discussion of lessons learned from the Teacher to Teacher program.

- The Teacher to Teacher program provides multiple perspectives and access to numerous resources. The interns are given an opportunity to immerse themselves in several different perspectives that give rise to ownership of their teaching philosophy. They have layers of support where constant feedback and dialogue is provided. The purpose of this feedback and support is, as Goodlad suggests, to produce a caring, confident, and competent teacher. This endeavor has been accomplished with the efforts of both formal and informal mentoring.
- The Teacher to Teacher program provides a mechanism to disperse information on best practices in both practical and theoretical areas. The Teacher to Teacher mentors model, team teach, and dialogue constantly with the interns throughout the first year. The informal mentors share information with the interns when appropriate and necessary. This approach is designed to empower the interns by enabling them to seek out knowledge and to act accordingly through participation in an action research project and an induction course.
- The Teacher to Teacher program provides universities and school districts with a plan to choose quality mentor teachers who best fit individual school and community needs. However, each community school is a reflection of the greater community, and the values and beliefs of that particular community must be taken into account.
- The Teacher to Teacher program provides a strong link between the professional community of a university and public schools. This ongoing relationship reacquaints teacher educators with the reality of being a teacher in today's classroom. Also, it provides the teacher educator with a more holistic view of public education classes as opposed to focusing on a specific methods course.

- This process gives teacher educators, administrators, and mentors the opportunity to go outside their areas of expertise and challenge their perceptions and beliefs. Simultaneous renewal is a result of many stakeholders involved in the Teacher to Teacher program.
- All stakeholders must be committed to the mission of the program. It is time intensive, problematic, and laborious. However, the end results are positive. The interns are staying in the profession, are feeling supported, and are achieving self-efficacy sooner and with more confidence than traditional first-year teachers.

References

Goodlad, J. 1990. *Teachers for our nation's schools.* San Francisco: Jossey-Bass.

———. 1994. *Educational renewal: Better teachers, better schools.* San Francisco: Jossey-Bass.

Huling-Austin, L., S. Putnam, and H. Galvey-Hjornevik. 1986. *Model teacher induction project study findings.* (Report No. 7212). Austin, TX: University of Texas at Austin, R and D Center for Teacher Education.

Lipton, L., B. Wellman, and C. Humbard. 2001. *Mentoring matters: A practical guide to learning-focused relationships.* Sherman, CA: MiraVia, LLC.

National Commission on Teaching and America's Future. 1996. *What matters most: Teaching for America's future.* New York: Teachers College, Columbia University.

National Research Council (NRC). 1996. *National science education standards.* Washington, DC: National Academy Press.

Odell, S., and D. Ferraro. 1992. Teacher mentoring and teacher retention. *Journal of Teacher Education* 42 (3): 200–204.

Stonesifer, B. H. (personal communication, September 30, 2001).

Van Manen, M. 1986. *The tone of teaching.* Richmond Hill, Ontario, Canada: Scholastic.

ASIST: An Induction Program for Science Teachers

Nancy C. Patterson, Gillian H. Roehrig, Barbara Austin, and Julie A. Luft

Nancy C. Patterson and **Gillian H. Roehrig** coordinated Project: ASIST as graduate students at the University of Arizona. Dr. Patterson is currently an assistant professor at Bowling Green State University. Her research interests include induction program design, beginning teacher change, and teacher turnover. Dr. Roehrig is an assistant professor at San Diego State University, where she continues to work with beginning teachers and conduct research in undergraduate science education. **Barbara Austin** was a high school physics teacher and is currently a graduate student at the University of Texas at Austin. **Julie A. Luft** is an associate professor at the University of Texas at Austin. Dr. Luft designed Project: ASIST and served as the program director. Her work in science teacher education currently focuses on beginning teachers and multicultural science education.

Concern about the increasing shortage of teachers, particularly in the areas of special education, mathematics, and science, has created a national call for induction programs to support beginning teachers (Darling-Hammond 2000; National Commission on Mathematics and Science Teaching for the 21st Century 2000). A recent report from the National Commission on Teaching and America's Future estimates that 30 percent of new teachers leave the profession within the first five years (Darling-Hammond 2000), while a recent National Science Teachers Association (NSTA) survey reveals that over 30 percent of younger science teachers are considering leaving the profession (National Science Teachers Association 2000). Our newest teachers are leaving the profession at an alarming rate. Next to the retirement age group, teachers aged 25 to 29 show the highest rate of attrition at 10 percent (National Center for Education Statistics 1997a). Based on these data and the increasing need for new teachers that has expanded from 2.5 million in the early 1980s to 3.3 million early in the next decade (Darling-Hammond 2000), it appears that the demand for teachers may not be met.

In light of nationwide teacher shortages, the authors of this chapter look at beginning teacher support as one possible response to the problem of beginning teacher attrition. The chapter begins by briefly reviewing the current state of induction programs internationally and in the United States. Next, the literature regarding induction program development and format is presented. The project Alternative Support for Induction Science Teachers is then discussed as an example program. Concluding the chapter are remarks about the future of induction programs for science teachers.

Status of Induction Programs

Induction programs have proliferated over the past two decades, both internationally and in the United States (Darling-Hammond 1998; Neuweiler 1988). The Pelavin Research Group (1997) recently reported on the rapid increase of induction programs in 11 countries in the Pacific Rim, Europe, and Asia. These programs are initiated by government agencies and often entail mandatory participation by beginning teachers. In the United States, fifteen states have mandated induction programs and six states have proposed or are piloting induction programs (National Commission on Teaching and America's Future 1996), while over 300 schools and colleges of education provide post-bachelor's degree programs (Darling-Hammond 1998). As a result of the increase of induction programs nationally, over half of American teachers report participating in a formal teacher induction program (National Center for Education Statistics 1997b).

Amidst this proliferation of induction support, there are inconsistencies among programs. For example, there are fundamental differences in funding and organization. Programs in the Pacific Rim are commonly funded through a combination of sources and are organized and enacted by multiple authorities (Pelavin Research Group 1997). Specifically, it is not uncommon to have national and local funds collectively supporting induction programs and to have a school, a district, or a state agency directing the program. Program funding and organization also varies in the states (Huling-Austin 1987). Authors of the National Association of State Directors of Teacher Education and Certification (NASDTEC) (2000) report indicate that 26 states, as well as Washington D.C., have teacher induction programs, with an additional two states planning programs, yet only 18 of the 26 are state-mandated. Of these, only 15 state legislatures cover some or all of the costs of teacher induction (NASDTEC 2000). In those states that do not have mandated induction programs, individual districts are responsible for the implementation of their own programs.

There are also variations in the structure of induction programs. One major difference is the inclusion of an evaluation component. International programs tend to have evaluation built into the program more often than do programs in the United States (Britton et al. 2000). Another difference is the duration of time that an induction program is available to a beginning teacher. In the United States, programs vary greatly in length and duration, with some programs lasting three days and others continuing for three years. International programs tend to last throughout a school year and over several years. Another variation is the purpose of induction programs. Some have the sole purpose of socialization, others have a goal of supporting specific methodologies, and many consist of combinations of both.

The design and rationale for induction programs should be grounded in educational research. It is generally agreed that induction programs should be configured to draw upon the "learning to teach" and teacher induction literature (Huling-Austin 1992). This research can guide teacher educators' understanding of the purpose and function of "quality" induction programs (Gold 1996; Hoffman et al. 1986; Huling-

Austin 1990; Odell 1986). Huling-Austin (1990) suggested that such programs should be developed to improve teaching performance, increase retention, promote personal and professional well-being, satisfy mandated requirements related to induction, and transmit the culture of the school. Yet many programs do not have a sound rationale that directs their format and purpose, and as a result they do little more than serve as mandatory inservice hours that are neither beneficial nor useful to beginning teachers.

However, the increased dialogue surrounding induction programs has brought forth new paradigms for these programs. One such change is the creation of induction programs that are tailored to the special needs of secondary teachers (e.g., Geva-May and Dori 1996; Luft and Patterson, in press). In science, such programs are responding to educational research that highlights the specific needs of beginning secondary teachers, and the goal of creating a seamless transition from the preservice program to the first years of teaching (Adams and Krockover 1997; Emmer 1986; Loughran 1994; Simmons et al. 1999). This focus ultimately helps to retain science teachers, enhance their performance, and improve their personal and professional well-being. These are critical areas in a time of demand for science teachers.

An Example Program: Alternative Support for Induction Science Teachers (ASIST)

Background

Alternative Support for Induction Science Teachers (ASIST) was developed in response to the number of science teachers who were leaving the profession in southern Arizona and to help recent graduates draw upon their preservice knowledge in their first years of teaching. ASIST is in its fourth year and is currently offered through the College of Education at the University of Arizona. Any first-, second-, or third-year science teacher can participate for up to three years or until his or her third year of service. Recently, beginning teachers have been encouraged to participate in a graduate degree program after two years of ASIST participation. ASIST has an administrative structure that is composed of various educators from the community, including university science educators, mentor science teachers, and graduate assistants. University and school district educators provide ongoing support to participants through monthly meetings, visits to classrooms, a trip to a national or state conference, and ongoing electronic dialogue. A comprehensive discussion of this program format can be found in Luft and Patterson (in press).

Over the years, 58 beginning science teachers have participated in ASIST. They come from several school districts in southern Arizona, and they have varying educational backgrounds, ranging from emergency state certification to university graduate programs that result in state certification. For their participation in the program, teachers receive district re-certification hours or university credit provided by their districts.

ASIST is grounded in the research literature and developed in response to the established needs of beginning teachers. While there are many needs of beginning teachers and several considerations that need to be attended to in designing an induction program, ASIST has two important areas that are the focus of this chapter: (1) ASIST as a discipline-specific program, and (2) ASIST as a program that is rich in opportunities for reflective practice. These components are focal points for the following discussion.

ASIST as a Discipline-specific Program

The importance of socialization of beginning teachers into the existing professional culture of schools is widely recognized (Atkinson and Delamont 1985; Gold 1996), and it is the traditional focus of most existing induction programs. This view of induction programs is evident in the work of Gold (1996). Her earlier work focused exclusively on the socialization of beginning teachers, while her later review argued for the need for both instructional and personal-psychological support. It was her assertion that effective support is multidimensional, including discipline-specific induction in addition to induction for teacher socialization. Advocating a similar position, Feiman-Nemser (1992) posited that discipline-related issues as well as management issues must be addressed for beginning teachers.

As the number of underqualified teachers in mathematics and science entering the profession increases (Ingersoll 2001), there is a need to develop induction programs that emphasize the discipline of science education. Such teachers lack a major or minor in a subject area, have little or no pedagogical training, or are teaching out of field. Ingersoll found the percentage of public high school teachers in science without a major or minor in science to be 18 percent and without certification in science to be 18 percent. Another dimension to this problem is the preparation of science teachers. Even for those teachers with a science background, often their specialization is narrow and they may be teaching in an unrelated field. It is not uncommon for a teacher with a biology major to teach a general science course, which encompasses biology, physics, chemistry, and Earth science. While induction programs need to address the unique needs of beginning teachers, they also need to incorporate support that is related to the discipline of science education.

ASIST was developed to address the unique discipline needs of the science teachers who participate in the program. The science teachers in ASIST come from a variety of teacher-training programs (or no training program) and frequently teach science courses in which they do not have a major. Their initial needs are often finding lessons or curriculum that is aligned with the goals of the course and with school district, state, and national standards. As a result of these needs, the National Science Education Standards [NSES] (NRC 1996) are used frequently in the program. In directing the discipline component of the program, the ASIST staff draw on the "science as inquiry" standard that states students should identify research questions, design and conduct experiments to answer these questions, develop explanations, think critically about the relationship of evidence and explanation, and communicate their findings (NRC 1996). Ultimately, this standard is the backbone of the program and is integrated in several different components that are part of the professional development process for the beginning teachers.

There are several ways in which the "science as inquiry" standard is integrated into the program. One of the most obvious inclusions is during the monthly workshops. These Saturday sessions are led by science educators and mentor teachers in the project, and last at least four hours. During each session, which is held on campus or in a participant's classroom, there is a demonstration or modeled lesson that draws on various aspects of the standard. For example, during one session, participating ASIST teachers learned how to generate student questions about natural phenomena. At the end of the lesson, staff and participants process the structure of the lesson and the connection of question generation to the NSES (NRC 1996) and conceptualize a new lesson that can be used in the upcoming weeks in the classrooms of the beginning teachers.

Another way in which the "science as inquiry" standard is incorporated into the program is through the local and regional conference trip. All ASIST participants can attend a local or regional science education conference (whichever is closer). They are joined by ASIST staff, who attend conference sessions with them and point out useful classroom resources in the exhibition hall. During these interactions, staff offer helpful advice about the presentations and materials that emphasize a "science as inquiry" position. In addition, they suggest useful instructional methods that are appropriate for the participants' courses and suitable resources for their standards-based classrooms.

Finally, to ensure that beginning teachers have access to the complete standards, and all of the standards documents, all project participants receive the NSES (NRC 1996) and a copy of *Benchmarks for Science Literacy* (American Association for the Advancement of Science 1993) from their districts.

ASIST as a Reflective Program

Reflection is critical in order to develop into a successful teacher. It is one mechanism by which teachers enhance their understanding of subject matter, pedagogy, student learning, and the social context in which schools operate and exist. Even Dewey (1933) recognized the importance of reflection when he stated that active and careful consideration about one's actions is an important part of teaching. More recent discussions describe the varied contributions of reflection to the development of a teacher. Zeichner and Liston (1996), for example, suggest that reflection enables teachers to examine, frame, and solve dilemmas in the classroom; take an active role in their professional development; and increase their awareness of the knowledge and assumptions they bring to teaching. Of course, the emphasis in each area varies, depending on the experience and background of the teacher and the environment in which he or she teaches.

The induction period is a critical time in the development of beginning teachers, as their beliefs and practices take shape as they gain instructional experience (Kagan 1992; Simmons et al. 1999). Unfortunately, these beliefs and practices may align with instruction that is not advocated by the NSES (NRC 1996). Simmons et al. (1999) found that beginning science teachers reverted back to traditional practices as they faced classroom realities. Luft, Roehrig, and Patterson (in review) found that in the presence of a discipline-specific support program, the beliefs and practices of beginning teachers were more student-centered than those of their peers who did not participate in the program. One way to facilitate teacher development toward constructivist instruction, which is aligned with standards-based instruction, is through the reflection on one's beliefs and practices (Richardson 1994, 1996). If beginning science teachers are going to refine their beliefs and practices in ways that are conducive to students learning science in standards-based ways (e.g., student-centered instruction, constructivism), then induction programs need to provide opportunities for such reflections.

The ASIST program is planned to offer numerous opportunities for beginning teachers to reflect on their practices, student learning, and the social context of schooling—important components of reflection (Zeichner and Liston 1996). For example, during the monthly workshops, mentor teachers meet with small groups of beginning teachers to discuss "life in the classroom." The beginning teachers talk with the mentor teachers about failed lessons and problems with students. The mentors' intention is solve some of the beginning teachers' dilemmas along with fostering a deeper understanding of their practice. Ideally, the immediate needs of the beginning teachers are met so that they can contemplate, analyze, and understand the impact of their instruction on students.

Observations are also included in the ASIST program in order to foster reflection among the beginning teachers. All beginning teachers are visited monthly in the classroom by an ASIST staff member. The purpose of the visit is defined by the beginning teacher, but it most often consists of the staff member observing the teacher's practice. Typically, the beginning teacher and the staff member agree on an area to focus on during the lesson. The staff member takes notes during the lesson regarding this area, and after the lesson both the teacher and the staff member discuss the identified topic. The processing session is geared to allow beginning teachers to discuss their experiences, gather insight from the staff member, and contemplate the impact of the lesson on student learning. In addition, all beginning teachers have release days to visit other beginning teachers or the mentor teachers in the program. These visits allow beginning teachers to compare and contrast their practices with those of their peers and the mentor teachers, and ultimately expand their understanding of student learning, instruction, and social contexts.

Another opportunity for reflection occurs through the listserv. The beginning teachers in the program participate in discussions that are moderated or self-initiated. In a moderated discussion, staff members pose pertinent questions for the beginning teachers to discuss. Questions and comments follow, with assistance from the moderator, to create a lively discussion that examines such issues as assessment, traditional curriculum, and inquiry instruction. Self-initiated discussions occur when the beginning teachers pose questions to the listserv. The teachers are often seeking suggestions or resource information on topics such as talking to parents, finding materials locally, and getting copies of successful lessons.

What Is the Impact of the Discipline and Reflection Focus?

There are several areas to consider when developing an induction program; in this chapter we discuss just two—discipline and reflection. The evaluation of the program in these areas has been summative and primarily for the sponsors of the program. For a majority of the program participants, the program has been valuable and they would recommend it to their peers. The beginning teachers have indicated that they have found the instructional suggestions regarding science, the classroom visits, and the discussions with peers and mentor teachers to be the most valuable aspects of the program. In addition, over 75 percent of the participants felt the focus of the program enhanced their understanding of science instruction. These basic reports indicated a successful program.

The research associated with the program has been more extensive and has explored the discipline focus of the program. In one study, Luft, Roehrig, and Patterson (in review) compared the practices and beliefs of beginning science teachers in the ASIST program to the practices and beliefs of beginning teachers in a generic induction program and no induction program. The results of this study revealed that beginning science teachers in a discipline-focused program implemented more standards-based lessons than did their peers in the two other programs, and they also incorporated fewer worksheet and textbook lessons than did their peers. Even with a small sample size, the results suggested that discipline-focused induction programs are an important part of the professional development of science teachers. Such programs can maintain the practices advocated during initial certification courses and reduce the tendency of beginning science teachers to use non–standards-based practices.

In another study, Roehrig and Luft (in review) examined the feasibility of having ASIST teachers implement inquiry-based lessons in their classrooms. Guiding this study was a desire to understand what barriers ASIST teachers encountered in implementing standards-based practices, such as inquiry. An understanding of the nature of science and scientific inquiry, content knowledge, pedagogical content knowledge, teaching beliefs, and concerns about management and students were found to have an effect on the implementation of inquiry among the beginning science teachers. Furthermore, it was found that these factors work collectively in different degrees to influence instruction as opposed to independent factors that singularly influence practice. For example, one teacher with a science background may be hindered by perceptions of student ability, while another teacher with few concerns about students may be constrained by a lack of content knowledge. This study reinforced the need for induction programs to provide several types of support, including discipline-specific support.

Final Comments

Quality induction programs that support beginning secondary science teachers need to be situated within the discipline and to be rich in opportunities for reflective practice. These focal areas assist beginning science teachers in developing their practices and in understanding science instruction. With such an emphasis, beginning teachers can clarify and refine their knowledge of science instruction and fortify their disposition towards standards-based instruction. In addition to the professional growth and personal well-being afforded by such a focus, beginning science teachers may be more likely to remain in the classroom beyond a few years. As such, induction programs are a relatively short-term investment with long-term results.

References

Adams, P., and G. Krockover. 1997. Concerns and perceptions of beginning secondary science and mathematics teachers. *Science Education* 81: 29–50.

American Association for the Advancement of Science. 1993. *Benchmarks for science literacy: Project 2061*. New York: Oxford University Press.

Atkinson, P., and S. Delamont. 1985. Socialization into teaching: The research which lost its way. *British Journal of Sociology in Education* 6(3): 307–22.

Britton, E., S. Raizen, L. Paine, and M. Huntley. 2000. *More swimming, less sinking: Perspectives on teacher induction in the U.S. and abroad.* Retrieved June 30, 2001 from *http://www.wested.org/wested/pubs/online/teacherinduction/*

Darling-Hammond, L. 1998. Teacher learning that supports student learning. *Educational Leadership* 55(5): 6–18.

———. 2000. *Solving the dilemmas of teacher supply, demand, and standards: How we can ensure a competent, caring, and qualified teacher for every child.* Retrieved July 30, 2001 from *http://www.tc.edu/nctaf/publications/solving.html*

Dewey, J. 1933. *How we think*. New York: Heath.

Eisenhower Mathematics and Science Foundation. 1998. *State higher education support for beginning teachers*, from *www.ed.gov/inits/teachers/eisenhower*

Emmer, E. 1986. Academic activities and tasks in first-year teachers' classes. *Teaching and Teacher Education* 2(3): 229–44.

Feiman-Nemser, S. 1992. *Helping novices learn to teach: Lessons from an experienced support teacher* (No. 91-96). East Lansing: Michigan State University, National Center for Research on Teacher Learning.

Geva-May, I., and Y. Dori. 1996. Analysis of an induction model. *British Journal of In-service Education* 22(3): 335–56.

Gold, Y. 1996. Beginning teacher support: Attrition, mentoring, and induction. In *Handbook of research on teacher education*, ed. J. Sikula, 548–94. New York: Macmillan.

Hoffman, J., S. Edwards, S. O'Neal, S. Barnes, and M. Paulissen. 1986. A study of state-mandated beginning teachers programs. *Journal of Teacher Education* 37(1): 16–21.

Huling-Austin, L. 1987. *Assessing the impact of teacher induction programs: Implications for program development.* Paper presented at the American Educational Research Association, Washington, DC.

————. 1990. Teacher induction programs and internships. In *Handbook of research on teacher education*, ed. W. Houston, 535–48. New York: Macmillan.

————. 1992. Research on learning to teach: Implications for teacher induction and mentoring programs. *Journal of Teacher Education* 43(3): 173–80.

Ingersoll, R. M. 2001. Teacher turnover and teacher shortages: An organizational analysis. *American Educational Research Journal* 38(3): 499–534.

Kagan, D. 1992. Professional growth among preservice and beginning teachers. *Review of Educational Research* 62(2): 129–89.

Loughran, J. 1994. Bridging the gap: An analysis of the needs of second-year science teachers. *Science Education* 78: 365–86.

Luft, J., and N. Patterson. In press. Bridging the gap: Supporting beginning science teachers. *Journal of Science Teacher Education*.

Luft, J., G. Roehrig, and N. Patterson. In review. Contrasting landscapes: A comparison of the impact of different induction programs on beginning secondary science teachers' practices and beliefs.

National Association of State Directors of Teacher Education and Certification (NASDTEC). 2000. *Report of teacher education and certification*. Washington DC: NASDTEC.

National Center for Education Statistics. 1997a. *Characteristics of stayers, movers, and leavers: Results from the teacher follow-up survey: 1994-95*. Washington, DC: U.S. Department of Education, Office of Educational Research and Improvement.

————. 1997b. *America's teachers: Profile of a profession 1993-1994*. Washington, DC: U.S. Department of Education, Office of Educational Research and Improvement.

National Commission on Mathematics and Science Teaching for the 21st Century. 2000. *Before it's too late: A report to the nation from the National Commission on Mathematics and Science Teaching for the 21st Century*. Washington, DC: U.S. Department of Education.

National Commission on Teaching and America's Future. 1996. *What matters most: Teaching for America's future*. New York: Teachers College, Columbia University.

National Research Council (NRC). 1996. *National science education standards*. Washington DC: National Academy Press.

National Science Teachers Association (NSTA). 2000. Survey indicates high teacher turnover, job dissatisfaction. *NSTA Reports!* 3: 5–6.

Neuweiler, H. B. 1988. *Teacher education policy in the states: A 50-state survey of legislative and administrative actions* (No. 296 997). Washington, DC: American Association of Colleges for Teacher Education.

Odell, S. 1986. Induction support for new teachers: A functional approach. *Journal of Teacher Education* 37(1): 26–29.

Pelavin Research Group. 1997. *From students of teaching to teachers of students: Induction programs around the Pacific Rim*. Washington, DC: U.S. Department of Education.

Richardson, V., ed. 1994. *Teacher change and staff development process: A case in reading instruction*. New York: Teachers College Press.

Richardson, V. 1996. Role of attitudes and beliefs in learning to teach. In *Handbook of research on teacher education* (2nd ed.), ed. J. Sikula, 102–19. New York: Macmillan.

Roehrig, G. H., and J. A. Luft. In review. Constraints experienced by beginning secondary science teachers when implementing scientific inquiry lessons.

Simmons, P. E., A. Emory, T. Carter, T. Coker, B. Finnegan, and D. Crocket. 1999. Beginning teachers: Beliefs and classroom actions. *Journal of Research in Science Teaching* 36: 930–54.

Zeichner, K. M., and D. P. Liston. 1996. *Reflective teaching: An introduction*. Mahwah, NJ: Lawrence Erlbaum Associates.

Honoring Adult Learners: Adult Learning Theories and Implications for Professional Development

Susan Mundry

Susan Mundry is co-director of the National Academy of Science and Mathematics Education Leadership at WestEd. She also conducts research and develops products on professional development, including *Teachers as Learners,* a video library of teacher learning in science and mathematics. She is co-author of *Designing Successful Professional Meetings and Conferences in Education: Planning, Implementation, and Evaluation* (2000) and *Leading Every Day: 124 Actions for Effective Leadership* (2001).

More than any other species, people are designed to be flexible learners and active agents in acquiring knowledge and skills. (Bransford, Brown, and Cocking 1999, xi)

Think about a time as an adult when you *really* learned something well. What made this learning so powerful? Was it an informal or formal learning setting? What motivated you? Did you learn with others? Were you able to transfer the learning to other situations in your life?

If you are like many adults, you had a clear personal or professional purpose to learning what you learned, you engaged with at least one other person as you learned, and you felt challenged and supported. These are just a few of the conditions that can support adult learners. When it comes to adults, many factors influence whether and how they will learn—one size does not fit all. The characteristics of powerful learning are very personal and one of the best ways to ensure effective learning is to clarify how you learn and what kinds of learning environments work best for you.

Those of us who design learning experiences for others must consider carefully the styles and preferences of different adult learners and factor these into learning designs. It helps to know one's audience. What experience and background do they have? What do they know well and what do they need to know better? What assumptions do they hold about what they are learning? In what contexts will they use their learning? Most importantly, designers must clarify the purpose for the adult learning. More than anything else, knowing a person's reason for learning influences the content and process of the learning.

Over the past two decades, U.S. educators and policy makers have implemented a variety of programs aimed at increasing teachers' knowledge and skills. From these efforts, we have learned a great deal about what constitutes effective adult learning for educators, as well as the attributes and principles of best practice in professional development (Sparks and Hirsh 1997; Guskey 1995; Loucks-Horsley et al. 1998; Hawley and Valli 1999; NCTAF 1996). Most notably, effective professional development programs have these characteristics:

- Focus on building content knowledge, knowledge of children, and understanding of teaching
- Foster collegiality and collaboration
- Promote experimentation and risk taking
- Involve participants in decisions about as many aspects of the professional development experience as possible
- Provide time to participate in, reflect on, and practice what is learned
- Provide leadership and sustained support
- Supply appropriate rewards and incentives
- Reflect knowledge of adult learning and change
- Enhance student learning
- Integrate individual, school, and district goals
- Integrate both organizationally and instructionally with other staff development and change efforts in the school district.

In this chapter, I focus on the eighth characteristic listed above—*Reflect knowledge of adult learning and change.* I review a classic adult learning model and introduce contemporary thinking about adult learning and the change process.

Adult Learning Theory
Androgogy
Nearly thirty years ago, Malcolm Knowles (1973; Knowles, Holton,and Swanson 2000) introduced the theory of adult learning called *androgogy*. He was one of the first to suggest that teaching adults is very different from teaching children. The theory of androgogy, the science and art of learning in adults, is based on six assumptions about learners. Below are the six assumptions and commentary on how I see them influencing the design of professional development for science teachers today.

- *Adults need to know why they need to learn something before they learn it.* Learning for the sake of learning—or worse, learning to fulfill someone else's purpose—just doesn't work for adults. That is why it is essential for all adult learning programs to be clear about their purpose. What do we need to learn and why, and how will we know when we have been successful? To support such purpose-driven professional development, providers must create ongoing opportunities for adults to assess their needs and then design learning opportunities that are directly linked to those needs and areas for growth.
- *Adults have a concept of themselves as responsible for their own decisions and will resist situations in which others impose their will.* Adult learning needs to

provide opportunities for self-directed experiences. Contemporary professional development programs that involve teachers in planning the program and/or that provide ample time for working on one's own plans and ideas encourage adults to take initiative and draw on their need to be self-directed. In recent years the emergence of learning groups, peer support groups, and electronic-based learning communities has created new opportunities for self-directed learning. The Internet's ability to bring knowledge on virtually any subject to a self-directed learner at the push of a button promises many more opportunities for adults to exercise self-directed learning.

- *Adults have rich and diverse experiences.* Adults vary in their motivation, needs, background, learning style, interests, and goals. Professional development programs are enriched when they capitalize on adults' vast and diverse experiences. Using techniques such as case studies, problem solving, and group discussions helps adults connect new learning and insights to their own experiences. In recent years learning theorists have discovered that the process of learning involves connecting new knowledge to that which one already knows and understands. This underscores the need to create opportunities for adults to bring their own thinking, opinions, and ideas into the learning process. Constructivism and transformative learning, two learning theories described later in this chapter, are related to the idea that learners' prior experiences greatly influence their learning.

- *Readiness to learn affects adult learning.* We've all heard the term "teachable moment," which refers to that time when someone reaches a point of needing or being ready to understand some new information or lesson. Adults are more likely to engage in learning when they are at these teachable moments—they know they need to learn in order to cope effectively with their real-life situations. In education the real-life pressure of closing the gap between achieving and nonachieving students is creating such a readiness for many teachers. For years teachers were reinforced to continue doing what they were doing because "enough" students mastered the knowledge and skills they taught. With recent requirements for and commitments to educating all students, teachers are looking for ways to cope with this challenge. The old ways don't work, and teachers are ready to engage with new ideas.

- *Adults' orientation to learning is life-centered or problem-centered.* Adults learn most effectively when concepts are presented in the context of real life. This principle is also often referrred to as situated learning—the learning is situated in real-life applications and materials. Based on this idea, effective teacher professional development uses problem-oriented simulations, engages teachers in learning subject matter in the ways that it will be taught, and uses real classroom materials such as the teachers' own curriculum and student work as the focus of professional development.

- *Adults are motivated to learn by internal pressures.* Adults are motivated more by their own need to improve performance than by external pressures imposed by someone else. Translating this to the educational arena, teachers' motivation to learn comes more from their desire to enhance their performance and increase outcomes for students than from external rewards, bonuses, and mandates. This characteristic of adult learners makes it important that teacher learning be connected directly to increasing classroom performance and measuring student outcomes.

The principles or conditions for adult learners defined by Knowles (1973) hold true today. In addition, more is known about how people learn that informs the design of professional learning experiences for adults, as discussed in the following sections on constructivism and transformative learning.

Constructivism

A theory of knowledge and learning that has revolutionized the way we think about learning is *constructivism*. This theory is based on the idea that learning is a very active process through which the learner interacts with new information and experiences and processes these through his or her own prior knowledge and beliefs (Bruner 1966). Learning comes about from thinking through and often struggling with problems and situations to come to new understanding. The learner interacts in a very active sense with ideas and experiences, rather than passively taking in facts or memorizing data (Bransford, Brown, and Cocking 1999). Constructivism defines knowledge as culturally and socially mediated, temporary, and developmental (Brooks and Brooks 1993.) We learn through what we already know and believe, and much of this is culturally based. Our culture influences what it is important to learn and what knowledge is valued.

Rather than seeing learners as a "blank slate" to be filled up, constructivists see learners as having lots of prior knowledge and experience through which they develop new understandings. People who use this model of learning draw upon the ideas learners already hold and help them connect new ideas to their current ones. This practice is apparent in student classrooms when teachers kick off a new lesson by asking students what they already know about the lesson topic. This helps the teacher to assess student understanding so he or she can build bridges to new ideas. In children and adults alike, learning experiences need to create connections between new and prior knowledge.

According to Jonassen (1994), learning environments that reflect constructivism are complex and multidimensional—they avoid learning that is oversimplified and narrow. In such an environment, one would rarely see memorization or fact learning without attention to meaning making. For example, the information might be discussed in terms of how different learners experience the information and what it means from their point of view (e.g., culture and prior experiences). Even in situations that call for a correct response, different approaches to solving the problem or generating the response are valued.

Designs for learning in this way consider the very individual nature of learning and provide time and support for learners to reflect on and make meaning for themselves. Learners might be asked, How would this play out in your situation? Is this always true? When wouldn't it be?

Real-world, authentic tasks that help learners contextualize and apply learning also characterize the constructivist learning design. As noted above, learners who learn while engaged in their real work increase the likelihood that they will transfer their learning back into their real-work situations. Finally, in the constructivist model, learners are placed in collaborative, not competitive, experiences with other learners (Jonassen 1994).

Adults have substantial prior knowledge and experience upon which to draw. Their knowledge helps them learn new things and reject or block some learning. If new ideas and information do not easily connect to prior knowledge, they are easy to reject. Learners need bridges between the new ideas and what they already know and they need experiences that create a need for them to learn. The next section discusses how people can come to transform their thinking when what they are learning or see the need to learn is not aligned with how they currently think and what they believe.

Transformative Learning

Educators, scientists, and psychologists have come to understand more about how individuals construct their own knowledge and connect new ideas and concepts to prior knowledge (Bransford, Brown, and Cocking 1999). Based on this, we now know more about the processes through which people transform their basic assumptions and restructure their frameworks for learning. This model of learning is called *transformative learning* or *critical reflection* (Mezirow 1991, 1997; Brookfield 1995). Like constructivism, it is based on the idea that the expectations we hold, greatly influenced by our cultural assumptions, directly influence the meaning we create for ourselves. Adults apply their frame of reference, including their habits of mind and their points of view, as a filter to all new knowledge and experiences (Mezirow 1991, 1997). Our frames of reference help us to make meaning, but they also can distort information and constrain thinking by blocking us from changing our beliefs even when data or experiences we have that seem valid contradict what we already know.

Transformative learning involves

(1) Critical reflection on assumptions supporting a problematic belief... its source, nature and consequences, (2) engagement in discourse ... to arrive at a tentative best judgment upon which to act until new perspectives, evidence or argument are encountered that are found to be more justified..., (3) reflectively and critically taking action on the transformed frame of reference, and (4) developing a disposition for critical reflection on one's own assumptions and those of others. (Marsick and Mezirow 2002, 2)

A number of experiences can lead adults to revise or transform their frames of reference. One way is through critical reflection, whereby adults become conscious of their behavior and choices and what they say about the assumptions held. They may challenge ideas or assumptions that they hold—usually in response to some information or situation that creates dissonance for them—or deepen their understanding of how that assumption is working for them. In a learning situation when an adult is faced with information that is contrary to his or her prior knowledge or beliefs, the person will experience *dissonance*. The information does not fit with what the person knows or believes and he or she doesn't know how to resolve the lack of fit. This makes people uncomfortable and most adults struggle to resolve the dissonance quickly. One of the most common ways adults resolve dissonance is to reject the experience or information that caused the dissonance. By rejecting the experience that causes the dissonance they relieve themselves of the need to change their way of thinking.

This has happened often in education with regard to student learning. Educators believe they have taught certain concepts; the student is tested and is shown to lack understanding. If a teacher believes her job is to teach the subject, not necessarily ensure that the student learned the subject, she will not experience any discord in seeing that the student failed the test. However, if the teacher is holding herself accountable for the students to master the subject matter, the test results will cause discomfort. Questions and reflection will lead the teacher to want to find better ways to teach and assess student learning in the future. When teachers see that what their students learned is not necessarily what the teachers think they taught, they can be truly shaken. Their equilibrium is disturbed and they are open to revisiting and possibly reconstructing their beliefs about teaching and learning (Thompson and Zueli 1999).

Because the new high standards for learning for all students call for profound changes in deeply held beliefs, knowledge, and habits of practice, transformative learning is needed throughout the education system (Thompson and Zueli 1999). New teachers not only need to develop skills to teach to high standards, but must also learn how to engage in critical reflection regularly. They need ongoing opportunities to become aware of their assumptions about teaching and learning and of what they know and believe and how it is affecting their practice.

Because the education reform movement calls for fundamental changes in teaching and learning, transformative learning is the goal of many of the adult learning experiences provided to teachers. Yet, such experiences are often not designed in a way that supports adult learners to transform their thinking. According to Thompson and Zueli (1999), professional development for teachers that promotes transformative learning needs the following five conditions:

1. The experience creates *cognitive dissonance*; information or experiences such as examining actual practice and student work create an alternative view of the current thinking. Learners confront information that doesn't match their own belief or information. Since the learners cannot reconcile the new information with what

they already know and believe, they must struggle to make sense of the new experience or information. A good example is the teacher who has serious doubts that students can learn science through inquiry. By engaging in a quality inquiry experience herself, the teacher deepens her own understanding of science, possibly opening the door to the belief that students could learn this way. That is where she begins to experience some dissonance. Her own experience as a learner challenges her long-held view (based on her own K-16+ learning experience) that students learn best through lecture, reading, and demonstration. Her experience of learning through inquiry may increase her readiness to consider the possibility of using inquiry methods in her own classroom. However, other things this teacher knows or believes still predispose her to resolve her dissonance by rejecting the idea that students can learn through inquiry. This is especially true if she has only had one experience of learning through inquiry. Her knowledge of classroom management issues may lead her to conclude that while you can learn through inquiry, it is too time consuming and disruptive in the classroom. In this case, the teacher may leave the inquiry experience having been enriched, but still reject the idea that students can learn through inquiry. The professional development succeeded in creating some dissonance, but not in transforming the teacher's belief that inquiry is a viable instructional method.

2. That is why transformative professional development also must provide *time and support for teachers to resolve the dissonance* by working over a sustained period with a coach or mentor. To reach resolution of cognitive dissonance, adult learners must have support and be able to engage in critical reflection over time. In the example above, the teacher needs the opportunity to talk with other teachers and an experienced coach or mentor about the value of inquiry-based learning, and she needs support to resolve the very real classroom management concerns she has. Her mentor can also continue to provide information or experiences that reintroduce the dissonance until the teacher begins to transform her own thinking.

3. The dissonance-creating and dissonance-resolving experiences need to be *connected to the learner's own context*. When teachers have no prior experience doing or understanding inquiry teaching, it will not help to show them that inquiry works in science and medical research laboratories or even to give them a personal experience with inquiry. They need to have direct experience seeing how the method works with their own students. Professional development programs may start by helping teachers see how students like their own benefit from inquiry, but until teachers are supported to try out inquiry with their own students, they are unlikely to transform their thinking. Teachers need a mentor who will help them reflect on their use of the new practice and get to a deeper understanding, over time. In a collegial arrangement the transformative learner engages in critical reflection that is data-based and challenging. In school settings teachers observe each other and each other's students to gather data on teaching and learning. They then discuss what they see—collegially, yet critically. The term "criti-

cal friend" has been used to describe groups of teachers who come together in this way to examine student work and practice with a focus on school improvement. This method, first developed by the Coalition of Essential Schools, features clear norms that focus the critical reflection on teaching and learning (Glickman 2002). Such norms are necessary since the kind of professional discourse that enables teachers to create and resolve dissonance and bring about transformative learning does not usually come about spontaneously (Thompson and Zueli 1999).

4. A fourth condition for transformative learning is *the development of new practices that are in line with the new ideas teachers are constructing.* As teachers deepen their understanding of how inquiry works to build student understanding in science, they are ready to adopt new practices to support their new beliefs. They will discover that the curriculum materials they are using no longer fit their new conception of teaching, or that the schedule they have for teaching science needs to be adjusted, or that they need a plan for acquiring and replenishing materials used by students engaged in inquiry. The role of the mentor, coach, or facilitator at this point is to help the teacher adopt the new practices they need to effectively use inquiry in the classroom. As mentioned above, the suggested approach is for the learner to be linked to an experienced mentor. The mentor and teacher work together to identify and learn new practices. They might view videotapes to see how other teachers facilitate the inquiry process, observe other teachers, and/ or have demonstration lessons. This ongoing support enables the teacher to move from the transformation in beliefs or knowledge to change in practice.

5. The transformative learning process continues by *ensuring that learners have the opportunity to become aware of new issues and problems, gain new understanding from these, and cycle back through the process* of cognitive dissonance, resolution, and change in practice related to the new understanding (Thompson and Zueli 1999).

Many teacher learning programs that aim to transform beliefs about teaching and learning still fall far short of providing all five of these critical conditions for transformative learning in adults. Some programs create the conditions for cognitive dissonance, but don't provide the ongoing support and pressure to resolve the dissonance by transforming thinking. Others create collegial work groups, but they lack the data-driven, critical reflection needed to unseat old habits and beliefs. Teaching is a highly complex undertaking that requires this cycle of continuous reflection, learning, and challenge for transformative learning.

The Change Process

Those of us working to promote effective teacher learning must keep in mind that learning is very much about change—changing beliefs and practices. As noted earlier, we will not create the kind of deep changes in practices called for in the national standards without helping teachers as learners reflect on and transform their beliefs about teaching and learning.

A highly useful framework for understanding the process people move through as they change and try out new practices is the Concerns Based Adoption Model (CBAM) (Hall and Hord 2001). CBAM grew from the original work of Frances Fuller thirty years ago. She wished to understand the stages prospective teachers went through as they developed their expertise as teachers. She discovered that new teachers went through a predictable pattern of changes in their concerns from the beginning of their teacher placement to the end of their practicum experience.

Later the model was adapted and developed to describe the change process teachers move through as they adopt and use new practices. The model documented the stages teachers move through as they change their practices and the concerns they express at each stage. At the beginning of learning something new, teachers have personal concerns and information needs. They want to know what the innovation is and how it will affect them. If teachers move ahead with the change, they then develop concerns about how to use the innovation. At this point they need professional development focused more on the "how to" and less on the "what" of the innovation.

As teachers integrate the use of the innovation into their practices and it becomes more routine, their concerns shift to being focused on impact. They need help at this point looking at the results of the change and whether the desired student learning is occuring. They may later "refocus" by shifting their attention to whether a new practice is needed or whether they need to make adjustments to the ones they are using. Hall and Hord (2001) pointed out that teachers can become stalled at any point on the continuum and abandon their use of an innovation unless they have learning experiences designed to address the particular concerns they have at the time. If teachers have informational and personal concerns, the "how to" session is not for them. If they are implementing the new program and having lots of problems, they need tailored assistance, demonstrations, and problem-solving sessions to help them use the innovation effectively. If they are grappling with what impact they are having, they need to work with others to examine student work and assessments. If they are beginning to refocus and consider changes in what they have been doing, they need to have time to examine data on what is working and why and make informed choices about the changes they will make.

The importance of paying attention to the change process is that it completes the picture of what is necessary for effective adult learning. Even when the conditions for effective adult learning and transformative learning outlined above are in place, learning is affected by what a learner's needs are at any particular point in the learning journey. Adult learning programs for teachers must be designed to support the learners wherever they are in the change process, continually adjusting as the learner develops.

As the science of learning continues to develop, we stand to learn more than ever before about how to best support learners. Designers of adult learning are challenged to create opportunities that reflect knowledge as complex and dynamic and the learner as an ongoing work in progress, capable of creative and complex thought and transformative change. We must not be naive about what it takes to create the conditions for teachers to be learners. No mandates, standards, or policies can take the place of teachers having frequent opportunities to work with other teachers and facilitators to reflect critically on their practices and to have access to the expertise and resources needed to deepen their knowledge of content, teaching, and children's learning.

References

Bransford, J. D., A. L. Brown, and R. R. Cocking. 1999. *How people learn.* Washington, DC: National Academy Press.

Brookfield, S. 1995. Adult learning: An overview. In *International encyclopedia of education*, ed. A. Tuinjman. Oxford: Pergamon Press.

Brooks, J. G., and M. G. Brooks. 1993. *In search of understanding: The case for constructivist classrooms.* Alexandria, VA: Association for Supervision and Curriculum Development.

Bruner, J. 1966. *Toward a theory of instruction.* Cambridge, MA: Harvard University Press.

Glickman, C. D. 2002. *Leadership for learning: How to help teachers succeed.* Alexandria, VA: Association for Supervision and Curriculum Development.

Guskey, T. R. 1995. Professional development in education: In search of the optimal mix. In *Professional development in education: New paradigms and practices*, eds. T. R. Guskey and M. Huberman. New York: Teachers College Press.

Hall, G. E., and S. M. Hord. 2001. *Implementing change: Patterns, principles and potholes.* Boston: Allyn and Bacon.

Hawley, W. D., and L. Valli. 1999. The essentials of effective professional development: A new consensus. In *Teaching as the learning profession*, eds. L. Darling-Hammond and G. Sykes. San Francisco: Jossey-Bass.

Jonassen, D. H. 1994. Thinking technology: Toward a constructivist design model. *Educational Technology* 34 (4): 34–37.

Knowles, M. 1973. 1990. *The adult learner: A neglected species* (4th ed.). Houston, TX: Gulf Publishing Co.

Knowles, M., E. F. Holton, and R. A. Swanson. 2000. *The adult learner: The definitive classic in adult education and human resource development.* Houston, TX: Gulf Publishing Co.

Loucks-Horsley, S., P. W. Hewson, N. Love, and K. Stiles. 1998. *Designing professional development for teachers of science and mathematics.* Thousand Oaks, CA: Corwin Press.

Marsick, V., and J. Mezirow, J. 2002. New work on transformative learning. *Teachers College Record.* www.tcrecord.org/printcontent.

Mezirow, J. 1991. *Transformative dimensions of adult learning.* San Francisco: Jossey-Bass.

———. 1997. Transformative learning: Theory to practice. In *Transformative learning in action: Insights from practice. New directions for adult and continuing education*, ed. P. Cranton, 5–12. San Francisco: Jossey-Bass.

National Commission on Teaching and America's Future (NCTAF). 1996. *What matters most: Teaching for America's future.* New York: Teachers College, Columbia University.

Sparks, D., and S. Hirsh. 1997. *A new vision for staff development.* Alexandria, VA: Association for Supervision and Curriculum Development and Oxford, OH: National Staff Development Council.

Thompson, C. L., and J. S. Zueli. 1999. The frame and the tapestry. In *Teaching as the learning profession*, eds. L. Darling-Hammond and G. Sykes. San Francisco: Jossey-Bass.

The Model Science Laboratory Project: Lessons Learned about Teacher Retention

Elnora Harcombe, Linda Knight, and Nedaro Bellamy

Elnora Harcombe is director of the Center for Education at Rice University, Houston, Texas, and has been director of the Model Science Laboratory Project since its inception in 1989. She is developing a similar project for high school with an emphasis on the ninth-grade science gatekeeper course (i.e., a required course that is difficult to pass and thus can close the "gate" to advancement for many students). She combines her Ph.D. (Yale) and research in neurophysiology with experience teaching at all levels in her current focus on ways to foster deeper thinking and learning in science.

Linda Knight is associate director of the Model Science Laboratory Project. Remaining in the classroom after receiving her Ed.D. (Indiana University), she guided students in publishing a quarterly journal, *Earth Focus*; was president of the Texas and National Earth Science Teachers Associations; received the Presidential Award for Teaching; and co-authored the textbook *Earth Science* (Harcourt Brace Jovanovich 1989; Holt 1994). Currently she is writing another textbook and coordinating nationwide student surveys of ozone and regional monitoring of a watershed.

Nedaro Bellamy is associate director of the Model Science Laboratory Project. She came to the Model Lab as a teacher resident in 1992 and since then she has given multiple conference presentations, led workshops around the nation, and published widely. She is pursuing an Ed.D. at Texas A&M University in information technology and is assisting in the development of science curriculum guidelines for the Houston schools in Project CLEAR (Clarifying Learning to Enhance Achievement Results, a project that elaborates on the Texas Essential Knowledge and Skills requirements.)

My year in the RML [Rice University/Houston Independent School District Model Science Laboratory] was life saving and kept me from leaving the profession.—SF

My experience at the RML bolstered my self-confidence as a teacher tremendously. I was able to try and experience a variety of things that even "veteran" teachers may not have done. By creating a program that practices what it preaches (self/real understanding through inquiry), the RML is able to allow teachers to see/develop for themselves what effective learning and teaching is about. That empowerment does not come in a can or with a set formula. It is a process of self-discovery, which the RML facilitates. The RML has made me a better teacher and allowed me to view teaching and myself as a professional in a profession. Such fundamental beliefs can only increase the retention of such professionals. —FA

The statements above are typical of comments from teachers—called "residents"—who have experienced a submersion year in the Rice University/Houston Independent School District's Model Science Laboratory Project. The intent of the project is to provide support, training, and time for teachers to refine their instruction of science to urban students in the Houston Independent School District (HISD). Although retention was not the focus, the teachers involved in the Model Science Laboratory Project over the past eleven years (1990-2001) have remained in urban education at a phenomenal rate, as shown in Table 1.

Table 1. Retention of the 82 Teachers Who Participated in the Model Science Laboratory from 1990 to 2001	
95.1 %	Have remained in education
74.4 %	Have remained in the Houston Independent School District
10.9 %	Are teaching in suburbs
74.4 %	Have remained in classrooms
7.1 %	Are in education administration

Along with the 95 percent retention rate over 11 years, the figures also indicate the extreme dedication these teachers exhibit toward urban children. Another remarkable fact is that many teachers remain with the challenges in the classroom, instead of moving into administration.

These teachers not only stay in the classroom longer, they are also more effective. Their focus on student thinking and their involvement in their own learning generate greater achievement on the Texas Assessment of Academic Skills (TAAS). Science is tested by TAAS only at eighth grade, so HISD has looked at yearly math scores on TAAS. Students taught by teachers who had been Model Science Laboratory participants showed significantly ($p < .01$) greater improvement in math scores than students in matched classes in the same schools. Even years after teachers had been lab residents, their students still made greater TAAS progress than their peers. Lab teachers do not teach math, but they emphasize experimental design, collecting data, graphing, and interpreting results, thus giving math skills a context. Similar results occur when we administer pre- and post-tests in science using a modified National Assessment of Educational Progress (NAEP) examination.

Most programs for teacher retention involve mechanisms to integrate new teachers into the profession. In this chapter, we hope to demonstrate that it is also important to include a *long-term* teacher enhancement component in any teacher retention program. It is imperative that school districts recognize and value the need to provide appropriate preparation, support, professional opportunities for leadership, and respect for classroom teachers. From our combined experience, we have concluded that if teacher retention is to occur, teachers should be provided an opportunity to develop the following:

- A personal sense of professionalism with all the accompanying respect and responsibilities
- A new focus on the understanding achieved by students as the ultimate measure of success
- An opportunity to learn in a constructivist environment
- Access to updated information on subject content, pedagogy, and technology in the school
- A safe and nurturing peer networking community
- A redefinition of what it means to be a teacher who is also a lifelong learner

What exactly is the program for which we have claimed high retention and strong impact on students? We have described our methodology extensively in Harcombe, Knight, and Bellamy (1998) and in Harcombe (2001), so the description provided here will be brief.

Each year, HISD middle school science teachers apply for eight positions in the program at the Model Science Laboratory. These eight teachers leave their schools for the year and report to work each day at the model lab, located in a middle school near the center of Houston. The model lab itself consists of only two rooms in this school—the lab classroom and another classroom that has been converted into an office with dividers between desks. Teachers have their own computers and telephones, and access to printers, a copier, a fax machine, and a special library collection.

The residents spend about half their time as teachers: teaching, analyzing the teaching, and preparing to teach. Our school is on a block schedule with four 90-minute classes one day (A) and another four classes on the alternate day (B). Thus, each pair of resident teachers instructs one A-day class period of regular students all year long. After two residents have taught their classes, they have the remaining three periods to discuss together the events in their classrooms, explore resources, and plan for future teaching.

The other half of the time, B-days, the residents become students and receive graduate credit from Rice University. Instruction is held in the model lab. Science content and pedagogy are taught in a constructivist manner so that residents may learn in the same way they are learning to teach. These courses are augmented by a variety of other activities, including observations of a diversity of teaching styles, mentorships with community scientists, case study of a student, field trips, guest lectures, attendance at professional conferences, and development and presentation of workshops for peers, as seen in Table 2. Each resident creates a final portfolio demonstrating personal growth and highlights.

The residents in the Model Science Laboratory are chosen primarily for their interest in students. Usually they apply but sometimes are nominated by their principal. They represent broad ranges in geography across Houston, years of teaching experience (1–30 years), age (23–60 years), ethnicity (white, African American, Hispanic, American Indian, Asian, African, Caribbean, and Pakistani), and level of science knowledge.

Table 2. Typical Two-Week Activity Schedule for Resident Teachers in the Model Science Laboratory

Week 1

		Monday	Tuesday	Wednesday	Thursday	Friday
A M		Teachers 1 & 2 teach class of students.	Science content class for teachers.	Teachers 1 & 2 teach class of students.	Pedagogy class for teachers.	Teachers 1 & 2 teach class of students.
		Teachers 3 & 4 teach class of students.		Teachers 3 & 4 teach class of students.		Teachers 3 & 4 teach class of students.
P M		Teachers 5 & 6 teach class of students.	Teachers observe and analyze an expert teacher in HISD.	Teachers 5 & 6 teach class of students.	Guest scientist presents research.	Teachers 5 & 6 teach class of students.
		Teachers 7 & 8 teach class of students.		Teachers 7 & 8 teach class of students.		Teachers 7 & 8 teach class of students.

Week 2

		Monday	Tuesday	Wednesday	Thursday	Friday
A M		Science content class for teachers.	Teachers 1 & 2 teach class of students.	Pedagogy class for teachers.	Teachers 1 & 2 teach class of students.	• Attend training in national programs, such as SEPUP (Science Education for Public Understanding Program), Fast Plants, FOSS (Full Option Science System), WET (Water Education for Teachers) • Take field trips • Present workshops • Go to conferences
			Teachers 3 & 4 teach class of students.		Teachers 3 & 4 teach class of students.	
P M		Interview student for case study or participate in writing class (to develop skills for writing for publication).	Teachers 5 & 6 teach class of students.	Technology class or interact with home school.	Teachers 5 & 6 teach class of students.	
			Teachers 7 & 8 teach class of students.		Teachers 7 & 8 teach class of students.	

The residents are required to return to their home schools after their year in the Model Science Laboratory, where they often experience an adjustment back into the real world. The model lab offers monthly meetings as refreshers and as a time for residents to reconnect with others who share their goals and dreams for students. The former residents develop additional workshop units that they present in the model lab during the fall semester while the new residents are learning.

Factors That Have an Impact on Retention

The Model Science Laboratory Project has demonstrated that there are seven factors that have a significant impact on teacher retention: professionalism, networking, developing conceptual understanding, understanding students, having a safe place to learn, lifelong learning opportunities, and time. We explore each of these factors below.

Professionalism

People are more likely to stay in a position longer if they feel successful and valued. To be successful, a person needs to have appropriate training for the position. Inner-city school populations and expectations have changed dramatically, but school systems seldom provide teachers with sufficient training for the new challenges. In the Model Science Laboratory we demonstrate a range of techniques that teachers can use to develop conceptual understanding in students and a variety of assessments that identify progress for both teacher and students. Furthermore, residents participate in many intellectual activities in the field of science education that enrich their professional self-esteem.

During the first year of the program, one resident exclaimed, "Thank you so much for giving me a computer! I was working with it on my kitchen table when some friends came in. Now they know I do important work." —AL This marvelous woman had performed miracles with inner-city students during the previous 30 years, but she had not been considered important by others until she had a piece of equipment! How can we possibly expect teachers to stay when they receive no recognition or respect?

Other residents cite a new sense of professionalism as a result of being in the program.

Being a resident teacher has made me recognize that teaching is not only a career, but also a profession. I have changed my belief about teaching. Once believing that teaching was a mediocre job with a two-month paid summer vacation, I now believe that teaching is the founding profession of ALL professions. Teachers develop the knowledge of nurses, doctors, policemen, trainers, household managers, lawyers, etc. —OW

I remember how shocked I was when I went to a grant-writing workshop and we were not treated as professionals. That was such a contrast to what I had become accustomed to in the RML. I became aware of how important it is to act professionally and to convey that I expect to be treated as a professional. I determined to learn more about improving my professionalism. —LR

Before I became a resident teacher, I was in sort of a rut because I wasn't thinking about the class I was teaching. The RML may have saved me in teaching. It came at a very opportune time. I was getting burned out where I was. The RML was a place where they "talk the talk and walk the walk." We were able to try new approaches just like a laboratory. We had living students there that we could work with. —NK

Networking

A major influence on teachers' sense of professionalism is their realization that other teachers have many valuable ideas to share and are also professionals. Suddenly, the highly paid speakers are no longer the *only* experts. Structuring a network of teachers with shared experiences through the Model Science Laboratory provides a vehicle to break through the fatal walls of teacher isolation. When teachers build trust and communication links, they create a personal safety net that helps keep them in the profession.

I believe one of the greatest impacts the Rice Model Lab has had on me as a teacher is that it has created a community of dedicated science teachers that I admire and enjoy working with, on both professional and personal levels. Having access to such a network enhances the enjoyment I derive from teaching and creates enthusiasm for trying out new ways of presenting information. —GG

The biggest thing RML did was helping me see that I have options. If I feel like something is frustrating, I can pick up a phone and call any one of this group and say, "I've got this going on. What do you think? Got any ideas?" I know teachers who are afraid to talk to anybody because the person to whom they talked will think, "Oh, she's a weak teacher," and that's not the way it should be. —JG

I have been through many projects since I began teaching. Now when I attend an in-service, I usually think, "This is bull because we tried this, thought about this, discussed this, and it didn't work. They are telling me that it will work and I don't think it will. Their approach doesn't take into account the students at all." —NC

I can never overstate the importance of other teachers in the program. —CT

Developing Conceptual Understanding

The Model Science Laboratory Project challenges teachers to focus on what the students understand more than on what they present. For many residents, this is a major reversal of their mind-sets about teaching, and many struggle over this change in perspective. They learn to draw on their creativity to narrow in on key concepts and to build their instruction around multiple assessments for understanding.

The RML training has greatly influenced the teacher that I am today. My background in teaching science was very traditional, and it worked with the community I taught in the affluent suburbs of Chicago. However, when I came to Houston's large classrooms with children of all abilities, I knew that the strategies I used before were not working. The RML training taught me to reach and excite the children's learning. I am positive that without the learning experiences I had at the model lab, I would either have left HISD or become a mediocre, struggling teacher. —CM

The RML made me more aware of the way my students think and prompted me to become more careful about finding out what they think and why, rather than assuming they will understand and correctly interpret lab results. I got really interested in the idea of misconceptions, questioning, and really talking to the kids: asking, not telling. Critical questioning is important in determining the depth of student understanding. Many students are capable of creating a seemingly logical, yet incorrect, structure to explain the world around them. Students become adept at giving the teacher the "right" answer. It takes careful questioning to uncover what the student truly thinks. —GG

I notice a striking difference between what my students remember when actively learning about a topic in contrast to what my students remember when merely discussing the information or doing worksheets about it. —NK

Understanding Students

Students learn best when they feel a sense of caring and attachment. Furthermore, when teachers monitor thinking rather than recall, it is useful to have a greater awareness of the students as individuals. Thus, each resident is required to do a case study of a student over a year. The overwhelming impersonality of the school culture becomes obvious when the residents shadow a child, observing a day from a student's perspective:

The classes were quiet, the expectations obviously well laid out and enforced. There were no noticeable discipline problems, no unruly students, no talking. There also was a noticeable absence of creative discussion, inquiry, ownership, and motivation. The students appear to be merely putting in their time and trying to make it through the day. It seems their reason for being here consists of the fact that there is nowhere else for them to be.

While reading Sizer's book (1984), I thought, "It really couldn't be that mindless, that awful." Was I ever wrong! I saw classes where the teachers held complete control, and little interaction was required or encouraged. Absolutely no emotions were involved. The teacher dispensed knowledge, and the students practiced it. Little was found in the classes to stimulate interest. Learning styles, multiple intelligences, and conceptual understanding are only words in these classrooms; no application of these theories is attempted. I now understand why students are surprised when you express interest in them. —DM

A Safe Place to Learn

Residents realize they must create a safe, nurturing environment for their students if they want serious learning to occur. Similarly, if teachers are to learn they also need a safe and nurturing environment. It is essential to take residents on an introductory retreat to work on team building, conflict resolution, setting goals, and constructive ways to talk to peers. The school culture of competitiveness and pettiness must be broken to help teachers defeat their strong fear of looking foolish if they ask questions or confront misconceptions. In the Model Science Laboratory, residents are evaluating the core of their profession and the guidelines by which they have operated.

Yesterday we talked about photosynthesis again, but everyone was sort of restless. I for one felt uncomfortable because I was beginning to realize the last time we had content class that I didn't know as much about photosynthesis as I thought I did. I felt uncomfortable because: (1) I should know because I teach science for a living; (2) Everyone else already knows everything about photosynthesis; (3) I'm an idiot.

It is so hard to put my ego aside and open my mind to learn something. I realize that this is a growth-inducing experience for me. It HAS to be because it is causing me pain and discomfort. —DC

DC needed the further reinforcement that came with successful learning in a constructivist manner. By the end of the unit, she wrote:

I feel overwhelmed by this job and everything that is available to me. There is so much to do and to learn, my brain is working overtime. Yet, I feel challenged and very active and alive. My life feels full in a way that I haven't experienced in a while.

Once she experienced the elation of learning photosynthesis in a concrete manner, she was able to lay aside her ego and open her mind to more learning without the struggle. Now, instead of feeling like "an idiot," just three weeks later, she felt challenged and alive. What a transformation. She made a similar reversal in her lesson planning, as did many others:

I was doing it all backwards. I used to think of activities first, and then tried to make them fit into what I was trying to teach. Now, I focus first on what I would like the students to learn, and then plan activities. This is just one example of insights I gained during the year at the Rice that have changed the way I teach. —DC

Lifelong Learning

Possibly the most exciting transformation to observe in the residents is when they realize it is safe to ask questions, and they can renew their personal interest in learning. Residents learn science through constructivist methods before they feel comfortable teaching with constructivist techniques. Teachers realize that to guide their students into deeper understandings, they themselves need additional instructional skills, methods for monitoring student thoughts, and a clearer understanding of the most important concepts of the material they are teaching.

When we tried new ways of teaching about the moon, I realized there were holes in my knowledge. My background knowledge in science has grown tremendously at the RML. I think it is really important to be competent and feel good about yourself as a teacher, and the RML gave me the chance to do that. —CM

The Rice Model Lab made me realize that I need to constantly change if I am to continue to be an effective teacher. After eight years, I continue to look for new ideas that will make my instruction better. —PW

Time

Time was a major factor in the program. Teachers had the time they needed to reflect on their classes, get feedback from observers, brainstorm effective practices, read about new philosophies, practice alternative methods, update science content, and make connections to the science community. Although these activities could theoretically be done while teaching in a regular school, the teachers are unanimous in claiming they needed the full submersion to be able to integrate all of this information. They would be too tired to think so intensely while teaching, and summers would not provide student feedback. If we wish to keep teachers in the profession, however, we must provide them with the extra time to grow, re-tool, and refresh their knowledge and spirits.

You never have time to explore when you are teaching. We worked a lot on the idea of conceptual change in the RML. I don't think that another staff development program could be as effective as the RML in making such changes. In the RML, when you come up with a new idea, you can try it, work on it for a while, and then try again to see if you can fine tune it and ingrain it in your thinking about teaching and planning. —JB

One luxury was time to develop lessons, throw ideas at each other, brainstorm, have feedback, and all the things that we normally don't have during a school year. Teachers need to have the time to be creative to make their classes interesting. Creativity doesn't flow on command. Too many teachers are in a rut; they are bored, tired, and exhausted. It is neat when you can get more than one person involved in lesson planning. Now I have gotten away from worksheets and it has made a big difference. —JG

In America, everyone seems to think that planning is incidental to teaching— that teachers can live without planning time and still be effective. Not only do teachers need more planning time, they also need more time to meet with other teachers and share ideas as we did in the model lab. —GG

Reasons for Leaving

It is as instructive to look at the reasons that people leave the teaching profession as it is to look at their reasons for staying. Income level was crucial for two residents. Another resident made the following comments:

Being in the RML might have made me even more dissatisfied. It might be good because it might spur me on to keep going and change things. It might just frustrate me so I'd say, "Well, that's it, I'll just go on and be a biologist again." I probably won't decide for a while, but it is in my mind because I saw how it could be. —CM [emphasis added]

Urban schools are a difficult environment for anyone who cares about students and their learning. The following comments show some frustrations from teachers still in the profession. The first quote suggests that there may be another departure soon.

The current environment is not allowing me to fulfill my ideals. As I return to my home school, I have many mixed feelings. I feel the burden of bureaucracy, lack of support, and detachment of a political climate that calls for more "accountability." Whatever that means, I feel it will lead to "blame the teacher." It seems that politicians and administrators make cavalier decisions that often create a negative impact. I will remain in education for now, and seek the best of what is around me. I will openly share with others and seek growth. Whether I stay in this assignment, or even this profession, only time will tell. Mark me in the "undecided" column. —JD

The RML builds you up so much that when you go back into a real school, you're frustrated. When you go back into a school where people still don't care about improving themselves, don't really want to improve their teaching, don't

really want to change at all and get better in whatever you're doing, that's disheartening. —TL

With a misplaced focus on tests instead of students, it is no wonder we forget that we are dealing with feeling people, like ourselves, who can be hurt, who need to feel loved, who want to perceive themselves as belonging and as learners. —NG

At school we have given students an episodic grasp of knowledge. They learn small bits of information and then shut that off and learn something else. It is not so much that we are not teaching but we are allowing no connections between what we teach. It is the difference between knowing something and knowing what it's good for. —DM

After witnessing the enthusiasm of children when they make a discovery, it is difficult to go back to an environment of control and mandated concentration on drills for the high-stakes tests.

Conclusion

Teachers who participated in the submersion year at the Model Science Laboratory have become more effective teachers (based on observations and student test scores) and have remained in the urban teaching force at a much higher rate than expected (HISD has a typically high urban teacher turnover rate). The expense of immersion enhancement is cost effective: HISD saved around $400,000 this year alone in sign-up bonuses, recruitment fees, and mentor stipends due to retention of Model Science Laboratory teachers. This figure does not account for the enhanced instruction of the residents. The retention occurred because residents had time and a safe environment in which to network with other teachers and learn new ways of teaching that focus on what students understand, in contrast to what teachers deliver. In the process the teachers developed the confidence, knowledge, and ability to become true professionals with all the responsibilities and authority the title conveys.

Acknowledgments

We wish to thank all of the resident teachers with whom we worked in the Model Science Laboratory Project during the past eleven years for permission to use quotes from their portfolios, interviews, and responses to questions about the model lab's impact on their decisions to remain in urban education. We also thank Dr. Joneen Hueni for use of some quotes from her doctoral dissertation (1999). Furthermore, we greatly appreciate the trust and support shown for teachers by The Brown Foundation, Inc., Rice University Center for Education, the Houston Independent School District, the multitude of community donors, and the National Science Foundation (Grant #ESI 91-55389).

References

Harcombe, E. S. 2001. *Science teaching/science learning: Constructivist learning in urban class-rooms*. New York: Teachers College Press.

Harcombe, E. S., L. B. Knight, and N. Bellamy, N. 1998. The Rice Model Lab: An opportunity for professional enhancement of middle school science teachers. *Science Scope* 21: 62–66.

Hueni, J. A. 1999. *The impact of an intensive yearlong staff development program on science teachers' perceptions of pedagogical change*. Ed.D. thesis, Texas A&M University.

Sizer, T. R. 1984. *Horace's compromise: The dilemma of the American high school*. Boston: Houghton Mifflin.

Beginning Teacher Mentoring Programs: The Principal's Role

Tom David

Tom David is the assistant superintendent of the Mattoon Public Schools in Mattoon, Illinois. He earned his graduate degrees (M.A. and Sp.D.) from Eastern Illinois University and Ed.D. from the University of Illinois. He is currently responsible for human resources, grants management, and professional development.

The U.S. Department of Education has predicted that two million new teachers will need to be hired during the first decade of the 21st century. The current teacher shortage—combined with a public clamoring for greater teacher accountability, a changing student population, and tough state standards—creates new and difficult challenges for teachers. In addition, an increasing percentage of students experience chronic and acute social and educational failure because of limited English proficiency, learning disabilities, or poverty.

All of these trends, along with the reality shock of facing their first job, lead beginning teachers to feel overwhelmingly stressed and isolated—both in the classroom and in their personal lives. These factors are taking their toll on the number of teachers who become disillusioned with teaching and drop out of the profession during their first few years. Fortunately, substantial research literature shows that effective mentoring programs can lower the attrition rate for new teachers and significantly facilitate their induction into the profession (Newhall et al. 1994).

Obviously no single program design can be implemented in all situations; however, the school principal must provide strong leadership whatever the mentoring program (Brock and Grady 1998). To implement effective mentoring programs, school principals must begin by focusing on their fundamental reasons for being educational leaders, their core values and beliefs about teaching and learning, and their visions for changing and improving education. These subjective elements greatly affect a program's design, its implementation, and its success or failure. Principals must create the conditions and design for an effective mentoring program; select, train, and support mentors; and continually evaluate and revise their programs based on feedback from mentors and their protégés.

The Purpose of Mentoring

It is essential for principals and their staffs to understand the purpose of their district's mentoring program. Types of programs include (1) orientation, (2) developing positive perceptions about the organization, (3) providing continuous staff development designed to improve teaching and learning, and (4) recruiting new teachers and retaining those currently employed. Fully developed programs typically serve multiple purposes; however, few program designers have sufficiently articulated the leadership roles that school principal should play in such programs. This ambiguity tends to foster multiple interpretations of the program's purposes. The absence of shared values and beliefs about the purposes of mentoring, coupled with the cultural norms of autonomy and isolation in teaching, tend to make many mentoring programs ineffective. A quality mentoring program can be designed to achieve a variety of purposes, but leadership makes all the difference. Clearly, the more expectations there are for mentoring programs to produce "results," the more resources and administrative supervision required, and the greater the dependence on research and best practice needed to achieve the desired results (Sweeney 1998). Good teaching does not just happen. Teachers must be hired who demonstrate the capacity to become excellent teachers, and then they must be provided with opportunities to learn and grow with the support of veteran colleagues. For this to happen effectively, principals must model and sanction the goals of their mentoring programs (Sweeney 1998). In the case of science teachers, principals must encourage and support instruction that is hands-on and inquiry based.

Creating the Conditions for Effective Mentoring

Teachers' values, beliefs, and actions are shaped by the structures, policies, and traditions of their workplace (Rosenholtz 1989). To the extent that school principals are capable of manipulating and controlling bureaucratic structures, interpreting and implementing policies, and shaping shared values and beliefs that influence the school social organization, they are capable of creating the conditions necessary to implement an effective teacher mentoring program. However, like so much else that goes on in schools, a program's success depends on the principal's active daily support. How can the principal create such conditions? Here are some suggestions for principals to consider when setting up new or improving existing mentor programs:

Communicate Beliefs, Values, and Goals

Principals should consult with the central office to learn as much as possible about the purpose and goals of their district's induction and mentoring program and also to learn the parameters of their discretion to modify the program. Principals must take the initiative to develop a clear expression of the core beliefs, values, and goals of their district's program. Mentoring programs that help beginning teachers become successful are developed with purpose and have an articulated vision statement upon which the program is based (Gordon 1991). To accomplish this objective, principals should speak out and behave in a manner that demonstrates a clear understanding of the learning environment, student needs, professional development needs of teachers, and a basic philosophy of management, all of which are informed by a sizable body of research literature and best practice. The principal should also convey to the science teacher his or her belief in and commitment to the importance of science in the curriculum. Moreover, the principal should promote a science curriculum that has safety as a focus; content that includes ethical and societal issues; and activities that engage students in experimentation and discussion of the findings.

Make Informed Decisions

Principals today must be able to view problems associated with planning, organizing, implementing, and evaluating mentoring programs from multiple perspectives. They must look at control, coordination, and accountability. They must also meet the needs of new teachers while attending to the good of the whole staff and balancing equity versus excellence issues. Principals must be able to arrive at sound, logical, and objective decisions that are grounded in research and best practice and that are agreeable to those affected. Here are some suggestions to guide principals in making good decisions as they develop new or improve existing mentor programs:

- Review the research literature on teacher mentoring.
- Talk with teachers, principals, and union officials in districts where successful mentoring programs have been implemented.
- Consult with university faculty who have knowledge of mentoring program development and implementation.
- Network with the state office of education.

Share Decision-Making

To create an environment favorable to the development of teacher induction and mentoring programs, the central office must foster the development of a democratic school culture where teachers are involved in decision-making processes that focus on teaching, learning, and student issues (Pajak 1992). Principals must assume a central role in this process by overseeing the direct administration of the mentoring program and by guiding a school committee (that includes science teachers) in the development and implementation of the program. Here are some suggested tasks for the principal on this committee:

- Articulate the purpose of mentoring, program design, and program components.
- Guide the committee in the development of an action plan that has objectives and time lines, assigns responsibilities, and includes an evaluation.
- Define the role and tasks of the principal, mentor, peer coach/instructional expert, teachers' union, and beginning teacher.
- Help the committee decide how mentors will be selected.

♦ Discuss how mentors and protégés will be matched.
♦ Plan mentor training.

Self Promote

The principal plays a crucial role in showing students, parents, and the community how the mentoring program helps support new teachers (Ganser 2001). Students may be curious about the relationship between a mentor and a new teacher. Parents need to understand the purpose of the mentoring program so they do not conclude that assigning a mentor to a "rookie" is an attempt to cover up poor teaching (Ganser 2001). To accomplish this task, principals should use a variety of media, such as writing articles for school newsletters, speaking on community radio programs, appearing on local TV talk shows, writing news reports for the local newspaper, posting information on the district's website, and speaking to clubs and service organizations.

Recruit and Hire Excellent Teachers

Excellent principals make a significant difference in their schools. They help all students meet or exceed minimum learning outcomes in the core curriculum by employing and mobilizing teachers who are committed to student growth and learning. Excellent teachers make a profound difference in the lives of students. Poor teachers, however, are enormously costly—not only in the time required to supervise, counsel, support, and evaluate them, the legal costs incurred in their dismissal, and the wasted salary but also in the cost of the educational deprivation in the lives of their students. Although school leaders cannot neglect to provide substantial support to marginal teachers, excellent teachers require far less help and are, therefore, a better investment. So, of course, districts must hire only the best teachers.

Mentoring programs are excellent recruiting tools. Many candidates, anxious about their first teaching job, will accept a lower paying job in a school district that offers them support over a position in a higher paying district that does not. During the interview, principals should talk with prospective teachers about their district's mentoring program.

Respect Confidentiality

It is paramount to the success of mentoring and induction programs that the relationship between the mentor and new teacher remain confidential. Principals should make it a point never to talk to mentors about the progress of new teachers. The temptation to ask a mentor, "How are things going?" is detrimental to the mentor/protégé relationship (Ganser 2001). Although it is essential that the mentoring program be assessed, a form of evaluation should be used that guarantees the anonymity of participants.

Manage Resources

Principals must develop specific ways to assess the needs of students and teachers; effectively use staff; efficiently use time; equitably acquire and allocate space, equipment, and materials; and wisely and prudently budget and distribute financial resources that are essential to the success of the mentoring program. Principals must be capable of managing these resources to provide incentives, recognition, and rewards; training for mentors; release time for mentors and their protégés; materials; and professional development for new teachers. Unfortunately, levels of funding in many school districts are inconsistent from year to year because of changes in state funding formulas, property tax value, school district leadership, budget priorities, and local politics (Laine 2000). As a result, mentoring programs are frequently the first victims of budget cuts. Unwavering financial commitment to mentoring programs sends a clear message to staff that support for beginning teachers is a priority.

Mentoring Program Design

Orientation

Regardless of whether a formal induction and mentoring program exists, there are plenty of things that schools can do to induct new teachers into the profession. For example, principals can introduce them to their colleagues and include them in social as well as professional activities. When resources allow, orientation programs are a great way to begin a process of socializing new staff into the school "family," values, and traditions. It is important that the orientation components and activities be decided upon several months before planning begins. For example, will there be district, building, and community orientations? Will key personnel be introduced? Will hepatitis B and blood-borne pathogen training be included? Will sexual harassment be addressed? Will copies of teacher handbooks, curriculum guides, and union contracts be distributed?

Principal's Role and Tasks

Beginning teachers know their principal will determine whether their contract is renewed, and so they anxiously seek feedback that they are performing satisfactorily. Principals often describe a conflict between their duty to evaluate all teachers on the one hand, and their desire to nurture beginning teachers on the other hand (Cole 1993). Mentoring programs can mediate this dilemma. Where mentoring programs exist, principals are responsible for evaluating teachers formally and the job of nurturing beginning teachers is delegated to others.

What should the role of the principal be in mentoring new teachers? Here are some things principals can do to induct new teachers into the profession:

◆ Champion the mentoring program.
◆ Oversee and be visibly involved in the mentoring program.
◆ Orient new teachers to school values, procedures, and cultural and social norms

(Sergiovanni 1995). Communicate school traditions and expectations for teaching and student learning (Brock and Grady 1998).

◆ Visit new teachers' classrooms regularly. Initiate conversation by asking questions and giving feedback about instructional matters (Hope 1999).
◆ Promote collegial relationships.
◆ Provide new teachers with role models besides their mentors and peer coaches.
◆ Maximize new teachers' success by reducing their duties and responsibilities.
◆ Assign new teachers only within disciplines they are qualified to teach.
◆ Reduce new teachers' isolation by assigning them to well-equipped classrooms that are close to the mainstream of the school (Brock and Grady 2001).
◆ Provide new teachers with professional development opportunities that center on their immediate needs.
◆ Provide teachers hired in late summer with additional support and time to prepare to teach.
◆ Ensure that there are adequate resources to support mentoring program goals and activities.

Mentor's Roles and Tasks

Program goals will determine the roles and tasks of mentors and have a great influence on mentor selection. Will mentors be expected to help beginning teachers acquire professional knowledge and skills or just socialize them to their culture and acquaint them with local policies, politics, and procedures? According to conventional wisdom, novice teachers must be frequently observed, evaluated, and given substantial instructional guidance; provided opportunities to observe veteran teachers who model best practice; and be actively engaged in an ongoing dialogue with other teachers about instructional matters. In the case of a science teacher, the mentor also should be aware of the National Science Teachers Association's position statements (*www.nsta.org/position*).

Despite the essential needs of beginning teachers, however, few mentor teachers have the time, experience, or skill to accomplish such tasks satisfactorily, and, even with training, are often strongly opposed to evaluating their peers—even informally. Furthermore, those teachers best suited to mentor their inexperienced colleagues may not wish to do so. It is ill-advised to assign mentoring responsibilities to teachers who do not want to perform such duties. Mentors are best used in a supportive role while someone else evaluates novice teachers.

What are some rewards and incentives principals can provide veteran teachers that will encourage them to volunteer to become mentors? Here are some ideas to consider:

◆ Offer stipends, release from added responsibilities, a reduced teaching load.
◆ Recognize mentors and protégés with special luncheons, media releases, lapel pins.
◆ Provide quality training for mentors.

- Schedule the mentor's and protégé's work days so they coincide.
- Plan and schedule periodic meetings between the mentor and protégé.
- Offer professional development opportunities that mentor and protégé can attend together.
- From time to time, bring groups of new teachers and mentors together in social situations where they can talk shop and develop social bonds.
- Establish an electronic network among mentors and protégés.

Peer Coach's Role and Tasks

Anyone with knowledge and skill in the areas of clinical supervision, counseling, research in effective teaching practice, beginning teacher concerns, and theories of adult learning may perform the function of a peer coach. It is essential that the relationship between new teachers and a peer coach, not unlike that of the mentor and new teacher, be a confidential one. Novice teachers need opportunities to discuss questions and problems that arise in the course of their work and receive feedback from an expert without fear of reprisal. The role of the peer coach is different from that of the mentor. The peer coach tends to focus on matters of pedagogy, curriculum, and classroom management, whereas the mentor, more often than not, becomes a "go-to" person to answer questions about school procedures, to be a friend, or to be someone to provide moral support when things do not go as planned. When choosing a peer coach, here are some considerations:

- The peer coach must be an expert in matters of teaching and learning, classroom management, and curriculum. In order to be especially helpful to a beginning science teacher, the peer coach needs to be an expert in the uses of a variety of techniques, including cooperative learning groups, computer simulations, laboratory investigations and experiments, lab write-ups, hands-on activities, and demonstrations.
- The peer coach must be able to relate to, understand, and communicate with others in a way that contributes to harmonious relationships and goal accomplishment. This person also must be able to provide intervention in an atmosphere of mutual respect.
- The peer coach must be highly respected by the veteran staff and be able to become an ambassador for the program.
- The peer coach must be very flexible, adapting his or her schedule to that of several dozen new teachers.
- The peer coach must be able to commit to several hours of direct contact with each new teacher—observing, counseling, and coaching.

Mentor Selection

When principals choose mentors themselves, they should do so in accordance with the goals and purpose of the mentoring program (Sweeney 1994). If the mentor selection involves a committee process, principals should be the facilitator of a nominal group process. For example, the principal should influence how mentors are chosen by steering the mentor selection committee in the development of criteria, review of applications, and selection of mentors (Ganser 2001). Unfortunately, it is often impossible to select an excellent mentor because there are none available that have the essential qualities or skills to become a successful mentor (Brock and Grady 1998). Furthermore, mentors hold personal convictions about their role as mentors (Saunders, Pettinger, and Tomlinson 1995) that are probably unknown to most principals. Even if principals were aware of the preconceived beliefs of their teachers in their role as mentors, mentor training, as typically designed, is unlikely to change mentors' orientations. Some schools remedy this situation by employing a peer coach and by differentiating the roles and duties of the peer coach and mentors. Other schools assign several new teachers to a single mentor. When this alternative is used, mentors need to be released from their teaching duties in order to fulfill their mentoring responsibilities.

What should a principal consider when selecting mentors? Here are some ideas to consider:

- Choose mentors who teach in the same grade range (i.e., primary or intermediate) or subject area as that of their protégés.
- Select mentors whose teaching schedules and planning or lunch periods coincide with those of their protégés.
- Select mentors who work in close proximity to their protégés (Ganser 2001).
- Choose mentors who have been teaching for at least five years (Sweeney 1994).
- Choose mentors who are highly skilled teachers and who have earned the esteem of their colleagues.
- Choose mentors who can develop and maintain positive and trusting relationships with others (Brooks 1996).
- Choose mentors who have high expectations of their students.

Professional Development Activities for New Teachers

Many teachers would say that professional development in their districts has had little, if any, effect on their teaching practices or on student learning (Sizer 1992). In fact, in spite of an abundance of information that is available about what constitutes good professional development (Darling-Hammond and McLaughlin 1996; Little 1993; Thompson and Zueli 1997), traditional inservice activities tend to be disconnected from issues of curriculum and learning and lack continuity (Cohen and Ball 1999). Principals are the primary staff developers because they have the greatest control over what happens in their schools. They create the context in which professional development is promoted or discouraged (Marczely 1996). Principals should make certain that all inservice activities, including those in their mentoring programs, are sensitive to how adults learn best. A successful mentoring program should have the following characteristics (Marczely 1996):

- Professional development that targets teacher competencies, validated by research, and that has as its ultimate goal improved student achievement
- Professional development that is classroom-centered, focused on instructional development, and allows teachers to grow as professionals without leaving the classroom
- Professional development that is personalized, rather than consisting of common activities for all participants

Program Assessment

Mentoring programs should be continuously and systematically assessed from the beginning. Rather than waiting until the end of the school term, mentoring program assessments should be administered after each activity and also periodically throughout the year. Beginning teachers typically experience an emotional low point after only a few months on the job. Surveys conducted at this time may provide valuable information that will help determine the support necessary to help them maintain and sustain the necessary enthusiasm. The perceptions of other stakeholders should be considered too. Current and former mentors, peer coaches, and other staff can provide valuable information about activities, materials, training, or support activities that were especially effective for them. All program evaluations should ensure the anonymity of respondents.

Program assessment should focus on program goals and implementation, determining the difference between intended and actual outcomes. Principals should document programs' successes to provide convincing evidence to policy makers that mentoring new teachers is returning substantial dividends on their investment. Programs should be changed to reflect what has been learned from assessments.

References

Brock, B., and M. Grady. 1998. Beginning teacher induction programs: The role of the principal. *The Clearing House* 71 (3): 179–83.

———. 2001. *From first year to first rate* (2nd ed.). Thousand Oaks, CA: Sage.

Brooks, V. 1996. Mentoring: The interpersonal dimension. *TeacherDevelopment* (Feb.): 5–10.

Cohen, D., and D. Ball. 1999. *Instruction, capacity and improvement.* Research Report RR–043. Philadelphia, PA: University of Pennsylvania, Consortium for Policy Research in Education (CPRE).

Cole, A. L. 1993. *Problems and paradoxes in beginning teachers' support: Issues concerning school administrators.* Paper presented at the American Educational Research Association, Chicago.

Darling-Hammond, L., and M. McLaughlin. 1996. Policies that support professional development in an era of reform. In *Teacher learning: New policies, new practices,* eds. M. McLaughlin and I. Oberman. New York: Teachers College Press.

Ganser, T. 2001. The principal as new teacher mentor. *Journal of Staff Development* 22(10): 39–41.

Gordon, S. 1991. *How to help beginning teachers succeed.* Alexandria, VA: Association for Supervision and Curriculum Development.

Hope, W. C. 1999. Principals' orientation and induction activities as factors in teacher retention. *The Clearing House* 73(1): 54–56.

Laine, S. W. M., with C. Otto. 2000. *Professional development in education and the private sector: Following the leaders.* Oak Brook, IL: North Central Regional Educational Laboratory.

Little, J. 1993. Teachers' professional development in a climate of educational reform. *Educational Evaluation and Policy Analysis* 15(2): 129–51.

Marczely, B. 1996. *Personalizing professional growth.* Thousand Oaks, CA: Corwin Press.

Newhall, A., K. Bergstrom, N. Brennen, K. Dunne, C. Gilbert, N. Ibarguen, M. Perez–Selles, and E. Thomas. 1994. *Mentoring: A resource and training guide for educators.* Andover, MA: The Regional Laboratory for Educational Improvement of the Northeast and Islands.

Pajak, E. F. 1992. A view from central office. In *Supervision in transition,* ed. Carl D. Glickman, 126–38. The 1992 ASCD Yearbook. Alexandria, VA: Association for Supervision and Curriculum Development.

Rosenholtz, S. J. 1989. *Teachers' workplace: The social organization of schools.* New York: Teachers College Press.

Saunders, S., K. Pettinger, and P. Tomlinson. 1995. Prospective mentors' views on partnership in secondary teacher training. *British Educational Research Journal* 21(2): 199–218.

Sergiovanni, T. J. 1995. *The principalship* (3rd ed.). Needham Heights, MA: Allyn and Bacon.

Sizer, T. 1992. *Horace's school: Redesigning the American high school.* Boston: Jossey-Bass.

Sweeney, B. 1994. *A knowledge base of best practices for mentoring.* Wheaton, IL: Resources for Staff and Organization Development.

———. 1998. *Developing high impact induction programs and mentoring practices.* Wheaton, IL: Resources for Staff and Organization Development.

Thompson, C., and J. Zueli. 1997. The frame and tapestry: Standards-based reform and professional development. In *The heart of the matter: Teaching as a learning profession,* ed. G. Sykes. San Francisco, CA: Jossey-Bass.

Three Approaches to Retaining Science Teachers: How a District, School, and Individual Teacher Can Help

Jennifer L. Fong

Jennifer L. Fong is a winner of the 2001 Presidential Award for Excellence in Mathematics and Science Teaching and the 2000 RadioShack National Teacher Award. She is currently an administrator at Mission High School in San Francisco, where she has taught science and was the science department head. Ms. Fong received her M.A. from Stanford and B.A. from Yale. A Bronx native, she also taught science in the New York City Public Schools.

Bright-eyed and enthusiastic, new high school science teachers in urban school districts are often hired at the last minute on emergency credentials. Most have no teaching experience, nor have they completed any teacher credentialing course work. Assigned the worst classes and given multiple preps, new science teachers are often alone, without the support of a veteran teacher. When it comes time to plan lessons and find lab equipment, they spend a lot of time reinventing the wheel, trying to locate basic resources. The result? A burned-out science teacher who quits teaching within five years of entering the profession.

There is a different way. School districts, schools, and individuals can each approach science teacher recruitment and retention from their own perspectives. In this chapter, I discuss examples of programs that educators on each level can use. In each case, the programs rely on building a relationship between new and veteran teachers and giving new teachers both a time to reflect on their practices and a person with whom to reflect. While these approaches actively support the *new* teacher, helping them to grow as professionals, each approach also results in a positive experience for the veteran teacher. Thus, the veteran teacher also avoids burnout and is encouraged to take on leadership positions within the school, which is critical to science teacher renewal.

What a School District Can Do
In 1998–99, the Graduate School of Education (GSE) at the University of California at Berkeley (UCB), the San Francisco Unified School District (SFUSD), and Lawrence Berkeley National Laboratory (LBNL) collaborated on a pilot project called Scien-

tist-to-Teacher (later renamed REPLICATE). Scientist-to-Teacher was designed to induct new science teachers into the profession, using an on-site training and mentoring program (Garcia and Harris 1998). The essence of the program was to pair two new science teachers with a veteran science teacher at the same school and encourage reflective inquiry on the part of all three. Thus, the veteran, or master practitioner, becomes responsible for the training and success of the new teachers.

The name, Scientist-to-Teacher, came from the program's idea to recruit scientists from industry, train them to become teachers on-the-job, and support them with a mentor teacher on-site by releasing both the new teacher and master practitioner for one period each day. A medical doctor training model was used. Just as first-time doctors (interns) are trained in hospitals by experienced doctors, the new science teachers were trained in the school by the veteran teachers. Anecdotal evidence from the initial twelve pilot teachers indicated that new teachers felt supported and confident about their teaching (Diehl et al. 2000). I served as the lead master practitioner for the San Francisco Unified School District (SFUSD), helping to coordinate with UCB. UCB's role was to hire a director to run the pilot program. The director made the contacts with SFUSD and helped the schools set up the master practitioner-intern relationships.

Unlike preservice teacher credentialing programs, Scientist-to-Teacher was designed to credential teachers as they taught full-time. Other inservice teacher intern programs exist between a school district and a local university; in these, teachers teach full-time on an emergency credential while taking course work for a regular teaching credential. Scientist-to-Teacher added a unique piece to this inservice training: on-the-job training and mentoring for one period per day, not just student teaching. Two interns and one master practitioner were released 0.2 FTE for the interns to learn on-the-job from the master practitioner (total of 0.6 FTE). (FTE means "full-time equivalency." A 1.0 FTE is 100 percent full time, which means teaching five periods. Since the interns were released 0.2 FTE they were released 20 percent of full time or one teaching period.) The master schedule assigned the same planning period to all three teachers (see Figure 1). In their meetings the interns and veteran teacher followed a syllabus, similar to that of a methods class, and discussed teaching techniques, assessing students, and adapting lessons, using the California Standards for the Teaching Profession to guide growth, observation, and reflection. Twelve SFUSD teachers participated (eight as interns, four as master practitioners); six of the eight interns were still teaching four years later.

Figure 1. District Level—Example of Teachers' Schedules Using Scientist-to-Teacher Model*

Period	1	2	3	4	5	6	7
Intern #1	Biology	Biology	Prep	Physiology	Biology	Prep	S-to-T meeting
Intern #2	Prep	Chemistry	Chemistry	Prep	Physical science	Physical science	S-to-T meeting
Master practitioner	Biotech-nology	Prep	Biology	Biology	Prep	Biology	S-to-T meeting

*Assuming a standard schedule has five classes and two prep periods.

Another feature of this model was recruiting people from industry to a secondary school teaching career. Naturally, such a move represented a significant career change. Not only were industry scientists being asked to give up higher paying jobs; many people in their position would object to losing a year's salary to take credential course work to enter a profession that pays significantly less than their former profession. The latter factor was mitigated by the fact that in the Scientist-to-Teacher program, new science teachers could immediately make the transition from industry to teaching without having to take time off for schooling.

Another critical component was the on-site relationship between the master practitioner and the intern. Scientist-to-Teacher interns were expected to observe master practitioners' classrooms and to participate with the master practitioner in lesson planning and preparation for laboratories and demonstrations. Therefore, interns benefited from all of the experiences of the master practitioners, who modeled excellent teaching and lesson preparation and offered advice about interns' teaching. The interns learned systems for record keeping, grading, and storing laboratory materials. Evaluative data indicate that interns found their daily meetings with other interns and master practitioners critical to their support system; the meetings provided opportunities to complain, to vent, and to share successes. In the following year without the release time, the interns, who were now second-year teachers, said they felt more isolated and less supported than they had felt the year before. In addition, the master practitioners said they felt a greater sense of commitment to the profession, and they subsequently took on more leadership roles at their schools.

Because it was a pilot project, Scientist-to-Teacher did not actually credential any teachers. The collaboration between SFUSD and UCB consisted primarily of arranging for release time on-site and weekly meetings of all teachers to discuss issues relevant to a teacher induction program. The curriculum was not formalized, although there were plans to seek accreditation and additional funding. A full program was expected to include two or three summers of credential course work, as well as two weekly after-school courses per semester, and, of course, the release times (which would substitute for the "observation," "methods," and "student-teaching" components of a traditional credentialing program).

A school district may consider using a "release time" model for both interns and master practitioner as used in the Scientist-to-Teacher pilot, either as a component of an intern credential program or as part of a beginning teacher–mentor teacher program. There is a considerable investment of time (0.6 FTE per site) and money, but districts would eventually save money by producing science teachers who were better prepared and could be expected to stay in teaching longer. The Scientist-to-Teacher project was supported in its development year by an Arthur Vining Davis Foundations Grant. Support for ongoing development of REPLICATE was provided through the Stuart Foundation.

What a School Can Do

A second approach to retaining teachers can be implemented on a school level, without any additional funding. Using the master schedule as an asset, a school can support and retain new science teachers. Historically, new teachers are given the worst schedules because the veterans usually get priority in choosing which classes to teach. Thus, new teachers usually get ninth graders, frequently the most difficult group in terms of classroom management. New teachers also get two to three preparations, while veteran teachers are assigned only one or two preparations. New teachers might also be given the chore of rotating from room to room, while veterans teach all five classes in the same space. Mission High School in San Francisco, where I have been a science teacher and an administrator for six years, has been actively trying to retain new teachers using the master schedule as a tool. Whenever possible, new teachers are given five classes of the same subject (only one preparation), or, at most, a mixture of two different subjects (two preparations), if the second course has a clearly developed curriculum. New teachers are already overwhelmed just teaching one subject; giving them three different subjects to teach is a recipe for burnout. They spend so much time preparing for their next subject that they have little time to reflect on what was successful in their first subject. One preparation allows time to focus on refining and improving a lesson—even within one day of teaching the same lesson multiple times.

Common planning periods may also be used, so both the new teacher and a veteran teacher teaching the same subject can meet several times a week during the school day (see Figure 2). If a teacher's day consists of seven periods, five are spent teaching, one is a preparation period, and the other is common planning time (CPT). The new teacher has a designated time to meet with the veteran teacher for advice with lesson planning, dealing with students, or testing experiments ahead of time. CPT can provide a source of support for the new teacher and reduce his or her feeling of isolation. During CPT, new and veteran teachers discuss their students, reflecting on successes and failures.

Figure 2. School Level—Manipulating the Master Schedule to Create Common Planning Time (CPT)*

Period	1	2	3	4	5	6[a]	7
New teacher	Biology	Biology	Prep	Physiology	Biology	CPT/Prep	Physiology
Veteran	Biology	Prep	Biology	Biology	Health	CPT/Prep	Biology

*Assuming a standard schedule has five classes and two prep periods.
Note: The new teacher has only two different kinds of courses (biology and physiology) while the veteran teacher has three different kinds, one of which is the same as the new teacher.
[a]During 6th period, the new and veteran teachers can meet to plan lessons.

This model has a positive impact on collegiality in a department, as two teachers have time to meet and get to know one another. It creates a support system for both, whether their concerns are related to teaching or to their personal lives. Teacher applicants who are considering offers from different school sites are often attracted to this model because they recognize that they will be supported during their first year of teaching.

What an Individual Can Do

Finally, individual, veteran teachers can welcome and support new teachers. We know that, unfortunately, some veteran teachers discourage new teachers without meaning to. Some veterans are resistant to change and are dismissive of new teaching methods that new teachers are trying. Their attitudes are pessimistic about students, teachers' salaries, and education in general. Some veterans will ask a new teacher why he or she chose teaching instead of a more lucrative career, thus creating a negative atmosphere within a science department. Furthermore, some veteran teachers are reluctant to share their laboratory experiments and materials with newer teachers who, because of their inexperience, may be unable to properly care for the supplies—thus forcing new teachers to have to create their own inventory of experiments and materials.

However, there are also many veteran teachers who actively support their newer colleagues. Veteran science teachers who had a supportive mentor when they entered the profession often feel the need to play the same role for a new teacher. Sometimes a veteran teacher who did not have a mentor recognizes what a help a mentor might have been and so decides to take on this role for a new teacher. For whatever reason the veteran teacher becomes a mentor, the school and the district need to support that teacher, either with a stipend or a release day and substitute teacher for the veteran or new teacher to observe the other.

Veteran teachers can share equipment, lab materials, and lesson plans; they can also open their classrooms for the new teacher to observe and gain ideas. It is critical for veterans to make themselves available to the new teachers with little judgment or bias.

Finally, if individual teachers feel they have the responsibility to help induct a new person into the profession, they will usually pass on to this new teacher a feeling of responsibility for the next generation of teachers. When the new teacher becomes a "veteran" in three to five years, he or she will feel a responsibility to look after a new teacher, and a cycle of learning is created. Teaching becomes a profession in which the training of new members is a responsibility all teachers must assume.

References

Diehl, C., J. Harris, D. Barrios, J. Fong, and H. O'Connor. 2000. *Teachers training teachers: Four perspectives on an innovative mentoring program for intern science teachers.* Presented at American Educational Research Association (AERA) conference.

Garcia, E., and J. Harris. 1998. *Single subject Scientist-to-Teacher internship.* (Concept paper written while Eugene Garcia was dean of the Graduate School at the University of California-Berkeley.)

Mentoring for Professional Renewal: The Kentucky Experience

Sharon Brennan

Sharon Brennan is an associate professor in the Department of Curriculum and Instruction and the director of field experiences and school collaboration at the University of Kentucky. Her primary interests include teacher assessment and professional development.

Teachers know the power of mentoring because they understand the connection between relationships and learning. Most can cite numerous examples of how seemingly disadvantaged students succeeded because someone they admired took an interest in them by providing just the right measure of faithful support, persistent guidance, and sometimes even "tough love" needed to spur growth.

Most teachers are mentors by instinct. They are frequently drawn to the profession because they care about helping others as much as they care about the subjects they teach. They often serve as mentors to their students, and they enjoy providing support and advice to new colleagues, sharing "trade secrets," and even telling stories about lessons attempted that went awry. But too often, the mentoring that prevails in schools is superficial or, at best, anecdotal—that is, the mentor and new teacher simply chat about events in their classrooms without focusing on ways to change their practices. While it is important to provide emotional support to welcome new teachers into the schools, this kind of mentoring often fails to address real curricular issues in ways that promote growth and encourage longevity.

To encourage new teachers to stay in the profession and to help them succeed, mentoring must be about much more than making them feel comfortable or confessing failures that may seem amusing in retrospect but, in fact, caused concern at the time. Although nurturing represents a very important aspect of the mentor's role, it is not sufficient to address the situation faced in today's schools in which unprecedented numbers of teachers are retiring and inadequate numbers are filling their shoes. The problem is particularly acute in science. In fact, a nationwide survey conducted by the National Science Teachers Association (NSTA) conducted in 2000 shows that well over one-third leave the profession within the first six years. Gerald Wheeler, NSTA's executive director, underscores that point: "… continuing job dissatisfaction among teachers poses a serious threat to efforts to raise student achievement. Qualified science teachers will always be in short supply unless schools and communities address science teachers' reasons for being dissatisfied in their careers" (National Science Teachers Association 2000).

Good mentoring can help reverse these trends, but only if it aims to do more than simply provide technical assistance or help new teachers feel they are part of "the group." For mentoring to realize its full potential, it must be done consciously with a clear set of goals, strategies, and techniques aimed at helping the novices grow.

The Role of Experienced Teachers

Like math teachers, science teachers have many other employment options, so the early years of teaching are even more critical than for those in other disciplines. The job needs to be interesting and challenging if these young people with a range of choices are, ultimately, to choose teaching. Who better to lead the way and guide the growth process than experienced teachers?

Indeed, the hope for increasing efficacy and retention of new teachers lies in the willingness of veteran teachers, who are often leaders in their field, to get involved. Veteran teacher-leaders have considerable expertise to offer new teachers. They generally have a passion for their subject; they want their students to find it interesting; and they know what does and does not work in the classroom. Although most novice teachers have acquired sufficient knowledge and skill to teach their subject, their approach is often mechanical, according to studies that have analyzed new teachers' performance (e.g., Reynolds 1995; Westerman 1991). Expert teachers, who reflect continuously about the impact of their actions on students and know how to shift gears accordingly, can help new teachers move from a step-by-step approach to more flexible, student-centered strategies.

Thus, one important reason to serve as a mentor is that it fulfills a professional responsibility. An even more compelling reason, however, is that the experience can actually be renewing for veteran teachers who may or may not realize how much they have to offer or how much they might gain. In Kentucky, where there has been a mandated teacher internship program for 18 years, mentors frequently report that they have learned a great deal from their protégés, or mentees. Mentoring helps them reexamine their own methods. Others have pointed to the value of collaborating about professional issues as a reason for serving in this capacity (Brennan, Thames, and Roberts 1999). The reports in Kentucky are supported by other accounts. One researcher describes the experience of a mentor teacher who said he became a better writing teacher through his supportive role (Feiman-Nemser 2001). Thus, by helping new teachers address their problems, the mentor addressed some of his own.

Unfortunately, however, mentoring does not always have this kind of impact. As several researchers have discovered, mentoring is often superficial, merely helping the new teacher adapt to the prevailing school culture with little attention to practice (Feiman-Nemser 2001; Gratch 1998; Little 1990). In fact, mentoring can be counterproductive when it perpetuates ineffective practices or reinforces "norms of individualism and noninterference" (Feiman-Nemser 2001, 28). The key to success, according to these and other reports of effective mentoring (e.g., Fairbanks, Freedman, and Kahn 2000; Haas 2000; Leiberman 2000), is the ability to keep the focus on issues related to teaching and learning. As mentor and mentee address various learning dilemmas, they build a long-term partnership that can have far-reaching implications.

The kind of collaborations that emerge from these partnerships have the potential not only to reverse trends of isolation, but also to transform the school culture by altering relationships within the school. Partnerships created in mentoring relationships can stave off loneliness while strengthening practice. This seems especially important now, considering the current environment of heightened accountability and high attrition in our schools. However, given the many demands placed on teachers, the process needs to be formalized and well supported if it is to result in success.

Mentoring New Teachers in Kentucky

Kentucky policy makers have generously supported a formal induction program for new teachers for the past 18 years. Mentoring represents a cornerstone of this statewide initiative known as the Kentucky Teacher Internship Program (KTIP). The legislation that created KTIP in 1984 was drafted in response to policy reports released early in that decade expressing concern about declining teacher quality. (See, for example, the National Commission on Excellence in Education (NCEE) (1983) report, *A Nation at Risk: The Imperative for Educational Reform.*) KTIP was designed to address teacher quality issues related to teacher efficacy and retention by establishing a structure that both guides and assesses the work of first-year teachers. Mentoring and assessment serve as natural companions in the KTIP process.

Key Program Features

A primary goal of Kentucky's internship program is to help new teachers, called "interns," learn to analyze the impact of their instruction on student learning through careful planning and continuous reflection. Every intern works under the supervision of three experienced educators (i.e., a mentor teacher, a teacher educator representing a neighboring university, and the school principal) who make up the intern committee. The program structure ensures regular, systematic guidance and assessment throughout the year, which is divided into three assessment cycles. During each cycle, committee members work with the intern both individually and collaboratively to analyze and confer about assessment data collected during observations and reviews of the intern's portfolio material. Among the documents placed in the portfolio are plans, assessments, samples of student work, and reflections about instructional impact.

Since final assessment is based on progress toward meeting nine teacher standards determined by the Education Professional Standards Board (EPSB) (the state's governing body for teacher certification and accreditation of teacher education programs), conferences, by necessity, focus on progress toward meeting these standards. The standards, and the benchmarks or performance criteria that accompany them, describe areas of teacher responsibility: designing and planning instruction, creating a positive learning climate, implementing and managing instruction, assessing student learning, reflecting about teaching, collaborating with others, seeking relevant professional development opportunities, demonstrating knowledge of content in the classroom, and using technology appropriately. Although interns are fully certified to work independently in their own classrooms during this first year of internship, they must demonstrate that they have met all nine standards by the end of the year in order to have their certificates renewed.

One key program feature is the plan used to monitor the intern's progress toward meeting the standards during the year. This important document, referred to as the Professional Growth Plan (PGP), is maintained by the intern with guidance from the committee. The PGP lists strengths and growth areas; it also outlines steps the intern has agreed to take to improve instruction. This growth plan is refined as the year progresses to reflect the committee's assessment and the intern's progress toward addressing identified growth areas. Through written plans, conferences, and committee meetings, interns are expected to explain their instructional decisions and discuss how they have refined their plans to improve learning of even the most reluctant students. Just as standards establish the goals of the program, this built-in process of documenting assessment through a formal growth plan establishes a habit of reflection and self-evaluation that most educators agree is vital to successful teaching.

Mentoring represents a second important feature of KTIP, not only because the program structure creates a means for each committee member to work closely with the intern individually, but also because of the built-in mechanism for collaboration. Intern and committee members work together in a supportive way during the committee meetings that are held after each observation cycle; they discuss specific aspects of progress and consider updates on the PGP. For most participants, this is the kind of trust-building and open communication that leads to a sense of collegiality.

A third key feature of Kentucky's program is the mandated training for mentors. All committee members must complete training in both the mentoring and assessment functions before they are allowed to serve on an intern's committee. This ensures that everyone working with the intern has been introduced to the same concepts about what is needed to provide effective mentoring and is grounded in the assessment process. Currently, the training is face-to-face, workshop style, but the state is developing an online version that will make the training more accessible.

Components of Mentor Training

Preparation for mentoring is woven into all aspects of the training process. Other aspects of training allow prospective committee members to learn about all program features, including policies, procedures, and assessment tools.

Mentor preparation begins with self-reflection to help prospective mentors think about their own practices in very specific terms. Prospective mentors are asked to provide concrete examples of their successes and disappointments in relation to the teacher standards. This allows them to practice the kind of reflective skills they will be expected to foster in their mentees and brings practices that frequently remain hidden in the subconscious into their consciousness. Since this is a written exercise, they can file it as a reference document to use as they begin to work with the intern. The self-reflection component is carried out in training in two parts. First, participants reflect generally about their practice (i.e., discussing goals for their students, broad strengths, and challenges they are facing). Then they review the intern assessment form and generate examples of what they do in practice that relates to those specific standards and benchmarks that make up the assessment. They are advised to discuss this reflection with their interns during the initial, get-acquainted meetings to break the ice and develop rapport. Trained mentors are also given a tip sheet for conducting initial meetings, which provides useful ideas and suggestions for getting started, such as browsing the Web with the intern to locate teaching resources and reviewing the state curriculum documents.

The heart of mentoring preparation is learning how to guide interns' reflection about plans, instructional activities, and portfolio entries that are used to document progress on the standards and promote growth. To do that, prospective mentors complete a series of exercises in which they review lesson and unit plans, analyze video-clips of instruction, and develop strategies for conducting conferences. During training sessions they form teams to discuss their findings and practice conferencing skills. They also view tapes of mock conferences to evaluate different conferencing techniques. Question prompts are interspersed throughout all exercises to stimulate reflection. For example, after viewing video conferences, prospective mentors are asked to think about whether and how the mentor depicted on the tape facilitated reflection and to compare their notes with what they saw discussed. Questions are posed such as, Did you identify the same growth areas as those described by the mentor? Do the findings discussed change your thinking about your approach?

In mentor training, as in the internship program itself, emphasis is placed on guiding the planning process. Over the years, committee members have reported this as a significant problem area for new teachers. Reports indicate that interns have difficulty articulating clear goals for learning (i.e., central questions to address during lessons and units of study to build conceptual understanding) and explaining assessments they will use to measure learning outcomes, particularly at the beginning of the year. Assessment procedures are either omitted from written plans or vaguely described (e.g., "walked around the room to check for understanding"). In addition, reflections tend to be rather shallow with little or no reference to assessment data (e.g., "students were attentive and seemed to enjoy the lesson"). Mentors report that plans are strengthened by coaching and practice. Since planning drives assessment for at least three of the nine standards (designing, assessing, and reflecting about instruction), time is spent helping the mentor learn to coach the planning process. Training addresses both assessment and coaching of the planning process by having participants review plans and then pose questions that require them to show how they would present their data to an intern in a conference. Representative questions include, How would you conduct a conference based on your review of this plan? What growth areas would you address? What strategies would you use to accomplish your goals?

Practical exercises like the ones described here are used throughout the training process to help mentors transform abstract ideas about mentoring into concrete strategies for practice. While this approach might seem unnecessary or simplistic, KTIP participants do not, as a rule, have well-honed mentoring skills. This may be, in part, due to the culture of isolation in which teachers are simply not accustomed to discussing their practices with colleagues.

Resources to Extend Mentor Training

To build on the foundation laid down in training and to encourage collaboration throughout the year, the Education Professional Standards Board (EPSB) has posted a variety of resources on its website: *http://www.kde.state.ky.us/otec/epsb/*. Web resources include specific tips for mentoring, questions to prompt reflection during conferences, resources related to teaching and learning, and research reviews of effective practice related to the standards. In addition, mentors can access state curriculum documents to use when helping interns with curriculum planning.

In addition to the resources provided by the EPSB, the University of Kentucky regularly offers a graduate level course to help mentor teachers further develop their skills. Course participants learn to use a variety of assessment instruments, develop peer-coaching techniques, and examine their own practices through reflective essays in which they discuss their teaching philosophies and goals for mentoring. An excerpt from one student's essay nicely summarizes the goals of the KTIP model for mentors to set clear goals and engage in the kind of reflection that leads to renewal. Jones (2000) wrote the following:

> *I don't presume to have time-tested, sure-fire answers to all of the questions about teaching, but I do have the enthusiasm to grow with a new teacher. I enjoy the renewal of listening to another person's fresh ideas and want to encourage new teachers to try to create themselves with ardor. I do recognize that it takes more than a good heart to be a good teacher, and that is where my goals and expectations come in. I believe that when expectations are clearly defined, the student is more at ease and more successful. I consider organization, planning skills, patience, and resourcefulness to be the pillars to success as a teacher. (3)*

Markers of Success

KTIP has flourished because of the sturdy structure built by reform-minded policy makers almost two decades ago and because policy makers have consistently supported developmental initiatives since that time in order to keep the program aligned with changes in the field. As a result, multiple assessment tools have been developed that are compatible with the one developed by the Interstate New Teacher Assessment and Support Consortium (INTASC) (1992). Similarly, the training has focused more on helping mentors strengthen their skills in modeling reflective practices, analyzing assessment data, and developing strategies to communicate clearly with their interns during conferences.

Although KTIP's structure addresses much of the research about teacher development and mentoring, data to support its effectiveness are very limited. To date, no research has been conducted that documents the actual impact of mentoring on the development of new teachers. The only program-specific evidence comes from two surveys of participant perceptions. [See McCormick and Brennan (2001) for a more detailed discussion of the survey data.] While these surveys and numerous anecdotal reports suggest that participants view the program as a catalyst for growth, systematic research is clearly needed to ascertain the impact of this program on novice learning.

Characteristics of Effective Mentoring Programs

Without strong research backing, policy makers and others might question the need to formalize the mentoring process and the need for mentors to concentrate so much attention on instructional analysis. After all, haven't veterans always given novices emotional support without the imposition of a formal structure?

Formalizing the process is necessary to counteract the normative culture—that tendency toward noninterference that discourages new teachers from sharing their concerns (Huling-Austin 1990; Lortie 1975). A good mentoring program can transform the culture from one of isolation to collaboration as educators discover the benefits of learning together. Through collaboration, mentor and mentee can address accountability pressures for student learning as they share their successes and disappointments and examine specific aspects of practice with which the new teacher is struggling. The teachers described in reports by Bliss and Mazur 1996; Haas 2000; Leiberman 2000; and Zeek, Foote, and Walker 2001 all found that examining instructional dilemmas helped them improve their own practices. While these studies have not analyzed teacher growth directly, the consistency in participant reports represents a good beginning.

In addition, these reports, and others, underscore the importance of self-reflection in mentoring. Simply knowing the ingredients of effective mentoring won't accomplish the desired goals unless that knowledge is translated into practice. Even the most dedicated mentors who *think* they are taking a reflective stance may discover that they are not, as was the case in a study reported by Randi Stanulis (1994). In interviews with the researcher prior to beginning the mentoring relationship, the mentor in this study described her role as one of asking questions to stimulate thinking rather than telling the mentee what to do. However, when viewing videotapes of her mentoring conferences, she quickly discovered that she was giving advice with lengthy explanations rather than asking questions to make the intern think. It took some deliberate work and reflection on her part to change this unconscious habit. This case vividly shows the power of programs that use concrete activities to develop mentor expertise.

All the mentoring programs described here have built in a mechanism for self-reflection. Although they differ somewhat in their approach to mentoring, they share other common characteristics: they all (a) seek to improve instruction, (b) encourage collaboration that extends to the larger learning community, and (c) report benefits for the mentors. Taken together, these reports provide good evidence of what is needed to maintain high-quality mentoring programs that are aimed at keeping good teachers in the profession. Feiman-Nemser (2001) noted other important elements when she aptly pointed out that the quality of mentoring depends on "how the mentors define and enact their role, what kind of preparation and support they receive, whether mentors have time to mentor, and whether the culture of teaching reinforces their work" (28).

The mentoring programs described in this chapter have enjoyed strong support and have defined the mentoring role as one that focuses on instructional issues. The mentor whom Feiman-Nemser (2001) studied had university and district support and was given time to carry out his role. The Kentucky program provides training, time, and ongoing support for its mentors. What these and other programs need now is systematic research showing the long-term benefits of focused, reflective mentoring. Such plans are underway in Kentucky, where the EPSB is putting an evaluation system in place that will become an integral part of the KTIP process. Since the majority of states now have mandated induction programs (Sweeney and DeBolt 2000), the time has certainly come to show convincingly that focused mentoring translates into better teaching and more satisfied teachers. Program evaluation is a key component.

References

Bliss, T., and J. Mazur. 1996. Common Thread Case Project: Developing associations of experienced and novice educators through technology. *Journal of Teacher Education* 47(3): 185–90.

Brennan, S., W. Thames, and R. Roberts. 1999. Mentoring with a mission. *Educational Leadership* 56(8): 49–52.

Education Professional Standards Board (EPSB). *http://www.kde.state.ky.us/otec/epsb/*

Fairbanks, C., D. Freedman, and C. Kahn. 2000. The role of effective mentors in learning to teach. *Journal of Teacher Education* 51(2): 102–12.

Feiman-Nemser, S. 2001. Helping novices learn to teach: Lessons from an exemplary support teacher. *Journal of Teacher Education* 51(1): 17–30.

Gratch, A. 1998. Beginning teachers and mentor relationships. *Journal of Teacher Education* 49(3): 220–27.

Haas, K. 2000. From teachers to teacher mentors through staff development. *MultiMedia Schools* 7(1): 42–46.

Huling-Austin, L. 1990. Teacher induction programs and internships. In *Handbook of research in teacher education,* ed. W. R. Houston, 535–48. New York: Macmillan.

Interstate New Teacher Assessment and Support Consortium (INTASC). 1992. *Model standards for beginning teacher licensing, assessment and development: A resource for state dialogue.* Washington, DC: Council of Chief State School Officers.

Jones, D. B. 2000. [Student's essay about mentoring]. Unpublished raw data, University of Kentucky.

Leiberman, A. 2000. Networks as learning communities: Shaping the future of teacher development. *Journal of Teacher Education* 51(3): 221–27.

Little, J. W. 1990. The mentor phenomenon and the social organization of teaching. In *Review of research in education*, ed. C. Cazden, 297–351. Washington, DC: American Educational Research Association.

Lortie, D. C. 1975. *Schoolteacher: A sociological study.* Chicago: University of Chicago Press.

McCormick, K. M., and S. Brennan. 2001. Mentoring the new professional in interdisciplinary early childhood education: The Kentucky Teacher Internship Program. *Topics in Early Childhood Special Education* 21(3): 131–49.

National Commission on Excellence in Education (NCEE). 1983. *A nation at risk: The imperative for educational reform. An open letter to the American people. A report to the nation and the secretary of education* (ED226006). Washington, DC: U.S. Government Printing Office.

National Science Teachers Association (NSTA). 2000. *NSTA releases nationwide survey of science teacher credentials, assignments, and job satisfaction.* Available *http://www.nsta.org/369.*

Reynolds, A. 1995. The knowledge base for beginning teachers: Education professionals' expectations versus research findings on learning to teach. *Elementary School Journal* 95(3): 199–221.

Stanulis, R. 1994. Fading to a whisper: One mentor's story of sharing her wisdom without telling answers. *Journal of Teacher Education* 45(1): 31–38.

Sweeney, B., and G. DeBolt. 2000. A survey of the 50 states: Mandated teacher induction programs. In *Quality mentoring for novice teachers,* eds. S. Odell and L. Huling, 97–106. Washington, DC: Association of Teacher Educators and Kappa Delta Pi.

Westerman, D. A. 1991. Expert and novice teacher decision-making. *Journal of Teacher Education* 42(4): 292–305.

Zeek, C., M. Foote, and C. Walker. 2001. Teacher stories and transactional inquiry: Hearing the voices of mentor teachers. *Journal of Teacher Education* 52(5): 377–85.

Recruitment and Retention of Secondary Teachers in New York State

Kabba E. Colley

Kabba E. Colley is co-director of the Secondary Science Teacher Education Program and an assistant professor of science and technology education at Queens College, The City University of New York. Dr. Colley previously served as director of evaluation for the Global Laboratory Project, an innovative secondary science curriculum developed by TERC, Inc. He has also held research positions at the Northeast Regional Educational Laboratory and the National Center for Improving Science Education.

A number of reports have indicated that the nation's public schools are suffering from a severe shortage of certified teachers (National Commission on Teaching and America's Future 1996; AAEE 2001; Gursky 2001). This shortage is particularly severe for public schools located in major urban centers such as New York City and Los Angeles. The most common reasons cited for the shortfall are increasing student enrollment, more teachers retiring, and legislation for smaller class sizes (Marrow 2000). Some researchers have noted that the shortfall "is largely a result of too many teachers prematurely exiting their jobs" (Ingersoll 1999, 33). In other words, the shortage is due to the inability of schools to retain teachers for longer periods.

This shortage of certified teachers has led school administrators to rely on uncertified teachers, substitute teachers, or out-of-field certified teachers to fill teaching vacancies (Ingersoll 1999). In some states, new regulations have been passed to allow for alternative routes to certification and provide incentives for those who are already in the system and for career changers to work toward certification. Despite these efforts, the shortage of certified teachers in public schools is cited by many as one of the main reasons that some students in public schools have lower academic achievement (New York State Education Commissioner 2000). This claim has been challenged by Goldhaber and Brewer (2000), who conducted a study on high school teacher certification status and student achievement and found that students who were taught by certified mathematics teachers had better test scores compared to students with uncertified mathematics teachers. However, they also noted that "contrary to conventional wisdom, mathematics and science students who have teachers with emergency credentials do no worse than students of teachers with standard teaching credentials, all else equal" (141). The researchers cast doubt on the claims that certification leads to better-performing teachers and noted that their research showed little evidence for that claim. Darling-Hammond, Berry, and Thoreson (2001) reviewed the Goldhaber and Brewer (2000) study and found a number of methodological flaws. For instance, in the subsample of the data that Goldhaber and Brewer used, most of the teachers had similar qualifications; further, they found that teachers who had more educational training showed better student achievement. Darling-Hammond, Berry, and Thoreson (2001) also cited numerous studies that linked student achievement to teacher training in content area, education course work, professional development, and certification.

Although the shortage of certified teachers varies among fields, those hardest hit are science and mathematics (AAEE 2001; National Commission on Mathematics and Science Teaching 2000; National Research Council 2000). Similarly, urban school districts tend to experience the greatest shortage of certified science and mathematics teachers because they are usually ill funded, with large populations of students who are traditionally underserved (Hewson et al. 2001). Further, urban school districts sometimes have to deal with social problems such as unemployment, crime, violence, dilapidated infrastructure, political pressure, negative media coverage, and limited resources—all of which can discourage new teachers from staying in the system.

This chapter examines how one urban school district in New York State recruited and retained its secondary science teachers. For reasons of anonymity, the district is called the Cabral School District. It consists of several educational municipalities and is considered one of the most ethnically and racially diverse districts in New York State. The district's school population is about 265,000, with a per-pupil expenditure of around $8,000. About 56 percent of the students are classified as free/reduced lunch students, and the student-teacher ratio is estimated at 16:7. The study discussed in this chapter was guided by the following research questions: (1) How does the Cabral School District recruit secondary science teachers? (2) What strategies does the Cabral School District use to retain and renew secondary science teachers? and (3) What factors hinder the recruitment, retention, and renewal of secondary science teachers in the Cabral School District? The researcher was also interested in whether the state education policy that places certified teachers in high-need urban school districts promoted or hindered the Cabral School District's own needs to recruit, retain, and renew secondary science teachers. The data for this study came from two main sources: interviews of informants from different levels of the district and a review of district and state education records. The chapter begins with a brief review of the literature and a discussion of the context in which the study took place. These are followed by a description of the methods used. Discussion of the findings and possible policy implications make up the rest of the chapter.

Context

Like many states in the United States, New York is in the middle of a major education reform, unprecedented in its education history. At the heart of this reform is the implementation of standards at various levels of the education system. In July 1998, the New York State Board of Regents adopted a major policy document, *Teaching to Higher Standards: New York's Commitment* (New York State Board of Regents 1998). In this document, the regents identified four "gaps" in the state education system and proposed solutions to closing them. The gaps are:

(1) New York State does not attract and keep enough of the best teachers where they are needed most; (2) not enough teachers leave college prepared to ensure that New York's students reach higher standards; (3) not enough teachers maintain the knowledge and skills needed to teach high standards throughout their careers; and (4) many school environments actively work against effective teaching. (2)

The regents also cited some interesting statistics about teacher recruitment, retention, and renewal. For instance, they noted that in the next 10 years, 50 percent of the teaching work force in New York State will be eligible for retirement. In addition, of 21,500 teaching/pupil personnel certificates issued in 1996–97, only 5,900 of the newly certified teachers were hired. Eleven percent of New York City's teachers are not certified in the areas they teach, compared to 4.5 percent statewide. Furthermore, New York City teachers' median salary is about $45,000, compared to $63,000 for teachers in the neighboring counties of Nassau, Suffolk, Westchester, Putnam, and Rockland (New York State Board of Regents 1998).

The New York State Board of Regents proposed several solutions to these gaps in the state education system. It is beyond the scope of this chapter to describe all the proposed solutions. However, the ones that are relevant to the research discussed here include establishing a teacher incentive program to attract qualified and certified teachers to high-need schools and requiring all new teachers to (a) be educated in the liberal arts and sciences, (b) complete a major in the subject they will teach or a major in one of the liberal arts and sciences for those entering the field of early childhood teaching or middle childhood generalists, (c) be prepared to teach to the student learning standards, and (d) complete multiple field experiences that enable them to teach all students. In addition, the regents proposed that special education teachers must have content knowledge equivalent to the preparation of regular classroom teachers. They also proposed the creation of alternative teacher certification programs for those who enter teaching from another career, as well as the re-registration of all teacher education programs to comply with state standards and regulations. Teacher education programs are required to ensure that at least 80 percent of their preservice teachers pass the required certification examinations.

Reactions to the current education reforms are mixed. Some say that even though the regents may have been motivated by good intentions, without increasing salaries, providing the necessary resources, and restructuring schools even the most qualified and dedicated teachers will become frustrated and leave the profession (Feldman

2002). Some of the teachers in various New York City schools feel their hands are tied. They complain that the state wants them to uphold high standards but is not willing to invest enough in resources. Others welcome the reforms because they see them as an opportunity to rid the profession of incompetent teachers, who make the teaching profession unattractive. Regardless of the differing opinions about the reforms in New York State, one thing is clear: The regents are absolutely serious.

Against the backdrop of these reforms, it is worth mentioning that two major events occurred in New York City recently that have affected the education scene across New York State and will continue to do so indefinitely. The first was a major court decision in which a group of parents, educators, and community activists sued the state of New York (*Campaign for Fiscal Equity v. State of New York* 2001) and the second event occurred September 11, 2001. In the first instance, on January 10, 2001, Justice Leland DeGrasse of the New York Supreme Court in Manhattan found that New York's school funding system was unconstitutional and failed to provide New York City's students with a "sound basic education." He also ruled that the state's school funding system violated federal civil rights because it disproportionately harmed New York City's minority students, about 73 percent of the state's total minority population (Keller 2001; Saunders 2001). The ruling gave the state approximately eight months to propose a remedy for the situation. Although most in the education activist community are hopeful that the ruling will lead to major changes in the way schools are funded in the state, the governor is appealing the case, and it could be a long time before the case is settled.

The significance of September 11, 2001 is that besides being a major tragedy, it also created new problems and challenges for New York and its citizens. For instance, both the governor and the mayor of New York City have announced that budget cuts are imminent, and some things will have to be sacrificed. Some in the education community fear that vital resources will be diverted to national security issues. Regardless of what the situation is, implementation of the regents' education reform program is going ahead.

Method

The method of research employed was a qualitative case study, which was chosen because the main aim of the researcher was to gain understanding of a contemporary issue and how individuals within a system responded to it. According to Yin (1994), a case study is more appropriate when the research operation concerns "contemporary sets of events over which the investigator has no control" (9). This study of an urban school district focuses on the complex interactions of people and issues within a particular context. It is a "bounded system," which, according to Stake (1994), is one of the distinguishing features of a case study.

The sampling technique used to select participants for the study was purposeful sampling, which allows the researcher to select participants who were directly involved with the research issue and likely to provide maximum and relevant data, as opposed to selecting participants who may or may not meet the needs of the researcher (Patton 1990; Merriam 1998). Prior to conducting the study, permission was obtained from various educational administrative areas within the district. The participants who agreed to take part in the study were the following: one assistant superintendent, three district school science coordinators, two district personnel/human resource directors, four assistant principals for science, and five science teachers. Nine of the participants were women, and six were men. Of these, two were African Americans, two were Hispanic Americans, one was an Asian American, one was an Arab American, and nine were European Americans.

Three semi-structured interview protocols were developed to interview the three levels of participants—that is, district administrators (superintendent, coordinators, and human resource directors), school administrators (assistant principals for science), and secondary science teachers. The interview questions were framed around the three main research questions (see below) and focused on recruitment policies, strategies of recruitment and retention, and factors that hinder the recruitment and retention process. All interviews were tape recorded and transcribed. Interview transcripts were sent via e-mail to participants for them to review and make any comments or changes. They were open-coded to determine emerging themes and patterns across different levels of participant and interview question. To ensure that the coding was valid, four colleagues with experience in qualitative research were asked by the researcher to recode segments of transcripts from different participants. There was little variation between the recoded segments and the researcher's. The coded data were then analyzed, using techniques suggested by Miles and Huberman (1994).

Findings

How does the Cabral School District recruit secondary science teachers?
One of the main findings from this study dealt with how the Cabral School District recruited secondary science teachers. The data showed that district administrators and school administrators differ in their strategies of recruiting secondary science teachers. In general, district administrators rely on job fairs, advertisement, outreach to local colleges and universities, the board of education employment office, referrals from alumni or retired employees, use of professional recruiters, and recruitment of foreign teachers from abroad. Below are examples of responses from district administrators.

Really the two basic ways that we handle our recruitment are by participating in job fairs—hosting our own job fairs that we conduct here at the district or at one of our schools or reaching out to colleges—and using the Internet.

We hold job fairs, where we announce it in the papers, and people who are on our list who have licenses are given invitations to attend the high school recruitment fairs. We have science APs from the different schools come down and interview the candidates, and they are hired on the spot if they feel the match is good between the prospective employee and the school. That's it, at the moment.

In contrast to district administrators, school administrators recruit secondary science teachers by word of mouth, résumés from applicants, referrals from the superintendent's office, and outreach to local colleges. In general, the superintendent's office plays an active role in the recruitment of secondary science teachers for the schools. However, these data do not reveal how the individual teachers are recruited. To find out how the recruitment process works, the teacher interview data were examined, and the results indicated two pathways to being recruited and hired as a secondary science teacher. The first pathway is speedy and is referred to as "rabbit recruitment," while the second is termed "turtle recruitment" because it is a slow process. The recruitment process for secondary science teachers in this district consists of three elements: luck, some networking, and personal initiative—as can be seen from the teachers' responses below.

"Rabbit Recruitment"

I actually went out and found my own job. I called different high schools, and I sent my résumé to different high schools. I was told that since I was certified, I would have to work in a SURR [Schools Under Registration Review] school. That's the new rule. I didn't go through the Board of Education for recruitment. I didn't go to any of the recruitment workshops they had. I just sent my résumé and went on interviews, and found my own position.

"Turtle Recruitment"

I became a school aide with a professor who also taught at this high school from our college, so I learned about this school from him, and then they needed to set up science labs and to have help in the science labs, so I took the position as a school aide to do that. Eventually, when I did get my license and got certified, they didn't have an opening right away. I worked in another school for a year, and then this year I was able to transfer in on what they call SBO Transfer—School Based Option Transfer List. It's published yearly, and it's for teachers to transfer within schools in the city. It gives the school the chance to interview the teacher candidate in front of a panel of about six representatives from the school. I went through that interview, and I was hired after the interview.

One of the areas of interest for this study was the level of awareness about district recruitment policy among district administrators, school administrators, and science teachers. Lack of awareness or understanding of a district's or state's recruitment policy may hinder recruitment efforts. On the other hand, when people are informed and educated about a particular recruitment policy, they are more likely to implement it accordingly. Analysis of the data suggests that district administrators were aware of the state's recruitment policy and were able to articulate it. For instance, one response from a district administrator on the policy was as follows:

We recruit by doing a number of things. Number one, we follow board of education policy. We attend board of education job fairs, which are up through the board of education. Where they advertise, not just science teachers, but all teachers. They're invited, and these are not only people who are certified, but people who are uncertified. Certified teachers in the areas of science and math and other shortage areas have priority in terms of going to schools that are considered to be SURR schools.

A review of New York State education documents indicated that there is a specific policy on recruitment and retention of certified teachers in public schools. According to the New York State Education Commissioner (2000), "the Regents' policy provides that schools may not employ unlicensed teachers after September 2003. Regents have further decided that no unlicensed teachers may be employed to teach in Schools Under Registration Review (SURR) after September 1999." This seems to be consistent with the above finding.

What strategies does the Cabral School District use to retain and renew secondary science teachers?

The findings on science teacher retention suggest that district administrators at Cabral School District differ in their strategies of retention when compared to school administrators. The former rely on or emphasize organizational structure and resources while the latter rely on personal support, professional experience, and trust. The three excerpts below represent the view of school district administrators on the retention issue.

Well, the bottom line is that you try to encourage them, like you do any other teacher. There are different policies. We provide mentoring; we provide staff development; we have new teacher workshops, which we provide for them.

We only keep the ones we want if we can help it, but we have extensive staff development. We have people going into the schools and working with them, and special programs for middle school science teachers.

We also provide a lot of professional development. We have a teaching and learning institute, where teachers are invited to come out for eight full school days and work with groups of teachers on new strategies, and how to really teach science in a way that's investigative, meeting the standards, and that's as exciting for the teachers as it is for the students.

A closer look at the above excerpts reveals a bureaucratic and impersonal attitude that underlies school district administrators' approach to retention. This is particularly true in the first two excerpts ("Well, the bottom line is..." and "We only keep..."). Whether or not this affects the retention of science teachers remains to be seen. As a science teacher educator, the researcher thinks that bureaucratic and impersonal attitudes may hurt more than help retention efforts. However, it is important to note that not all district administrators demonstrated this attitude toward secondary science teacher retention, as noted by this alternative voice among the school district administrators.

Well, this past year, one of the main things we've done to support all of our teachers is that we have put in a teacher-centered specialist at each school. This way, new teachers have someone in each individual school who can help them and walk them through many of the things they may find difficult or didn't necessarily anticipate were related to teaching—some of the little administrative factors that are attached to that. They give them guidance in classroom management.

In contrast to the district administrators, the school administrators at Cabral School District cited more specific, personal strategies for retaining science teachers. Below are examples of their responses.

What we do is offer mentoring for new science teachers whereby they're paired...with an established science teacher with an excellent record. They receive personal training from a teacher who really knows the subject matter and has a lot of experience teaching the type of students, at the age level, that they're going to be dealing with. We also provide them with in-house courses for advancement as far as getting the number of credits they need in order to get a permanent license. We give them a thorough type of preparation as far as the in-house mechanisms that we have for grading and for tracking students, so they're not lost when they start here. We publish a science department new teacher handbook that helps many of them, too. It's very difficult to survive the first year of teaching.

Not one science teacher has left me in five years. I never ask a teacher to do anything unless I've done it first. I respect my teachers! For a teacher to be an effective teacher, you have to feel good on your job, and you have to feel you're doing the best job that you can. I use myself as a model.

I try as much as I can to keep them teaching within their subject. That's one thing. I try to be available, always, to them, to discuss things. If they're unhappy, then I welcome them to discuss things with me.

School administrators retain their science teachers by focusing on the teachers' personal and professional needs. According to Darling-Hammond (1996), teachers who have access to professional support, networks, and a welcoming work environment are likely to stay in their schools.

When secondary science teachers were asked to talk about things that their schools do to keep or retain them, their responses correlated very strongly with the school administrators' responses about retention. For instance, one teacher noted:

They provided us with senior teachers. They are there if I need help, and they are very helpful and very sincere.... They also provided us with a resource book for the teacher. You can make your own lesson plans, worksheets, things that you can use to make the class more fun for your students. That's what I like.

Another teacher said:

You work with a resident teacher who's been teaching for a number of years, and you discuss teaching methods and philosophies with them. We meet once a week.

A common theme that emerged from the teacher data on retention was mentoring and the providing of teaching resources. All the teachers said that they were provided with a mentor or a senior teacher for professional support. The fact that mentors are provided to all the teachers could be a district policy. Mentoring is also the least expensive way of helping retain teachers in a resource-tight school environment.

What factors hinder the recruitment, retention, and renewal of secondary science teachers in the Cabral School District?
Two of the most common factors cited by participants as a hindrance to the recruitment, retention, and renewal of secondary science teaches were low salaries and the Board of Regents' policy requiring certified teachers to be placed in high-need schools. Other, less frequently cited factors were difficult school conditions, such as overcrowding; shortage of qualified candidates in science; teaching out of field; lack of leadership support; large class sizes; lack of freedom to decide classroom practice; and, as one teacher expressed it, "very little community spirit."

Conclusion

This study demonstrated that in one major urban school district, the recruitment, retention, and renewal of science teachers was conducted differently at the district and the school levels. Furthermore, district administrators, school administrators, and secondary science teachers hold different views of recruitment and retention. For the most part, school administrators and secondary science teachers share the same responses on issues of science teacher recruitment, retention, and renewal.

State recruitment policy as practiced by district administrators is different from that of school administrators. School administrators tend to focus on personal and professional needs to recruit and retain secondary science teachers while district administrators respond to bureaucratic and organizational needs. Most of the participants agreed that the state policy to place certified teachers in high-needs schools—well intended as it may be—imposes constraints on schools and prevents them from recruiting the certified secondary science teachers they need.

Throughout the study, participants were asked whether their schools or districts were experiencing a shortage of secondary science teachers, and the response was mixed. For instance, some participants noted that their schools were "excessing," meaning laying off secondary science teachers due to an excess, low student enrollment, or budget cuts. Other schools were losing teachers to more affluent districts because of better working conditions.

The teacher shortage problem is sometimes characterized as a retention problem. For instance, Marrow (1999) noted that the teacher shortage resembles a leaking swimming pool, with teachers as the water in the pool. He claimed that even though everyone notices that the water is leaking, we keep adding water to the pool. Instead of preparing new teachers who will eventually leave, Marrow suggested that we fix the leak first. This means providing rigorous training for preservice teachers and providing inservice teachers with better salaries, more professional development, and better working conditions. The words of Richard Riley, secretary of education in the Clinton administration, are relevant in this regard:

> We must take steps immediately to meet the current shortage of mathematics and science teachers. We also must invest wisely in the recruitment, professional development, and retention of these teachers if we are going to accommodate the explosion of knowledge in these fields, as well as the uninterrupted increase in school enrollments projected through this century.

Acknowledgments

The author wishes to thank the following colleagues and friends for their feedback and comments during various stages of preparing this manuscript: Dr. Eleanor Armour-Thomas, Dr. Randi Dickson, Dr. Rikki Asher, and Dr. Magnus Bassey of Queens College, CUNY; Dr. Andrea Bilics, Worcester State College; and Dr. Ira K. Thomas, Associate Director for Research, AACTE. Special thanks go to my wife, Dr. Binta M. Colley, York College, CUNY, for reading the final manuscript and to all my participants/informants.

References

American Association for Employment in Education (AAEE). 2001. *Job search handbook.* Columbus, OH: AAEE.

Darling-Hammond, L. 1996. The quiet revolution: Rethinking teacher development. *Educational Leadership* 53(6): 4–10.

Darling-Hammond, L., B. Berry, and A. Thoreson. 2001. Does teacher certification matter? Evaluating the evidence. *Educational Evaluation and Policy Analysis* 23(1): 57–77.

Feldman, S. 2002. A boost for good teaching. *New York Times,* Week in Review, 13 January, 7.

Goldhaber D. D., and D. J. Brewer. 2000. Does teacher certification matter? High school teacher certification status and student achievement. *Educational Evaluation and Policy Analysis* 22(2): 129–45.

Gursky, D. 2001. Supply and demand: Finding and training the teachers we need for the 21st century. *On Campus* 20(4): 10–11, 15.

Hewson, P. W., J. B. Kahle, K. Scantlebury, and D. Davis. 2001. Equitable science education in middle schools: Do reform efforts make a difference? *Journal of Research in Science Teaching* 38(10): 1130–44.

Ingersoll, R. M. 1999. The problem of underqualified teachers in American secondary schools. *Educational Researcher* 28(2): 26–37.

Keller, B. 2001. New York system of state aid thrown out. *Education Week* 20 (18): 1, 24.

Marrow, J. 1999. *Teacher shortage: False alarm.* PBS documentary. Available at *www.pbs.org.*

———. 2000. *Choosing excellence.* New York: Scarecrow.

Merriam, S. B. 1998. *Qualitative research and case study applications in education.* San Francisco: Jossey-Bass.

Miles, M. B., and A. M. Huberman. 1994. *Qualitative data analysis.* Thousand Oaks, CA: Sage.

National Commission on Mathematics and Science Teaching for the 21st Century. 2000. *Before it's too late: A report to the nation from the National Commission on Mathematics and Science Teaching for the 21st Century.* Washington, DC: U. S. Department of Education.

National Commission on Teaching and America's Future. 1996. *What matters most: Teaching for America's future.* New York: Teachers College, Columbia University.

National Research Council (NRC). 2000. *Educating teachers of science, mathematics and technology: New practices for the millennium.* Washington, DC: National Academy Press.

New York State Board of Regents. 1998. *Teaching to higher standards: New York's commitment.* Albany: New York State Board of Regents.

New York State Education Commissioner. 2000. *Report to the State Board of Regents.* Available at *http://www.nysewd.gov.comm./reg0007.htm*

Patton, M. Q. 1990. *Qualitative evaluation and research methods.* 2nd ed. Newbury Park, CA: Sage.

Saunders, S. 2001. Court ruling turns up heat on need for more school aid. *New York Teacher* 42(8): 3.

Stake, R. E. 1994. *The art of case study.* Thousand Oaks, CA: Sage.

Yin, R. K. 1994. *Case study research: Design and methods.* 2nd ed. Thousand Oaks, CA: Sage.

Index